Properties of Violence

GEOGRAPHIES OF JUSTICE AND SOCIAL TRANSFORMATION

SERIES EDITORS

Deborah Cowen, University of Toronto
Nik Heynen, University of Georgia
Melissa W. Wright, Pennsylvania State University

ADVISORY BOARD

Sharad Chari, London School of Economics
Bradon Ellem, University of Sydney
Gillian Hart, University of California, Berkeley
Andrew Herod, University of Georgia
Jennifer Hyndman, York University
Larry Knopp, University of Washington, Tacoma
Heidi Nast, DePaul University
Jamie Peck, University of British Columbia
Frances Fox Piven, City University of New York
Laura Pulido, University of Southern California
Paul Routledge, University of Glasgow
Bobby Wilson, University of Alabama

Properties of Violence

LAW AND LAND GRANT STRUGGLE
IN NORTHERN NEW MEXICO

DAVID CORREIA

THE UNIVERSITY OF GEORGIA PRESS
Athens & London

© 2013 by the University of Georgia Press
Athens, Georgia 30602
www.ugapress.org
All rights reserved
Designed by Walton Harris
Set in 10/13 Minion Pro

Most University of Georgia Press titles are
available from popular e-book vendors.

Printed digitally

Library of Congress Cataloging-in-Publication Data
Correia, David, 1968–
Properties of violence : law and land grant struggle in northern New Mexico /
David Correia.
xiii, 220 p. : ill. ; 23 cm. — (Geographies of justice and social transformation ; 17)
Includes bibliographical references (p. 207–214) and index.
ISBN-13: 978-0-8203-3284-0 (hardcover : alk. paper)
ISBN-10: 0-8203-3284-4 (hardcover : alk. paper)
ISBN-13: 978-0-8203-4502-4 (pbk. : alk. paper)
ISBN-10: 0-8203-4502-4 (pbk. : alk. paper)
1. Land grants—Law and legislation—New Mexico—Tierra Amarilla—History.
2. Alianza Federal de las Mercedes. 3. Tierra Amarilla (N.M.)—History. I. Title.
KFN4055.C67 2013
333.309789'52—dc23

2012034306

British Library Cataloging-in-Publication Data available

For Toni, Willa, and Harper

CONTENTS

	List of Illustrations *ix*
	Acknowledgments *xi*
INTRODUCTION	Property and the Legal Geographies of Violence in Northern New Mexico *1*
PROLOGUE	Yellow Earth *15*
CHAPTER 1	Colonizing the Lands of War *28*
CHAPTER 2	"Under the Malign Influence of Land-Stealing Experts" *47*
CHAPTER 3	The Night Riders of Tierra Amarilla *69*
CHAPTER 4	An Unquiet Title *84*
CHAPTER 5	The New Mexico Land Grant War *120*
CHAPTER 6	Terrorists and Tourists in Tierra Amarilla *146*
EPILOGUE	Rare Earth *167*
	Notes *181*
	Bibliography *207*
	Index *215*

ILLUSTRATIONS

William F. M. Arny   42

Map of El Rancho del Poso   89

Map of the Brusselbach Ranch   96

Map of the Mundy Ranch   107

"No trespassing" sign erected by
La Corporación de Abiquiú   127

Colonia Mejicana ad   132

Handcuffed José María Martínez being led
into the Tierra Amarilla jail   138

Tijerina after his arrest following the courthouse raid   139

The official FBI "Rabble Rouser Index" form for Tijerina   141

Amador Flores during a court hearing   161

Amador Flores and his son, Vincent Flores   162

Rafael Flores reacting to news about
his son's legal issues   163

Sign with image of Zapata along the road
into Tierra Amarilla   165

Entry gate to Canyon Ridge   168

View north from Canyon Ridge over
the Cañon Creek Gorge   170

View east from Canyon Ridge development   171

Trail sign marking the site of
Sheepherder's Monument   172

Map of the Jicarilla Apache land acquisition   179

ACKNOWLEDGMENTS

MOST ACKNOWLEDGMENTS, PARTICULARLY ONES written for scholarly books, start with something about how writing a book takes the support of a lot of people. It's true, of course, and I have plenty of people to thank and debts I can't possibly repay. But in writing this book I learned something else about this work. It can be awfully lonely. It requires months combing through archives alone; untold afternoons and evenings reading books, articles, and reports in seclusion; years drafting chapters behind a desk and a closed door; even more time revising, editing, and then revising again. And it's all done alone. Writing is a lonely thing indeed. Thankfully, along the way, I've had the privilege and joy of meeting, befriending, and benefiting from the companionship and help of some amazing friends, activists, and scholars.

Nik Heynen is an inspiring scholar and activist and the series editor for the Geographies of Justice and Social Transformation series, of which this book is a part, at the University of Georgia Press. This project would never have seen the light of day without Nik's interest in my work.

My colleagues in the Department of American Studies at the University of New Mexico have been nothing but supportive and inspiring. Amy Brandzel, Jennifer Denetdale, Alyosha Goldstein, Laura Gomez, Rebecca Schreiber, Michael Trujillo, Alex Lubin, Gabriel Meléndez, Vera Norwood, Irene Vasquez, Gerald Vizenor, and Peter White constitute an inspiring and wonderful faculty. In particular, I've had many conversations about this book with Alex. He's a good friend and a great scholar, and I hope this work reflects the kind of rigorous, politically committed scholarship that he practices. Alyosha and Rebecca have become good friends and mentors, and this book is better because of them. Special thanks to the chair of the department, Gabriel Meléndez. I've also had the good fortune to work with some fantastic graduate students at UNM, particularly Berenika, Miles, Sam, and Summer, whose intelligence and intellectual curiosity I greatly admire.

Beyond the Department of American Studies, I'm lucky to have colleagues at UNM like the folks in geography, particularly Mindy Harm Benson, Scott Freundschuh, and Maria Lane. Kate Lenzer did terrific cartographic work. The maps are her accomplishment. Bill Fleming, David Henkel, and Teresa Cordova in community and regional planning are old friends and mentors.

Thanks to Matt McCourt, Brad Dearden, and Cathleen McAnneny from the University of Maine, Farmington. Jennifer West and the *Santa Fe New Mexican* were generous in permitting me to use their photos in the book.

This book has benefited from the support and encouragement of friends and colleagues. I owe a debt of gratitude that I'll never be able to repay to Kay Matthews. She read and commented on every sentence that appears in this book, and it's better because of her. Andy Doolen carefully read several chapters. He's a great scholar and a great writer with the all-important critical eye. I always turned to him when I needed a tough appraisal. Jake Kosek's work and support have been an inspiration. He has been a friend and a cheerleader for this project. Lorena Oropeza is an incredibly generous and brilliant scholar and great friend. At least twice along the way, she sat me down, and together we mapped out a way to complete this book. Derek Krissoff at the University of Georgia Press has been remarkable for his patience and confidence in this project. Thanks also to Tad Mutersbaugh, who has served as a mentor of incomparable generosity. I learned from watching Tad that good scholarship, like so much else in life, is about putting in the hard work, every day, all the time. You need a few good ideas too, and Tad has those in spades. I hope this book rises to the level he expects of me.

Thanks to many current and former New Mexicans: David Benavides, Ike DeVargas, Em Hall, (honorary New Mexican) Eric Perramond, Richard Rosenstock, Jakob Schiller, Eric Shultz, and the late, great Mark Schiller.

I've presented portions of this project over the years at conferences of the Association of American Geographers, the Critical Geography Conference, and the Western Social Science Association, and at invited lectures and seminars at the Office of the New Mexico State Historian, the UNM history department lecture series, the UNM geography department colloquium, the University of Kentucky geography colloquium and the Environments and Societies workshop at the University of California, Davis. I thank Felipe Gonzalez, Matt Huber, Mazen Labban, Paul Matthews, Richard Nostrand, Rich Schein, Louis Warren, Diana Davis, Jody Emel, Jonathon London, Gavin Bridge, Saed Engel-DiMauro, John Hintz, former state historian Robert Torrez, and many others, for comments, conversations, or close reads at those and other events.

Thanks to my sister-in-law, Liz Bisbey-Kuehn, and my mother-in-law, Gretchen Kuehn, for their support, often in the form of child care, and encouragement. My sisters, Amy and Alison, and my parents, Robert and Elisa: thanks for your love and support.

I've spent months in archives all over New Mexico. Nancy Brown-Martinez, Beth Silbergleit, and Ann Massmann at the Center for Southwest Research at the University of New Mexico are terrific at what they do, and I'm grateful for their support on this project. The beleaguered staff at the New Mexico State Records Center and Archive in Santa Fe have suffered budget cuts and staff shortages and yet still manage the Sisyphean task of smoothly running a remarkable repository of New Mexico history. Many thanks also to the staffs of Fray Angélico Chávez Library in Santa Fe, the National Archives and Records Center in Denver, and the Rio Grande Archives at New Mexico State University in Las Cruces.

This project would not have been possible without the financial support of a number of institutions. Tobias Duran of the Center for Regional Studies at the University of New Mexico generously provided funding to hire a graduate student to transcribe interviews and help translate documents. Patricia Perea was the hard-working student who did just that. Former New Mexico state historian Estevan Rael-Gálvez and former assistant state historian Dennis Trujillo supported this project from the very beginning with money and enthusiasm. New Mexico is a better place for having had such sharp, dynamic, and creative leaders running the Office of State Historian.

Parts of chapter 5 were included in "'Rousers of the Rabble' in the New Mexico Land Grant War: Alianza Federal de Mercedes and the Violence of the State" (*Antipode* 40 [2008], 561–583). I received helpful feedback on this chapter from Melissa Wright and two anonymous reviewers. A section of "Making Destiny Manifest: United States Territorial Expansion and the Dispossession of Two Mexican Property Claims, 1824–1899" (*Journal of Historical Geography* 35 [2009], 87–103), appears in chapter 2. Graeme Wynne and two anonymous reviewers helped improve this article.

All that work, however, means, of course, that the price for this project has been paid largely by my family. I've dragged my wife, Toni, and our two beautiful daughters, Willa and Harper, from family and friends on multiple occasions as we've moved all over the United States. By the time we landed back in New Mexico in 2008, Willa and Harper had lived in four states, attended five schools, and moved in and out of six houses in seven years. Toni left her family, twice, and had to find, and quit, five jobs. They allowed me to disrupt their lives so that I could write this book. And they gave me this gift willingly (well, Willa was pretty mad about leaving Maine). This book is for them.

Properties of Violence

INTRODUCTION

Property and the Legal Geographies of Violence in Northern New Mexico

WHEN SPAIN IN THE SEVENTEENTH CENTURY and later Mexico in the early nineteenth century pushed colonial settlements north into lands controlled by powerful Indian nations in what is today northern New Mexico and southern Colorado, they did so by distributing millions of acres in scores of large common property land grants to landless sheepherders and agriculturalists. Over the course of more than two hundred years, Spain and Mexico launched thousands of settlers into a remote territory dominated by the Utes, the Navajo, the Comanches, and the Apaches. Colonial administrators did this because they viewed these borderland settlements as human shields that could guard valuable mining regions south of Santa Fe from powerful Indian nations.

When all of what is today the state of New Mexico was made part of the United States following the end of the U.S.-Mexican War in 1848, the United States agreed to recognize these land grants as preexisting property rights. Despite guarantees enshrined in the war-ending treaty, the late nineteenth century in New Mexico was a chaos of land speculation marked by dubious legal decisions that contributed to the dispossession of millions of acres of Spanish and Mexican common property land grants.

The history of the loss of common property land grants in northern New Mexico was largely unknown until the late 1960s, when Chicano activists and the heirs of numerous land grants came together to form an organization called La Alianza Federal de Mercedes. Alianza rejected the then commonly held notion that the only lands lost during the period of postwar property adjudication were illegitimate claims. Instead they advanced the explosive idea that millions of acres were stolen outright from legitimate owners and that the United States government was complicit in this wholesale property dispossession. The charismatic leader of Alianza, Reies Lopez Tijerina, organized the group through a series of provocative tactics. He threatened to seize private lands from ranchers, organized sit-ins on former land grants controlled by the U.S. Forest Service—an agency he described as an occupying force in New

Mexico — and attempted to make citizen's arrests of prominent political figures, including Warren Burger, the chief justice of the U.S. Supreme Court.

His tactics and rhetoric resonated with the thousands of living land grant heirs who populated scores of tiny hamlets and villages in the mountains of northern New Mexico. With that constituency Tijerina built Alianza on a promise that he alone could lead the heirs in their fight to reclaim the land grants. Through Alianza they would prove, he convinced many, that the large private ranches and huge federally owned forests that dominated, and still dominate, northern New Mexico were the illegal spoils of a colonial invasion. Rather than respecting treaty obligations, federal officials stood by, and sometimes joined in, as a vast land grab dispossessed hundreds of communities of their rightful property. According to Tijerina, because of the conspiratorial machinations of a gang of commercial speculators, duplicitous federal officials, corrupt public servants, and greedy territorial lawyers, the poor Spanish-speaking land grant communities of New Mexico had been robbed of their history. Their poverty was a monument to colonial greed. By the late 1960s Tijerina claimed that more than ten thousand dues-paying members had joined Alianza, including the wife of New Mexico's Republican governor.

Alianza's tactics culminated on June 5, 1967, when nineteen of its members, armed with pistols and shotguns, stormed the Rio Arriba County Courthouse looking for a district attorney named Alfonso Sanchez. Just days earlier Sanchez had ordered the arrest of eleven Alianza leaders after the group threatened to take over the nearly six-hundred-thousand-acre Tierra Amarilla land grant in northern New Mexico. The raiders, Tijerina would later explain, planned to liberate those arrested and place Sanchez under citizen's arrest. The raid turned into a pitched gun battle inside the courthouse. A New Mexico state police officer and the county jailer were shot, and two men, including a reporter covering the arraignment, were briefly kidnapped. Neither Sanchez nor the eleven arrested Alianza members, however, were in Tierra Amarilla that morning. Tijerina and the other raiders fled into the rugged mountains surrounding Tierra Amarilla. In the weeks after the raid, state police helicopters buzzed northern New Mexico's land grant villages, while National Guard tanks prowled the dirt roads of the Carson National Forest looking for the raiders.

The raid thrust New Mexico's colonial ("ancient," according to many in the press) property disputes into the national consciousness. Journalists, fascinated by Tijerina, rushed in to explain to an unbelieving public what was happening in northern New Mexico. Did the courthouse raid herald the start of a peasant revolution in the United States? Was Tijerina an agent of foreign powers? What motivated the thousands who joined Alianza and the select few who took up arms? The media microscope placed the raid — its causes and consequences — under intense scrutiny. Before June 5 few but the staunchest supporters of Tijerina knew much about Alianza and its explosive claims. After the raid Tijerina became a national figure in the Chicano movement and a sought-after speaker on civil rights.

Alianza's tactics impressed the most radical social activists, Tijerina's rhetoric galvanized the most conservative land grant heirs, and his fantastic claims of land loss eventually convinced the most skeptical scholars. The law, however, took another view. A growing repressive reaction against Alianza that had been building slowly prior to the raid gained momentum afterward. Alianza and Tijerina became central obsessions of FBI director J. Edgar Hoover and COINTELPRO, his covert counterintelligence program. FBI agents doggedly tailed Tijerina everywhere. When Stokely Carmichael invited Tijerina to speak at a Black Panther "Free Huey Newton" rally in Oakland, the FBI tagged along to record the event. When Nation of Islam leader Elijah Muhammad invited Tijerina to Chicago, FBI agents fed Hoover constant updates. When the Poor People's Campaign invited Tijerina to fill in for a slain Martin Luther King Jr. and join Ralph Abernathy and Jesse Jackson in the Poor People's March in Washington, D.C., in 1968, plainclothes agents snapped photos and recorded speeches. Hoover briefed federal agencies, including the CIA, on Alianza's exploits and dubiously claimed that Tijerina was a subversive foreign agent. Eventually Tijerina landed on the FBI's notorious Rabble Rouser Index, an elevation that made him an official target of Hoover's counterintelligence apparatus. Not to be outdone, the New Mexico State Police organized and deployed a secret paramilitary squad of agents provocateurs to infiltrate, undermine, and destroy Alianza.

The covert war waged by law enforcement agencies against Alianza and the land grant movement unfolded alongside a different, public response. Federal agencies lined up to offer solutions to what many considered the intractable poverty that defined life in northern New Mexico. Antipoverty programs, idled after the Depression, were restarted. The Office of Economic Opportunity expanded projects in New Mexico. The State of New Mexico commissioned a report called the *Land Title Study*, which carefully examined the question of fairness in the adjudication of preexisting Spanish and Mexican property claims in New Mexico. The report concluded that much of what Tijerina and Alianza had been saying was true. Corrupt federal officials aided in a pattern of land speculation that began during New Mexico's territorial period (1848–1912) and ultimately dispossessed scores of land grant holders of their common property.[1]

Scholarly interest in Alianza and in the claims partially confirmed by the *Land Title Study* culminated in a body of historical research in the years after the courthouse raid that further ratified the fantastic claims of land loss and property theft. Speculators in the nineteenth century had manipulated the law and federal courts to advance dubious legal theories. Historians found that more than 80 percent of all Spanish and Mexican grants were lost to legitimate claimants.[2] Historian, lawyer, and land grant scholar Malcolm Ebright showed that U.S. courts confirmed only 6 percent of land grant property claims.[3] This new land grant historiography told a story of the wholesale dispossession of Spanish and Mexican land grants at the hands of corrupt bureaucrats and unchecked land speculators. It was a much different history than the tourist-friendly myth of peaceful tricultural coexistence that New Mexico boosters preferred.

Historians, journalists, federal agencies, foundations, and legislators told the story of New Mexico's land grants in the wake of the courthouse raid as one authored by a single group, Alianza, and one man, Tijerina, who apparently single-handedly brought the land grant fight into the mainstream of the larger civil rights movement in the late 1960s. Tijerina remains a significant historical figure in both New Mexican land grant politics and the national civil rights movement, and in the nearly fifty years since the raid, nearly every aspect of the land grant struggle, the courthouse raid, and the Alianza movement has been examined.

But while the media, the government, and civil rights activists were caught up in the historical significance and fantastic possibilities implied by the raid (revolution? communist conspiracy? guerilla war?), the nineteen courthouse raiders were not interested in advancing the cause of national civil rights. Rather, they were engaged in a struggle over local property rights. In the days leading up to the raid, law enforcement officials in New Mexico had become increasingly convinced that Alianza planned a hostile takeover of the Tierra Amarilla land grant.

Of all the notorious conflicts that populate New Mexico's land grant history, Tierra Amarilla ranks among perhaps the most sensational and yet the least known. From early in New Mexico's territorial period, land speculators targeted Tierra Amarilla, a collection of small villages populated by smallholder ranchers and farmers along New Mexico's border with Colorado in a region rich with timber, mineral, and grazing resources. The names of the speculators who pursued Tierra Amarilla during the late nineteenth century read like a who's who of New Mexico's political and economic elite. Their dubious acquisition of Tierra Amarilla in the late nineteenth century created new millionaires, huge land barons, and lasting conflict. Resistance to these patterns of speculation in Tierra

Amarilla has been persistent and fierce. But the story of property dispossession in Tierra Amarilla is usually told as a nineteenth-century tale of land loss punctuated by an explosive but fleeting eruption of pent-up rage by Alianza and Tijerina in the 1960s. As a result, a more complicated history of land struggle and its contemporary manifestations has been obscured.

This book takes a different view. Though Tijerina talked the language of civil rights, the land grant movement that he popularized was a property rights movement. And though credit is usually given to Tijerina, he was not the first to reveal the consequences and contradictions of New Mexico's colonial past. The settlers and heirs of the Tierra Amarilla land grant were among the first to organize on a large scale and fight for the return of lands lost to outside speculators. As this book shows, they were among the first to identify the enclosures as a threat to common property land grant communities during the territorial period, the first to go to court to stop the patterns of privatization, and among the first to take up arms against the state and private ranchers.

Property and the Problem of Spanish and Mexican Land Grant History

Outside of the work of Alianza and a few other sensational stories, the long history of resistance to land loss in northern New Mexico and the particular tactics and rhetoric of that resistance is not well known.[4] According to most historians and scholars of New Mexico's land grants, the story of land grant dispossession is not one of active, sophisticated, and ongoing struggle. Rather, the land grant story is one of legal dispossession in the past in which the patterns of speculation and land loss during New Mexico's territorial period were a function of the almost impossibly contradictory and unresolvable conflicts that arose with the United States' arrival in the mid-nineteenth century, when the largely fee simple property rubric found in Anglo law collided with the common property relations of Spanish and Mexican law in New Mexico.

Ebright says it most emphatically when he declares, "The main reason for [land loss] was that the land grants were established under one legal system and adjudicated under another."[5] Historian Maria Montoya makes a similar, though more nuanced, argument. The failure of U.S. courts to properly translate Spanish or Mexican land policies stemmed from the commercial, colonialist motivations of the United States, in which the United States imposed new private property relations as a way to "establish a conquered, colonized, and dependent region."[6] Dispossession, according to Montoya, occurred because of contradictions in property law. "The U.S. legal system," she concludes, "could not incorporate the informal property regime that had evolved under Mexican law, and consequently the *peones* and settlers lost what few property rights they had established."[7]

According to this version of property dispossession, a cabal of cunning speculators understood and exploited these legal incompatibilities to their benefit.[8] It is a compelling argument. The early 1880s marked an era of speculation in New Mexico that exposed its isolated rural villages to finance capital and speculative investment. As railroads worked their way west, speculative investment surged into New Mexico from places as far afield as Amsterdam, London, and the major centers of East Coast U.S. finance. These economic forces transformed social relations, cultural traditions, production practices, and, ultimately, property relations.

Following the Treaty of Guadalupe Hidalgo that ended the U.S.-Mexican War, the United States undertook a lengthy adjudication process of Spanish and Mexican property claims throughout the newly acquired territory. Scholarly research has focused on the problems that confronted both U.S. officials and land grant settlers seeking patents to grants given under Spain or Mexico.[9] But this preoccupation with contradictory tensions in Spanish and Anglo legal codes, or with the unfortunate misapplication of legal standards, has reduced the study of land grant loss to a series of technical legal questions regarding treaty obligations and legal decisions. It takes the law for granted as a "given," a kind of container in which property struggles and ultimately dispossession took place.

Such a view is understandable because it is difficult to see property, as the legal geographer Nicholas Blomley puts it, as anything other than an object or a natural part of the landscape. Law and property appear to reflect the "order of things." Property appears self-evident and thus needs no close scrutiny. For this reason it is difficult to understand law or property as anything other than "apolitical, impersonal and inevitable."[10]

To critical legal scholars, this is a familiar depiction of law.[11] Rather than understanding law as an arena of conflict, historians of New Mexico's land grants often depict it as a taken-for-granted category, as part of the landscape — a geographical "fact" no different than the existence of the pine forests that blanket the mountains surrounding Tierra Amarilla. As Blomley notes, "Despite [the law's] manifest exclusions, expulsions, and violences, it appears equitable and benign."[12] This is how the law has been understood in New Mexico's land grant history. But taking law for granted as such obscures a more complicated view of property.

In this book I draw on the work of legal geographers and critical legal studies scholars in order to overcome this preoccupation with an overly legalistic explanation for property dispossession in New Mexico. I argue that the collision of two kinds of property law — common property versus private property — cannot explain land loss in New Mexico because law and property are not independent objects that operate on society and *cause* land loss. Rather, law is a site of social struggle where claims over property are constructed and contested. This struggle for New Mexico's Spanish and Mexican land grants, and the valuable natural resources found within their boundaries, was a struggle over the very meaning of property that played out in courts and on the ground.

It would be a simplification, however, to claim that property is not a legal object or category but rather a site of struggle. Property is interesting for its dual nature as both object and relation. The law describes private property as a bundle of "sticks" or rights that are conferred by law to a legitimate owner. These rights include the right to sell, rent, and exclude, among others, and those rights are enforced by the state. In this sense property defines a relation between an "owner" and a "thing." Property, in other words, as an object. But as Blomley notes, slyly tweaking the metaphor, property is "a bundle of sticks, with which one can beat one's neighbor."[13] In this sense property also defines contentious social relations *among people over things*. Property is therefore not only a legal right that defines a relationship between a person and an object, but it is also a set of social relations among people enforced by the state. Property, in other words, is about social ordering: who gets what, who gets excluded, and how.

The purpose of this book is to examine the struggle over that social order. I am interested in the political constructions and enforcement of various kinds of property relations in Tierra Amarilla, from the common property during the Spanish and Mexican period to the assertions of private property claims after the United States arrived. For this reason I begin the book by examining the role of Indian removal in the origins of the Mexican land grant of Tierra Amarilla. Spain and Mexico erased Ute and Apache claims to Tierra Amarilla in the mid-nineteenth century in a project that culminated in the 1860s and 1870s when the Bureau of Indian Affairs implemented aggressive policies of administrative and spatial control over nomadic Indians in New Mexico. The Southern Utes, an adversary of Spanish and Mexican authorities and settlers who repeatedly tried to settle Tierra Amarilla, became a particular target of Indian agents and political appointees after 1848. Because property is not understood as a form of political struggle, the interruption of Ute and Apache claims to Tierra Amarilla and the imposition of new forms of spatial and social control have been bracketed out of histories of land grant dispossession in New Mexico.[14] Far from unrelated, however, the removal of the Utes and the Apaches was a necessary condition for the establishment of Spanish and Mexican common property land grants in northern New Mexico. Indian dispossession began with Spanish and Mexican land grants and was finally accomplished through the negotiation of treaties and the forced removal of tribes by U.S. federal troops.

As I examine in chapter 1, land grant settlers in Tierra Amarilla were central players in this process. Mexican settlement in Tierra Amarilla required the broad adoption of policies and practices of Indian displacement that made common property land grants possible. The struggle over property in northern New Mexico, whether under Spain, Mexico, or the new U.S. sovereign, was a struggle predicated on Indian removal.[15] By placing the origins of Mexican property claims to Tierra Amarilla in the context of a colonial history defined by violent conflict over land and resources between common property claimants and various Indian societies in northern New Mexico, I offer an alternative framework to understand the struggle for Mexican property rights in that area. I believe this is an important clarification in the historical and social production of property claims, and the social struggle over those claims.

My purpose for doing this, however, is not to locate a legitimate property claim or undermine contemporary Mexican-derived claims to Tierra Amarilla. As I argue in this book, the settlers who moved north into the Indian borderlands of Tierra Amarilla were colonial subjects in ways similar to the Utes and the Apaches whom they displaced. Other than Montoya's book on the Maxwell land grant, however, the various studies of conflict over particular Spanish and Mexican colonial property claims in New Mexico have ignored the ways in which land grants were constituted in violent, colonial contexts and what this may mean for contemporary property claims in New Mexico. Close examination of the constitution and the struggle over property provides an opportunity to understand how colonialism worked on the ground, how settler colonialism displaced preexisting social relations, and how property ultimately came to be redefined as something in opposition to both Ute and Mexican claims.

In this book I focus on the particular histories and spatial patterns of property struggle in Tierra Amarilla. I demonstrate that Tierra Amarilla land grant settlers participated in the processes of Indian removal that made their claims possible, found themselves made colonial subjects similar to Utes and Apaches, were well aware of the efforts by speculators to enclose the commons, and organized sophisticated patterns of legal resistance against those seeking to transform Tierra Amarilla into private property. They organized, conducted research, and even, on occasion, took up arms to defend their claims. Their resistance included multifaceted challenges to the reified relations of private property. As the land grant heirs demonstrated through years of active resistance, it was not just elite political and commercial interests in territorial New Mexico who had a sophisticated understanding of the legalities and politics of property.

The heirs went to great lengths to stage public performances of their property rights. When judges dismissed their claims, they ignored the judges and enacted common property relations anyway. They erected fences around common pastures and cut down those on private ranches. When the courts found their claims lacking, they wrote new deeds and distributed property to their members. Histories of New Mexico's land grants may say that the land was lost in the nineteenth century, but common property persisted well into the middle of the twentieth century in a pattern that challenges stories of land grant dispossession as an historical event rather than an ongoing struggle. Ultimately their resistance to the law's construction of private property provoked a unified and repressive reaction from the police and various agents of the state.

The Violent Properties of Tierra Amarilla

The title of this book, *Properties of Violence*, reflects a central theme of the study. Violent clashes between Tierra Amarilla land grant settlers and Indian tribes established Mexican claims in the nineteenth century. Conflicts between heirs and Anglo ranchers transformed common property relations in the twentieth century, and conflicts between heirs and law enforcement officials have continued well into the 1990s. These conflicts have included night riding and fence cutting, pitched gun battles, and tanks rumbling along the rutted dirt roads of northern New Mexico. But these violent practices and events, I argue, are not merely the effects of property conflicts or the result of legal struggle. Rather the legal geographies of property in Tierra Amarilla reveal that violence is inherent to law and property.

I realize the incredulity some may bring to claims of law's and property's inherent violence. Law presents itself as anything but violent. It is supposed to be apolitical and based on universal rules and standards that stand in opposition to violence. Where would we be, after all, without law and the social order it ensures? According to this view, violence is the very antithesis of what is legal. I argue the opposite, namely, that violence is inherent to law, particularly property law. "All law which concerns property," legal scholar Robert Cover famously wrote, has a "violent base."[16] The violence to which Cover refers is the legitimating violence made possible through legal interpretations of rights. As Cover points out, legal interpretation necessarily concludes with legal decisions that often require force in their implementation. Whether in a sentence of death or a quiet title lawsuit, law, to be lawful, requires that it be enforced. "Naturally, one who is to be punished may have to be coerced," Cover observes. "And punishment, if it is 'just,' supposedly legitimates the coercion or violence applied."[17] In this sense law can only be said to expel violence from society because it monopolizes it. It is real violence hidden in plain sight.

Law, particularly property law, is defined, moreover, by practices of legal interpretation that Cover has described as "staked in blood." Legal interpretation appears disinterested but requires violent enforcement by legal agents, agents who the historian Charles Tilly reminds us, "specialize in inflicting physical damage."[18] Law's use of violence and its relation to social order obscure a central irony: violence is not the opposite of law but rather is essential to its operation. Violence "is domesticated, concentrated, rationalized, and deposited in law for safekeeping."[19] Violence cannot be explained away as an unintended effect of law but rather must be understood as a central "principle of property."[20] In the many lawsuits that dominated the struggle in the twentieth century, for example, judges constructed an entirely new history of property. As I show in this book, they reached back into the past and replaced histories of common property with private property. And these practices of legal interpretation were followed by patterns of violent enforcement by agents of the state.

The suspicion that violence lurks in the heart of law is not limited to critical legal scholars. Similar concerns preoccupied the German cultural critic Walter Benjamin in the 1920s. In trying to come to terms with the rise of Nazism in postwar Germany, Benjamin turned to an examination of the law's relation to violence and justice and the role of the police in what he called "law-making" and "law-preserving." He concluded that the "sanctioned" violence of the state laid bare the inherently violent nature of law. It is not possible, he concluded, to separate violence from law. However obscured from its origins and the forces that maintain it, the law owes its existence to violence, and violence is always either engaged in making law, in its origins, or in preserving it through the practices or threat of violent enforcement. "Lawmaking pursues as its end," he wrote "with violence as the means, what is to be established as law, but at the moment of instatement does not dismiss violence; rather, at this very moment of lawmaking, it specifically establishes as law not an end unalloyed by violence, but one necessarily and intimately bound to it, under the title of power. Lawmaking is power making, and, to that extent, an immediate manifestation of violence."[21]

To Benjamin law's violence revealed a central paradox. Violence is not just a method of enforcement but is also a means to reinforce the legitimacy of law in the face of other claims to truth. In its first instance the law appears in violent opposition to a competing claim to authority. The origins of law are therefore violent moments of rupture in which the law appears as both just and unjust. For French philosopher Jacques Derrida this paradox defines what he calls law's "mystical foundation of authority." For this reason challenges to private property are particularly threatening to the state. "What the State fears... is not so much crime or *brigandage*, as long as they transgress the law with an eye toward particular benefits, however important they may be. Rather the State is afraid of fundamental, founding violence, that is, violence able to justify, to legitimate ... or to transform the relations of law, and so to present itself as having a right to law."[22]

New Mexico is an ideal place to examine the struggle over law and property and the ways in which violence constitutes not only law and property relations but wider social relations as well. In the colonial context of New Mexico, the legal transfer of property from one group to another, whether Indian removal or Mexican dispossession, has depended on law's violence. And this violence has been at the heart of property relations. As the historian Ned Blackhawk has argued, violence has been central to the conflict over territory in northern New Mexico. The Spanish and Mexican societies that relentlessly coveted land along the Ute frontier and the Indian nations eventually dispossessed of those lands "remade themselves in response to the region's cycles of violence."[23] These cycles of violence not only constituted New Mexico's colonial borderlands societies but also, in a very direct way, created the conditions for Mexican, and later U.S., property claims for Tierra Amarilla. The legal theories that erased land grant property relations legitimated not only strictly private property claims but also sanctioned the physical violence necessary to accomplish this transformation.

Frances Leon Swadesh's seminal book *Los Primeros Pobladores* examines at length the violence that permeated frontier society in northern New Mexico, where slavery, kidnapping, and punitive raiding parties were central elements of everyday life. Swadesh examines the incomparable cruelty of frontier violence in terms that almost treat violence as a cultural form. I depart from Swadesh's culturalist explanation of violence, however, in order to argue that the violent politics of property in the long struggle for Tierra Amarilla suggest deeper truths, not only about New Mexico but also about the law, namely, that while the law can be said to mediate conflicts, it can also produce the conditions for those conflicts.

The dispossession of Ute and Mexican property claims was accomplished through the application of force and sustained through coercive systems of authority. To examine these violent legal geographies of property in Tierra Amarilla, I focus on key sites of law's violence and property's production: at the moments of property's legal origins; at the sites and struggles over legal and social legitimation of property; and when the actual use or threat of force imposes or sustains particular property rights.

The Plan of the Book

In the chapters that follow I trace the history of property struggle in Tierra Amarilla among Ute, Apache, Mexican, and Anglo claimants and follow the conflict into the contemporary moment as political struggles over property dominate current debates over development in northern New Mexico. I am interested in how, and to what ends, land grant heirs identified the law and the legal process as the focus of their active resistance to the loss of the commons. In ways dramatic and everyday, various claimants enacted and performed property relations as a means of directly reinforcing or challenging and overcoming the legal construction of private property on the land grant.

My focus on law and the legal system suggests that land grant settlers had a keen and sophisticated grasp of the law as both a means and a method of resistance. From the very beginning, in the 1860s, land grant settlers advanced an alternative sociolegal history of property in Tierra Amarilla that subverted the legal story of private property. They tapped into what they considered the dual nature of the law as, on the one hand, something that reflected the brute logic of repression and, on the other hand, a site for emancipatory resistance.

The prologue that follows this introduction describes the first efforts among Spanish authorities to draw Tierra Amarilla, Yellow Earth in English, into the orbit of Spanish colonial administration. In chapter 1 I examine not only the patterns and consequences of settlement in Tierra Amarilla in the early years of U.S. rule in New Mexico, but also the politics of law and property and the role of violence in the construction of property claims. The origins of Mexican property claims to Tierra Amarilla, I show, are found in a climate of political turmoil and escalating violence. Thus considerable effort in chapter 1 is given to understanding how these struggles resulted in Indian removal, which established the conditions for private claims to Tierra Amarilla.

In chapter 2 I follow a familiar arc in land grant studies. The story usually goes something like this: when the United States acquired Mexico in 1848, clever, conniving land speculators, aided by politicians, lawyers, and federal bureaucrats, stole millions of acres of common property from the many Spanish and Mexican community land grants in northern New Mexico. They took advantage of illiterate Mexican settlers who were ignorant of legal processes, could not speak English, and were oblivious to the legal dispossession going on around them. In this version of New Mexico's territorial history, land grant communities were the victims of a rat's nest of nefarious and conspiratorial characters who robbed land grant communities of their common lands. Through dubious tactics speculators employed every trick, legal or otherwise, to acquire vast acreages in New Mexico. As I try to demonstrate, however, this history is both a historical fact upon which generations of heirs have built opposition and a convenient fiction that imagines dispossession as an event rather than a historic and ongoing struggle.

Chapter 3 traces the beginnings of organized resistance to land speculation in Tierra Amarilla. In the second and third decades of the twentieth century, large commercial ranchers fenced the common pastures that local sheepherders depended on for their livelihoods. The entire region erupted in years of widespread rural violence characterized by fence cutting, barn burning, and physical violence and intimidation. Clandestine night riders cut fences and burned the haystacks, barns, and even homes of private ranchers and their political protectors. A secret organization called La Mano Negra (the Black Hand) claimed responsibility for this campaign of property damage. For more than a decade its members bullied wealthy newcomers and commercial ranchers and intimidated Anglo merchants and politicians in an attempt to reassert common property use of the grant. But the story of La Mano Negra, as I demonstrate, is only part of a much more complicated struggle over property and land grant resistance that revolved around increasingly racialized struggles over property and citizenship.

In chapter 4 I examine the legal geographies of resistance that began with the birth of an organization called La Corporación de Abiquiú, Merced de Tierra Amarilla (the Corporation of Abiquiú, Tierra Amarilla land grant). La Corporación seized property, wrote new deeds, and registered them with the county clerk. It tried to evict nonheirs and demanded financial compensation for encroachments on what it still considered the commons. It distributed property to members of La Corporación and it defended these new property rights with its own police force. The fascinating legal struggles of the 1930s and 1940s, struggles completely ignored in land grant studies, suggest that the land grant heirs were sophisticated legal actors and became effective at using the courts and the law in the struggle over property. La Corporación brought the issue into the courts on four occasions. I examine these court struggles in order to understand law as a site of social struggle and to understand how law replaced a history of common property in Tierra Amarilla with private property.

In chapter 5 I return to the land grant war provoked by the courthouse raid discussed briefly above. I pay particular attention to the secret history of state-sponsored and state-tolerated violence directed at land grant activists in New Mexico. The legal theories that erased common property relations legitimated not only new private property claims to Tierra Amarilla but also sanctioned the physical violence against land grant claimants during the 1960s. The FBI and the New Mexico State Police infiltrated land grant organizations and began active surveillance and counterintelligence operations against land grant activists in Tierra Amarilla as early as 1963.

In chapter 6 I tell the story of the Chicano political party La Raza Unida and a group called El Consejo de la Tierra Amarilla. La Raza Unida brought young Chicano political activists into contact with land grant heirs in campaigns against police violence and political repression in northern New Mexico. It argued that police violence reinforced the conditions of land loss for land grant communities and replayed colonial patterns of dispossession. The conflict erupted in 1989 when a Tierra Amarilla man named Amador Flores claimed a small parcel of land on the Tierra Amarilla land grant and declared it the common property of all heirs. A small number of followers, supported by a large army of sympathizers, dug foxholes, distributed booby traps around the property, and dug in for what became a fourteen-month standoff with police.

In the epilogue I examine struggles over the land that were unfolding as I was writing this book. Current conflicts over development and planning on the former common lands of the Tierra Amarilla land grant suggest that the context of land grant struggle is increasingly one defined by a depoliticized logic of the market and the language of rational planning. Comprehensive planning, premised on the logic of development economics, has effectively displaced questions of legal rights and social justice and shifted the conflict from a legal fight over the constitution of property rights to one preoccupied with technical questions regarding land development. I examine how these current development controversies in Tierra Amarilla have replaced the logic of the law as a key arena of social struggle, one that has so far proven much more difficult for land grant activists to navigate. As the struggle has shifted from property law to bureaucratic and administrative planning processes, new logics continue to obscure the politics of property on the Tierra Amarilla land grant.

PROLOGUE

Yellow Earth

WHEN THE SPANISH MISSIONARY-EXPLORERS Fray Atanasio Dominguez and Fray Francisco Silvestre Vélez de Escalante left Santa Fe on July 29, 1776, they and a small detail of military and civil aides labored north on familiar trade routes up dry mesas and through piñon-juniper forests alongside the Rio Grande's dense cottonwood *bosque*, or forest. The pair had been charged with opening a direct trading route that would link Spanish colonial New Mexico to new Spanish settlements in California. The route was crucial to the survival of Spanish New Mexico, where "powerful Indian societies controlled most of the territory New Spain claimed with its northern boundary."[1]

By the end of their first day on the trail, the party had reached the confluence of the Rio de Chama and the Rio Grande, the site where Juan de Oñate brought a wagon train of settlers and soldiers north from Zacatecas in 1598 to establish Spain's first permanent settlement in New Mexico. Oñate's short rule in New Mexico was marked by a relentless military campaign against Pueblo Indian communities up and down the Rio Grande. When the mesa-top pueblo of Acoma resisted Oñate's authority, he launched a three-day siege of the pueblo. Oñate's soldiers killed nearly two thousand members of the pueblo during the short battle and burned Acoma to the ground. The children who survived the slaughter were shipped off to convents in Mexico City. Adult women were enslaved. Spanish authorities hauled the few men who survived the "war by blood and fire" on a gruesome publicity tour of various other pueblos, where their public punishments, including the amputation of their right leg below the knee, served as a grisly warning to potential insurgents and sympathizers.[2]

The violence of Oñate's campaign put Spanish and Pueblo Indians on a collision course that exploded in 1680, when Pueblo villages along the Rio Grande conspired to eject the Spanish from New Mexico. In a violent uprising they routed Spanish troops and expelled Spanish settlers from the Rio Grande valley.[3] The Spanish reconquest twelve years later relied on new patterns of diplomacy and military authority in New Mexico. While diplomacy rather than brute force characterized the Spanish reconquest and largely resolved hostilities between Spanish settlers and Rio Grande Pueblos, volatile relations with the powerful equestrian societies that surrounded New Mexico threatened to once again undermine Spain's tenuous foothold in New Mexico.

Various Indian nations controlled huge swaths of what Spain considered its northern boundary in the New World. The Utes had displaced the Navajos out of the Upper San Juan Basin in the early eighteenth century and asserted political and military authority in a region stretching from Santa Fe into present-day southern Utah and central Colorado. Their equestrian prowess threatened more than Navajo political and economic power, however, as it also threatened Pueblo Indian communities and Spanish settlements along the Rio Grande Valley in New Mexico. The Utes attacked Taos in 1716 and, combined with the growing military and economic power of other equestrian societies such as the Apaches and the Comanches, posed a difficult challenge to Spanish settlements in New Mexico.

In 1749 the new Spanish governor of New Mexico, Tomás Vélez Cachupín, concluded that the only way to ensure Spanish security in New Mexico was to interrupt existing Indian alliances along the northern borderlands. He bristled at what he considered the shortsightedness of militarized Spanish policies governing frontier politics and argued for diplomacy alone as the key to peaceful frontier Indian relations. He pursued a policy of Spanish-Indian trading and found an ideal ally in the various Ute bands along New Mexico's northern border.[4] He exploited increasingly strained Ute-Comanche relations by establishing a 1752 peace accord with a Ute coalition and then restricted access to Ute lands in order to avoid unnecessary conflict. Eventually, the Spanish-Ute alliance proved to be an important countervailing force to Comanche and Navajo conflict and assured, at least temporarily, consistent and peaceful trade relations. "The conservation of the friendship of this Ute nation and the rest of its allied tribes," Cachupín explained to his Spanish superiors, "is of the greatest consideration because of the favorable results which their trade and good relations bring to this province."[5]

The strategy required a network of frontier trading outposts along the northern borderlands, linked to Santa Fe, where Spanish traders could establish trade relationships with Utes and other Indian nations. While Cachupín's diplomatic strategy insulated Santa Fe from borderlands conflict, violence along the northern borderlands increased. The trade that sustained borderlands villages like Abiquiú, northwest of Santa Fe, cemented close Spanish-Ute relations but also contributed to, and exacerbated, forms of borderlands violence. Trade relations were punctuated by violent conflicts and simmering animosities, exacerbated by a burgeoning slave trade. Despite diplomatic efforts, Indian aggression toward Spanish settlement reshaped the colonial geographies in dramatic ways as villages and pueblos throughout northern New Mexico were abandoned.[6] Brutal conflicts with the Comanches dominated 1770s New Mexico. In July 1773, five hundred Comanches attacked Cochiti, south of Santa Fe.[7] At the same time, frequent Navajo raids stretched Spanish defenses to the breaking point.[8] A state of constant war nearly drove the Spanish from New Mexico.

By 1776 Spanish authorities had lost faith in military or diplomatic solutions to Spanish-Indian conflicts and looked for other ways to stabilize colonial settlements. Between 1770 and 1800 ten major expeditions radiated out from Santa Fe in all directions in search of defensible trade routes to California as an alternative to the failed policies of Spanish-Indian trade enforced through military violence and diplomacy.[9] Utes, Navajos, and Comanches, among other Indian nations, responded by seeking new alliances of their own in increasingly tense efforts to oppose Spanish encroachments.

This was the political turmoil into which Dominguez and Escalante marched in July 1776. Despite a quarter century of close trade relations with the Utes, they knew very little about the geographies of Ute society north of existing Spanish settlements. At the time, seven distinct Ute bands controlled a vast western territory centered in the southern Rocky Mountains. Capote and Mouache bands occupied the southern edge of this territory adjacent to Spanish settlements north of Santa Fe. To the west the Weeminuche band occupied most of what is today southwest Colorado extending into present-day Utah. Four other bands extended Ute territory north and east of Colorado.[10]

On the morning of July 29 the expedition left the confluence of the Rio de Chama and the Rio Grande and trekked north toward Abiquiú. Abiquiú had been the linchpin in Cachupín's diplomatic strategy of Ute pacification. As the largest trading center northwest of Santa Fe, it served as a commercial hub linking the rest of New Mexico to Indian societies north and west. As Dominguez noted in his journal, "many heathens of the Ute nation" relied on seasonal trade fairs in Abiquiú that brought Indian societies and Spanish traders into economic and social relations that included not only the exchange of horses, furs, and agricultural products but also, as Dominguez noted, a bustling trade in human captives.[11]

Suspended between an expansionist colonial power and unyielding indigenous nations, Abiquiú was a site where conflict and commerce merged in a grim economy in Indian captives, often Navajos and Paiutes. Slave taking and trading played a central role in the complicated political economy of the Spanish-Indian borderlands, where human bodies proved to be valuable commodities for the frontier slave traders who served the slave-labor economy of northern New Spain. As the historian Ned Blackhawk notes, "Captives were overwhelmingly young women and children whose sexual and reproductive labor became essential to the colony."[12] But as Spanish settlements increasingly relied on slave labor (despite official Spanish condemnation of the practice), the Indian slave raiding that served those needs increased the instability of an already volatile frontier.

Abiquiú lay at the confluence of a radial network of trade routes that connected Spanish villages and brought Indian societies into New Mexico. None of these was more important than the routes through the Tierra Amarilla valley. The valley served as an important corridor through which Navajo, Comanche, and Apache bands traveled.[13] Likewise, Spanish traders and militia relied on the corridor for economic and military purposes. The valley was more than merely a trade corridor; Abiquiú sheepherders coveted the vast grasslands of Tierra Amarilla, and Capote Utes depended on the uplands for hunting and gathering.

Throughout the eighteenth century, scores of Abiquiú settlers ignored Ute claims and pestered Spanish authorities for permission to settle Tierra Amarilla.[14] The fact that permissions were never given, despite liberal settlement policies elsewhere in New Mexico, testified to the diplomatic importance Spanish authorities placed on the region. Permissions and plans for northern expansion into Tierra Amarilla remained off limits in the late eighteenth century. Even decades later, well into the 1820s, authorities remained concerned that settlement north of Abiquiú would inflame the Utes and topple Spain's, and later Mexico's, precarious place on the Indian borderlands. Despite the shift in diplomacy reflected in the purpose of the Dominguez and Escalante expedition, Abiquiú and Tierra Amarilla remained strategically important to Spain but beyond the ability of its sparse military to control.[15]

Dominguez and Escalante's party arrived in Abiquiú late in the afternoon of July 30. Though they were only days into a long journey, they lingered in the village, reluctant, it seems, to move further into Ute territory. Escalante provided no explanation in the official journal for the delay and instead wrote of long days spent attending mass and praying, perhaps nervous at the prospect of traveling north into Tierra Amarilla, a valley locals called "the lands of war," where Apaches, Navajos, and Comanches frequently swept down into New Mexico to raid Rio de Chama villages.[16]

The settlers whom Dominguez and Escalante encountered in Abiquiú were only a generation removed from conflicts that had nearly ended Spanish settlement in the region. Attacks and reprisals in 1746 between Spanish militias and allied groups of Utes and Comanches culminated in a devastating Ute-Comanche raid on Abiquiú in 1747.[17] In the aftermath of the raid, Cachupín's predecessor ordered the abandonment of Abiquiú and surrounding villages.

Cachupín later ordered settlers to return to Abiquiú, but the frightened settlers refused to return.[18] Desperate to reestablish Abiquiú as a trading center and military garrison, Cachupín found willing settlers among dispossessed, displaced, and "exiled Indian peoples from Hopi and other pueblos as well as northern Indian captives."[19]

Among the manifold effects of Indian slavery that troubled Spanish authorities, one was most pressing. What to do with the freed adults and the children of captive Indians acquired by ransom or obtained at the many trade fairs in and around Abiquiú? In the complicated caste and class society of colonial New Mexico, detribalized Indians, known as Genízaros, occupied a cultural borderlands, no longer members of Indian nations or citizens of colonial New Spain. Abiquiú became the only official Spanish property claim extended specifically to former Indian slaves and the children of former slaves.[20] Cachupín's elevation of Genízaros to property holders in the mid-1700s came not from egalitarian notions of fairness but rather from the practical politics of borderlands security. Genízaro Abiquiú became an important geographical and cultural borderlands village that linked Spanish and Indian societies in captivity and commerce.

Dominguez and Escalante finally left Abiquiú on August 1 and continued northwest along the Rio de Chama through grueling box canyons and rugged mesas until, in the afternoon of the first day, they turned north to follow a rising plateau into ponderosa pine forests. Rain halted their progress. The following day they traveled further into the high-elevation forests that floated like islands over the vast grasslands of the Tierra Amarilla valley. In the expedition's official journal, Escalante described hiking down into a wide valley unlike any he had seen elsewhere in northern New Spain, ringed by forested slopes and groves of white poplar. It was a valley with "abundant pasturage" with everything, he suggested, that a Spanish settlement would need.[21] The party decamped early on August 4 and hiked north through the valley in the shadow of the massive exposed granite face of what Mexican settlers would later call Brazos Peak, a solid and looming ridge that dropped like a curtain along the valley's eastern edge. In winter deep snow blanketed the ridges and spread out along the length of the peak, and in summer the wide valley was thick with grasses that Dominguez described as fields of flax.

As the expedition pressed further into Ute territory, its route became less direct. And as the weeks wore on, its official mission gave way to more personal, religious concerns. The Spaniards lingered for months in present-day Utah and Arizona, fascinated by the Indian societies they found. They lost interest in commercial trail blazing and devoted increasingly more effort to missionary pursuits. They never reached California. Illness and the frightening prospect of winter travel forced them back to Santa Fe. Their return in early 1777 coincided with increased Spanish-Indian conflict amid an official policy of Spanish retrenchment in New Mexico caused by a fiscal crisis that gutted Spanish administration throughout northern New Spain. Their expedition, as with all the others, failed to find useful trade routes. Stretched thin and lacking revenue, Spanish New Mexico was close to collapse as the budget for military preparedness and Indian diplomacy plummeted in New Mexico between 1789 and 1811.[22] New Mexico's Spanish authorities had few options with which to maintain peaceful Spanish-Ute relations. Without Spanish trade Ute bands saw no compelling reason to ally with Spain against other Indian societies.

The end of the Dominguez-Escalante expedition coincided also with more intense claims by Abiquiú settlers on the Tierra Amarilla valley. Though the use was not sanctioned through official property rights, Abiquiú's many sheep and cattle ranchers used Tierra Amarilla pastures for seasonal grazing and perhaps, like the Utes, for hunting. They built rough-hewn structures from piñon and juniper branches and fortified these with plaster made of local mud. These *jacales*, as they are still called, were surrounded by simple corrals that accommodated their small herds. Only suggestive traces of this historic use remain.[23] Within a generation, however, a growing clamor for land found its way into official requests for permanent settlements in Tierra Amarilla.

In 1814 a group of more than seventy Abiquiú residents petitioned the Spanish governor for a common property grant of land in Tierra Amarilla.[24] The request was rejected without comment. Six years later, more than sixty residents (many were holdovers from the first request) petitioned once again for a community land grant in Tierra Amarilla.[25] As with the 1814 application, no record exists of any official explanation for the rejection. Although the political agreements that limited expansion into Ute lands no longer existed, the rejections suggest that Spanish authorities may have hoped to limit settlement in Tierra Amarilla as a way to salvage Spanish-Ute relations. In the volatile political context of Spanish New Mexico in the early nineteenth century, the first two requests for land deep inside Ute territory in Tierra Amarilla provided few economic or political advantages to Spain.

Mexico declared its independence from Spain in 1821 and in 1824 promulgated new laws governing property distribution and colonization. The year 1824 also marked the third time that Abiquiú residents requested property in Tierra Amarilla. Despite recent changes in colonization policies, Tierra Amarilla remained off-limits for Abiquiú's growing population. The third petition, like the others, was rejected without comment.[26]

This third rejection must have been particularly frustrating for Abiquiú's many small ranchers. From a village of less than forty families in 1740, its population had grown to more than 1,700 in 1789 at the beginning of Spanish retrenchment and had reached 3,500 residents by the time Mexico declared its independence from Spain in 1821.[27] What was once an isolated frontier outpost surrounded by pastures, agricultural fields, and Indian societies was, by the early 1800s, a regional marketplace, a military garrison, and one of New Mexico's critical administrative centers. As Abiquiú's population grew, social divisions deepened. Hispanic elites increasingly enticed by land on the frontier appropriated Genízaro property. The land grabs also included individual alienations of common property through land sales from Genízaros to Hispanic elites. In defense of common lands, many Genízaro grantees filed lawsuits that charged two territorial governors, a local priest, and a man named Manuel Martínez with land speculation.[28]

Martínez was a prominent Abiquiú resident, a property owner with a large cattle herd, and connections to the colony's political and military class. Throughout his adult life Martínez, the man who would eventually secure an official claim to Tierra Amarilla, successfully navigated the tangle of Spanish and Mexican administrative authority with a skill rooted in a privileged economic and political position in borderlands society. Martínez had been party to the previous petitions to acquire Tierra Amarilla, always describing his need for land as necessary to accommodate his meager herds and current landholdings. Yet the fact that he owned private land at all placed him in a rarefied position in Abiquiú, a community comprised largely of landless laborers and weavers or sheepherders dependent on the common use of local pastures. He was linked by marriage to José María Chavez, a prominent Abiquiú resident and a man who served in military leadership under all three sovereigns: Spain, Mexico, and the United States.[29] Martínez's political connections were also a function of his fluency in Spanish and Mexican administrative governance and an ability to navigate the shifting territorial bureaucracies that governed the distribution of property along the frontier. Tierra Amarilla's official Mexican origins begin with Martínez.

Tierra Amarilla's Mexican Origins

The history of Manuel Martínez's efforts to secure a land grant in Tierra Amarilla is not a story of Tierra Amarilla's legitimate legal and social origins but rather a history of political efforts to impose durable property relations in a volatile borderlands region defined by overlapping and often complexly intertwined Mexican and Indian claims. Through much of the summer of 1832, Martínez circulated various petitions, appeals, and reports among political officials in which he made a new request for land in Tierra Amarilla. The record of this correspondence provides what appears at first blush to be an informal exchange between Martínez and various officials regarding the possibilities of a property claim in Tierra Amarilla.[30] Martínez was in fact closely following the legal requirements for property making codified in the Mexican Colonization Law of 1824 and the Regulations of 1828. The regulations streamlined the diverse frontier property-making practices in Mexico's northern territories. According to the colonization codes, all petitioners were required to direct requests first to the territorial governor, who was then required to turn to local political authorities for advice. Local officials investigated the requested grant of land for adverse claims, including rights reserved by Indian societies. If the subsequent report supported the petition, the governor directed the local political chief to place the settler or settlers in possession of property. If a grant was approved, the documents that registered this process — the petition, the report, and the granting decree — were combined into an official record known as the land grant *expediente*. The *expediente* served two mutually reinforcing purposes: first, as a story of property origins that chronicled the grant-making process, and second, as the legal patent to property.

The Mexican claim to Tierra Amarilla began in April 1832, when the Mexican territorial governor of New Mexico, Santiago Abreu, received Martínez's request. Unlike the three previous petitions, this one was a request for a private grant to Martínez "together with eight sons and some others who voluntarily desire[d] to accompany [him] ... in the name of the Sovereignty of the Mexican nation, to which [they had] the honor of belonging."[31] In the petition Martínez assured the governor that there were no adverse claims for the land and that his acquisition of the land would "not injure any third party." Finally, Martínez reminded the governor that the grant was desperately needed "for no other object than that of improving [his] situation," arguing, "Because although in this jurisdiction I have the use of some agricultural lands, it is evident that they are so worthless, old and exhausted; and by now even the most laborious effort is not enough to provide for even our minimum need."[32] The petition made no mention of previous petitions and ignored existing Ute claims. To do so would have been the undoing of the request as the governor would have been forced to reject the appeal.

Upon receiving Martínez's petition, Abreu, too busy, it seems, to provide the administrative oversight for official property making, passed the request along to the secretary of the territorial legislature.[33] The secretary turned to

Abiquiú for advice. Rather than direct the alcalde, or mayor, to investigate the claim and provide a recommendation, the secretary forwarded the request to La Corporación de Abiquiú, the locally elected assembly in the village. The members of La Corporación agreed that the land requested by Martínez should indeed be settled, but not by Martínez and his family alone. The lands, they argued, should be reserved as community property. The land that Martínez requested was dominated by an enormous valley "capable of accommodating five hundred families without property, and without any injury to third parties, leaving the pasture and watering places free to all the inhabitants of this jurisdiction of Abiquiú."[34] La Corporación, like Martínez, made no mention of a Ute presence in Tierra Amarilla.

Despite the favor La Corporación did Martínez by ignoring Ute claims, its recommendation threatened to upend his request for a private land grant. Martínez moved quickly and pressed his case for a private land grant with the governor. "It would certainly be unjust," he told Abreu, "that the stock raisers of Abiquiú should proceed to establish permanent stock ranges within the limits of the property I seek to obtain, under the guarantee that the grant was made on condition that the pasture and watering places should be common with those of Abiquiú, to be freely used to the injury of the proprietors, which will have no other tendency other than that of causing endless disputes and difficulties."[35]

Unwilling to adjudicate the matter himself, the governor formed a committee of prominent Santa Fe politicians and charged them with resolving the conflict between Martínez and La Corporación. The committee deliberated briefly and issued a short decision supporting the recommendation of La Corporación. The Tierra Amarilla land grant, according to the committee, should be distributed to all "who may join together" with the petitioner.[36] The territorial legislature accepted the decision of the committee and the recommendation of La Corporación de Abiquiú on the following day. The Mexican land grant of Tierra Amarilla was made official on July 20, 1832. In the decree the secretary of the legislature directed the alcalde to distribute small tracts of private farmland to "each of those who [would] unite with the petitioners" and directed that the rest of the grant — the pastures, watering places, roads, and forests — remain common property for the collective use of all whom the alcalde placed in possession.[37]

As a historical record the documents that traveled back and forth from April to July 1832 between Martínez, La Corporación de Abiquiú, the governor's Santa Fe committee, and the secretary of the territorial legislature describe the circumstances surrounding the first Mexican claim to property in Tierra

Amarilla. They tell a story that not only elevates Mexican claims over Ute claims but also erases altogether the presence and history of the Utes in the region and the violent history of struggle for property that preceded it. Reading history through the lens of the *expediente*, therefore, is to read a colonial presentation of property that obscures the dispossession of the Utes and, moreover, the role of Mexican authorities in using landless settlers as a tactic in an ongoing war of position with powerful Indian societies.

Although 1832 marks the date of the first Mexican claim to Tierra Amarilla, the Ute presence in Tierra Amarilla, ignored in the documents, made actual settlement impossible. A new escalation in conflict between Mexican militias and Capote Utes engulfed northern New Mexico in the early 1830s. Fearing for his life, the alcalde of Abiquiú refused to travel to Tierra Amarilla and perform the possession ceremony.[38] Despite the danger Martínez recruited a group of settlers and moved north from Abiquiú into Tierra Amarilla in the summer of 1832.[39] They abandoned the brief settlement, however, during a severe winter marked by constant Ute raids. Over the next fourteen years, until his death in 1846, Martínez would make a series of failed attempts to settle Tierra Amarilla. Little is known about the circumstances of these failed sorties into Ute-controlled Tierra Amarilla. No evidence exists to chronicle exactly who joined Martínez, how many attempts were made, and how fiercely the Utes resisted the efforts. What is known is that the settlers who moved north into Tierra Amarilla after 1832 marched directly into the teeth of a growing indigenous insurgency that by the early 1840s had forced the abandonment of all Mexican settlements along the northern border.

Throughout the 1830s and 1840s, landless settlers, desperate for land, settled deeper and deeper in Ute lands in places like Tierra Amarilla. These encroachments exacerbated tenuous Mexican-Ute relations and led to increased conflict that made settlements even more dangerous. The violent conflicts that foreclosed Martínez's plans to colonize Tierra Amarilla reflected a region-wide escalation in conflicts as Mexican authorities launched wave after wave of settlement campaigns into the region. The settlers who tried to colonize Tierra Amarilla in the 1830s risked their lives as the reluctant proxies of a borderlands power struggle. Although it is true that despite their limited agency they advanced the interests of Spanish colonial and later Mexican expansion at the expense of Ute claims to land, the history of Spanish and Mexican common property land grant settlement suggests that the settlers who moved into Ute lands during the Mexican period, overwhelmingly from the Genízaro land grant of Abiquiú, were not agents of conquest but rather subjects of colonial expansion in ways similar to the Utes.

Mexican Property Claims and Ute Conflict

Although the circumstances of various Mexican settlement attempts in Tierra Amarilla are unknown, the events and conditions of Mexican expansion in the region are well documented and provide a window into the violent struggle over property waged among Mexican settlers, Mexican elites, and various Indian societies in northern New Mexico. Four years after Governor Abreu created the Tierra Amarilla land grant in the mountains north of Abiquiú, he approved a similar request for property to other residents from Abiquiú. In March 1836 a group of more than three dozen settlers received a grant of land in the rugged southern San Juan Mountains east of Tierra Amarilla at a place called La Petaca. Unlike with Tierra Amarilla, the alcalde of Abiquiú agreed to travel to the grant and place the settlers in official ownership.

With snow likely still on the ground, the alcalde led Petaca's hopeful settlers northeast from Abiquiú into the Tusas Mountains surrounding Petaca. Although the Tusas Mountains lack the majestic peaks and high elevations of the dramatic Sangre de Cristo Mountains to the east, they include some of New Mexico's most rugged territory. High mesas thick with ponderosa pine forests drop suddenly down steep rocky slopes into remote canyons fed by small springs that cut narrow valleys. Though the terrain is similar to Tierra Amarilla, it lacks the vast and abundant pastures. The very name that the settlers gave the grant, La Petaca, refers to the rugged box canyons and narrow valleys. Despite the difficulty the terrain posed for travel, particularly in March, the alcalde led the group upcountry along small springs and watercourses that eventually feed into the Rio de Chama south of Abiquiú. One purpose of the land grant possession ceremony was to introduce the settlers to the boundaries of the grant, so the party hiked up and down the steep, forested slopes along ridgelines that took them in and out of the remote canyons defining the limits of Petaca. In the ceremony the alcalde explained that the rights that accompany property came with a set of obligations that defined both the settlers' legal relationship to the grant and to one another.

As they hiked through the narrow valley, the alcalde measured out long, rectangular lots that abutted a small river and stretched into the piñon-juniper uplands. He distributed one small private lot to each of the families in the party and explained that their continued private claim to those lots would be contingent on a set of obligations and performances related to common property. They had to dig and maintain ditches, called acequias, that divert water from the Rio Tusas for community irrigation. They were to lay down their fences in the fall and make dormant fields available for collective stubble grazing. They had to remain on the grant, defending their and their neighbor's land, for a period of five years. Only through performing these obligations would their private claims become fully vested. With the lots distributed and staked out, they hiked up the valley wall through rocky outcroppings onto the broad, forested mesas that surround the Petaca valley to the east and the west. There they walked the mesa-top boundary, leaving rock cairns to mark Petaca's borders. The alcalde made sure the settlers understood that "the pastures, forests, waters, and watering places [were] in common."[40]

While their lots along the river provided a homesite and a small agricultural plot, the commons supplied pasture to graze animals, hunt game, collect firewood, gather wildings, and find materials for homes and ranches. Given the politics and ecology of settlement in northern New Mexico, these were all activities that required collective effort and close cooperation. The *expediente* notes that Petaca's new property owners were so overcome by their good fortune that they "plucked up herbs, leaped, cast stones, and shouted with joy."[41] The ceremony and its culminating celebration served as a ritual demonstration of the personal and collective commitment required of Petaca's new settlers. But as in Tierra Amarilla Mexican hopes for a thriving village to serve as a bulwark against Indian attacks came up against the reality of bloody borderlands conflict.

Land grants settlers in Tierra Amarilla and Petaca became human shields in "a ferocious war" that raged between Mexico and Indian societies in northern New Mexico.[42] Petaca settlers told harrowing tales of sudden death from recurring Ute attacks amid repeated efforts by grantees to dig acequias and erect simple homes in patterns likely similar to what was happening in Tierra Amarilla. "[My father] said that there had been a grant there in 1836," reported one child of a Petaca grantee "but that it was not settled because the Indians were killing always dozens of people."[43] But the Petaca settlers, like those who tried to settle Tierra Amarilla, had few other options. They lacked land in Abiquiú, so they were forced to return again and again to the Ute-controlled Tusas Mountains. The difficult task of carving out an isolated village deep in northern New Mexico's rugged and densely forested mountains became a nightmare of endless work and constant Ute raids.

When Mexican expansion provoked Indian aggression in the 1830s, Mexico responded with more settlements and indiscriminate military violence. In 1836 a Mexican militia with more than eight hundred soldiers attacked a Navajo party suspected of raiding, killed twenty Navajos, and seized more than five thousand sheep.[44] After Ute aggression against Mexican settlements accelerated in 1844, Mexican settlers abandoned every land grant village north of Abiquiú and west of Taos.

When Steven Kearney and his Army of the West invaded New Mexico in 1846 to begin the U.S.-Mexican War and a U.S. occupation that would eventually culminate two years later in the transfer of all of New Mexico to U.S. control, Tierra Amarilla was a land grant in name only. Capote Utes had forced the abandonment of nearly all of northern New Mexico's many common property land grants. Permanent settlement by land grant claimants would not happen until the 1860s, more than a decade *after* U.S. control of the region, and would mark not the end of contentious property claims for Tierra Amarilla but the beginning of more than 150 years of nearly constant conflict over the Tierra Amarilla land grant.

CHAPTER ONE

Colonizing the Lands of War

IN FEBRUARY 1848 representatives of Mexico and the United States negotiated an end to the U.S.-Mexican War. The subsequent Treaty of Guadalupe Hidalgo proved costly for Mexico. The terms transferred more than five hundred thousand square miles to the United States, an amount that comprised nearly all of what is today the U.S. Southwest, including all of what would become the state of New Mexico. In the decades after the treaty was signed, a western migration of political appointees, bureaucrats, and technocrats flooded New Mexico, transforming political institutions in the new U.S. territory. The clubby territorial politics of U.S.-controlled New Mexico opened up the region to enterprising lawyers and land speculators who swarmed the territory during the 1870s and 1880s in order to invest huge sums in land purchases and natural-resources extraction. The many "politicians for revenue only," as one critic described them, fare poorly in histories of New Mexico's land grants.[1] In the compelling story of social transformation and land loss in postwar New Mexico, a cabal of speculators called the Santa Fe Ring prowled the territory for real estate investments and eventually dispossessed scores of land grant communities of millions of acres.[2]

Membership in the ring included every territorial governor until 1885, nearly every federal appointee with authority over land and resources throughout the nineteenth century, and scores of federal and territorial judges. Enterprising lawyers with connections to eastern investors tapped the ring's political networks as a way to "translate and mediate" the common property claims of subsistence settlers.[3] The history of the Santa Fe Ring is a story of waves of enclosures and dispossessions as its legal machinations converted common property claims into commercial investment opportunities for moneyed interests. At the heart of this transformation was the treaty, a document that all but guaranteed that Spanish and Mexican land grants would fall prey to predatory speculators.[4]

The story of New Mexico's territorial period is often told from the perspective of the ring, depicted as an ad hoc array of elites who, from a privileged political and economic perch, manipulated legal procedures, co-opted federal bureaucrats, and hoodwinked unwitting settlers. Spanish-speaking land grant communities, it seems, had little chance against these experts in "high finance, intricate legal arrangements, and the latest techniques of investment and exploitation."[5] By the end of the nineteenth century, the ring controlled the financial and political infrastructure of the territory and used this control to absorb huge investments in resources from Gilded Age investors in boardrooms from Boston and New York to London and Amsterdam. Within a generation these investors and their money had transformed New Mexico's land grant communities from remote agrarian outposts into critical nodes in the circuits of global capital. By the time New Mexico became a U.S. state in 1912, speculation and legal chicanery had stripped nearly 80 percent of all Spanish and Mexican land — millions of acres — from land grant settlers and heirs.[6]

But how did indigenous nations and Spanish and Mexican land grant communities of northern New Mexico experience this tumultuous period? What patterns of resistance did they offer to the land grab that threatened their lives and cultural traditions? These are questions that have preoccupied recent histories of colonial and postcolonial New Mexico. The many Indian societies and land grant communities that populated northern New Mexico were not the silent victims of colonial speculation but actively resisted these patterns and political agents in struggles over land and resources.[7]

This emphasis on social struggle, however, is not part of the many histories of Spanish and Mexican land grants in which the agency of Indian nations and land grant society disappear behind stories of powerful land speculators and Santa Fe Ring operatives.[8] The story of New Mexico's land grant struggle is often an account of the inexorable transformation from subsistence production to industrial extraction, from common property to private property, from Spanish and Mexican land grants to large private ranches. It is a story in which everyone but the sophisticated speculators and powerful ring members were pawns in a transformation wrought by legal and economic changes following the arrival of U.S. authority. According to Malcolm Ebright, "Hispanic land grant settlers, unfamiliar with Anglo laws and language and often not aware of court proceedings involving their land grants, had little chance of protecting their property."[9] It was a vast dispossession made possible by the law. Even if land grant settlers were familiar with Anglo commerce and could have somehow protected their claims from Santa Fe Ring speculators, they were still doomed. The potent legal edifice of private property made resistance impossible. "The reason for [land loss]," concludes Ebright, "was that the land grants were established under one legal system and adjudicated by another."[10]

Ebright's explanation describes the law as a relentless force of land dispossession in New Mexico during the territorial period. The common property claims of Spanish and Mexican land grants were simply inconsistent with the privileged private property relations introduced by U.S. administrators and courts and therefore could not survive the change to U.S. control. Land loss came like a wave that swamped existing legal practices. Indian nations and land grant settlers in New Mexico have often been portrayed as victims of the law, refugees from a common property history adrift in a sea of private property. Where speculators found ways to manipulate the law and take advantage of the divide between common and private property, all others spoke only the language of subsistence and never the language of the law. Power and agency resided with Santa Fe Ring members, who used the law as a way to transform the diverse practices and relations of Indian nations and Spanish and Mexican land grants into objects of commercial investment. "The problem of land grants in the American Southwest" argues historian Maria Montoya, "is largely a problem of translation."[11]

In this chapter I offer an alternative to a focus on law, legal translation, and elites in studies of land grant dispossession. Although I do examine the tactics and consequences of commercial speculation by the Santa Fe Ring in the next chapter, I focus here on a different set of actors. Here I examine the active and sophisticated patterns of resistance to speculation by Capote Utes and land grant settlers in Tierra Amarilla. In the face of new legal authorities and emerging commercial challenges, Utes and land grant settlers alike asserted, performed, and defended their diverse property claims against Santa Fe Ring speculators. The resistance of Capote Utes and the complicated legal struggles for property waged by land grant communities suggest that Indian and Mexican claimants did not mistake the law as an autonomous force mediating the struggle for property but rather understood law and property as a tool of resistance and a site of social struggle.

The Making of Property in Tierra Amarilla

A curious letter arrived in the office of New Mexico's surveyor general in July 1861.[12] "Mr. Surveyor General of the Territory of New Mexico," the letter began,

> The people who have colonized the well-known Tierra Amarilla have encountered some embarrassments and difficulties as a result of Don Francisco Martínez and his brothers who were the primary cause for many people to abandon their personal interests in a place in which many have devoted their lives in defense based on the promises of Mr. Martínez, promises that he made before he became the verified settler, promises that have been, and continue to be, ratified through

the toil and work of many poor men, and promises that have not been honored; although we have handled the matter with a sense of humor, we know well the damage that is being done to our interests, interests and rights we have acquired through our work in the aforementioned place; the people appeal to your authority to give your opinion regarding what rights we have in the Land Grant and the work that we have put; the tenth of this same month we will have a meeting in Tierra Amarilla, and we place our hope in the kindness of your consideration in our dispute and respond in a convenient manner.

No record of any response to the letter exists in the archives of the Office of the Surveyor General. Though the surveyor general was tasked with investigating Spanish and Mexican property claims in New Mexico, the letter was apparently of little interest to him. But despite official disinterest in the letter and its contents, the brief appeal is remarkable for a number of reasons. First, the letter demonstrates that at the very beginning of U.S. efforts to adjudicate Spanish and Mexican property claims in New Mexico the settlers of the Mexican land grant of Tierra Amarilla inserted themselves into the messy property disputes that would come to dominate territorial politics. It describes efforts to organize meetings and pursue strategic alliances with U.S. officials and articulates a brief but familiar theory on the origins of property and the various rights that accrue to legitimate property holders.

Second, the explicit claims and tacit assumptions in the letter offer an alternative telling of New Mexico's land grant history. While land grant scholars have narrated New Mexico's land grant history through a focus on speculators and federal officials, this letter offers a glimpse at a different story lurking behind the dominant narratives of powerful commercial interests and Santa Fe Ring political power. By following the clues offered in the letter, I examine how land grant settlers understood and asserted claims to property vis-à-vis U.S. property law and how they navigated the complicated adjudicatory structures placed in front of them.

Three themes appear in the letter and serve as the organizing structure of this chapter. The first theme relates to claims of legitimate property origins made by land grant settlers. Property, according to the letter, was a right acquired by certain people and "ratified through the toil and work of many poor men." The wording reads as though cribbed from the pages of John Locke's *Second Treatise of Government* (though perhaps more elegantly than Locke's), arguably the founding document of a version of U.S. liberalism preoccupied with limited government, private property, and market economies.[13] Locke's labor theory of property (property ratified through toil) was a familiar trope to U.S. property adjudicators, and more importantly, it was a theory that U.S. adjudicators assumed absent in Mexican notions of property. Indeed, most existing histories of New Mexico's community land grants focus on the importance of common property as a form that stands in stark contrast to the private property arrangements imagined to be imported into New Mexico by the United States after the war.

The letter suggests, however, that land grant settlers shared liberal notions of private property and even understood land grant common property in terms consistent with Lockean-derived liberal theory. As I examine in this chapter, the brief letter offers a clue that challenges a key premise in land grant historiography: the idea that New Mexico's common property relations were wholly incompatible with the private property relations imposed by U.S. property adjudicators after the U.S.-Mexican War. As I will argue, the theories of property among U.S. adjudicators and federal officials were not anathema to the land grant settlers' own understanding of property in Tierra Amarilla.

A second theme of the letter refers to the way property was structured and practiced in New Mexico. The writers make vague reference to certain "embarrassments and difficulties as a result of Don Francisco Martínez and his brothers who were the primary cause for many people to abandon their personal interests in a place in which many [had] devoted their lives in defense based on the promises of Mr. Martínez, promises that he made before he became the verified settler." The reference here is an important one. It refers to the very specific and unique ways that Tierra Amarilla settlers constructed legal and discursive strategies to assert and legitimate their property claims to skeptical U.S. authorities.

While the letter writers in the first theme offered a theory of property that supported their legitimate property claims, those claims, in order to be legal and compelling, required particular practices or performances of property that could demonstrate and confirm legitimate rights and claims. Property, as they understood it, required certain recognizable practices, and land grant settlers reconfigured these practices after the arrival of U.S. authority, in ways they hoped would conform to new legal and economic property relations.

A final theme reflects the notable voices and property struggles missing from the letter. Just as the original Tierra Amarilla land grant documents of 1832 made no mention of Ute or Apache claims to Tierra Amarilla — or even the existence of Utes and Apaches in Tierra Amarilla — so too does the 1861 letter ignore the existing and, as we shall see, powerful Capote Utes in Tierra Amarilla in 1861. While Tierra Amarilla's Mexican land grant settlers were seeking support from the surveyor general in political struggles over property in Tierra

Amarilla, they were also engaged in a violent struggle for land with the various Ute and Apache groups that maintained permanent settlements within the boundaries of the land grant. Land grant settlers in Tierra Amarilla worked both with and against various federal officials, particularly the many Indian agents sent to New Mexico, to undermine Ute and Apache claims in a violent struggle for property. The silences in the letter belie the violence that dominated local property struggles in the early 1860s. As I show in this chapter, land grant settlers in Tierra Amarilla required, even perhaps anticipated, the broad adoption of U.S. policies and practices of Indian removal as a means to protect common property claims.

On a Labor Theory of Property

The writers of the 1861 letter appealed directly to the surveyor general to make a defense of their property claims by virtue of it being "ratified by the toil and work of many poor men." The language echoes the liberal tradition on property elaborated by key Enlightenment thinkers, particularly English political philosopher John Locke.[14] Though Locke's writings were influential far beyond seventeenth-century England, it seems unlikely that the writers would have actually read Locke's *Second Treatise on Government*, his most explicit examination of the roots of property; books, particularly legal books, were an unusual luxury on New Mexico's frontier.[15] And yet the letter develops the same sensibilities and draws on the same political commitments to which Locke appealed when he published his immensely influential tract on the role of government and the theory of property in 1690. For Locke property was a natural right that one derived from "the labour of his body, and the work of his hands."[16] By natural right, nature, once transformed through human labor, becomes the private property of whoever transforms it and "labor was to be his title to it."[17] This new right, according to Locke, necessarily requires new kinds of property, particularly those that exclude "the common right of other men."

Locke's formulation of natural rights arranged as "life, liberty, and property" found its cognate in the U.S. Declaration of Independence's "life, liberty, and happiness." Both phrases refer to "natural rights," and although Jefferson's vocabulary in the declaration differed from Locke's explicit claim to property as a natural right, these Enlightenment notions of property, to which Locke contributed, served as the foundation for liberal notions of private property, markets, and capital accumulation in the development of U.S. colonial expansion.

Locke's version of property was also one that allowed for unlimited private appropriation. This liberal theory of property to which Locke contributed was at the heart of the waves of enclosures that transformed the patterns of common property land tenure in Europe beginning in the seventeenth century and in New Mexico beginning in the mid-nineteenth century. As E. P. Thompson writes of the eighteenth-century agrarian enclosures in England, this liberal version of property law became a key way in which "the land was laid open to the market."[18] U.S. property adjudicators in New Mexico in the late nineteenth century, and the institutions in which they served, considered common property land grants like Tierra Amarilla to be a violation of the liberal contract. The presence of common property, in other words, impeded the expansion of market exchange and stifled progress, thus marking a deep cultural pathology in land grant society.

Rectifying this state of affairs became the central task of administrators in postwar New Mexico. The solution for many was the steady migration of Anglo settlers into New Mexico and the slow transformation from common property land grants to private property smallholders. "For years," lamented New Mexico's territorial governor L. Bradford Prince in a speech he gave in 1891 on the prospects of economic development in New Mexico, "we have suffered under the incubus of unsettled land titles. The uncertainty which prevailed prevented sales and paralyzed enterprise."[19] Replacing Mexican common property tenure with strict, private property tenures, it was argued, would transform New Mexico into "the temple of civilization . . . reared upon the ruins of the past."[20]

The 1861 letter, however, challenges the very notion of common property as incompatible or in opposition to private property relations. It highlights the similarities rather than the differences between common property in Tierra Amarilla and the dominant mode of fee simple private property in U.S. law. Instead of privileging or defending common property or collective rights, the letter writers asserted a natural right to private property in Tierra Amarilla consistent with Locke's labor theory of property. The assertion appears as something more than merely political rhetoric. Private property and common property rights coexist, imply the letter writers, and in ways that complicate the story of property adjudication and land grant loss in northern New Mexico. That property rights in Tierra Amarilla included the kind of private claims in liberal formulations privileged by U.S. property authorities troubles the idea that land grant loss in New Mexico was a function of two contradictory kinds of property relations, private property versus common property, in irresolvable tension.

U.S. adjudicators saw no similarity between common property and private property. As the property theorist C. B. MacPherson has argued, however, common property relations and private property relations (1) can only be understood in relation to each other, (2) are both defined by individual rights, and

(3) are both consistent with liberal (Lockean) theories of property. MacPherson's view focuses less on the differences between common and private property and more on the similarities. Most importantly to MacPherson, both describe exclusive rights for individual claimants. "Common property is created by the guarantee to each individual that he will not be excluded from the use or benefit of something; private property is created by the guarantee that an individual can exclude others from the use or benefit of something. Both kinds of property, being guarantees to individual persons, are individual rights."[21]

The appeal to liberal notions of property by land grant settlers shares this view of property. In Spanish and Mexican land grants, private and common property land tenures were not understood as distinct and contradictory kinds of property relations. Common property, where it existed, was not an open access commons but rather a village-level resource in which a variety of spatial exclusions occurred at multiple scales (colonial, territorial, local) and drew in various subjects (political authorities, land grant settlers, Indian societies). Members of a land grant, for example, excluded nonmembers from the use of common resources and expected the state to enforce those exclusions. In a land grant that included common property, private property and common property existed only in relation to the other and served reciprocal and complimentary functions. Private rights to land in community land grants, such as the private home site, were an alienable property claim. These private rights were one of the key incentives that drew settlers into the northern borderlands. These valuable private claims, however, were not possible without various common property obligations such as digging acequias, sharing common grazing areas, and comanaging and using uplands for hunting and gathering. Land grant property relations, in other words, developed in relation to particular conditions and circumstances as a way to manage and exploit important resources within the unique challenges of settling a dangerous and semiarid region.[22]

Despite the importance of common property to community land grant reproduction, local land grant communities placed no emphasis on common property over private property. In theory and practice Spanish and Mexican land grants were entirely consistent with liberal notions of property. Under both Spain and Mexico, that portion of a land grant understood as the private property of an individual was a fungible commodity. Land grant members frequently sold land to outsiders who, upon purchase, entered into the common property tenure arrangements included in the transaction. Such an arrangement demonstrates that, as in all liberal property regimes, the rights of individual owners were paramount.

In every community land grant in New Mexico, private property combined with community property in ways that blurred any easy distinction between the two. Certain performances of common property, like the collective digging and maintaining of acequias, were also the material and legal conditions for private property. Likewise, to fully realize the benefits of small home sites and irrigated pastures and plots, land grant recipients engaged in the collective use and management of the commons. In other words, private property could not exist without these shared commitments to common property and vice versa. Each type of property relation, common or private, not only allowed for a diversity of production practices (agriculture, forestry, pastoralism, etc.) but also, more importantly, served as the very means through which the other could take place. The conditions of production required both common and private property. In the everyday lives of land grant settlers, the reductionist logic of U.S. private property made little sense. As implied in the 1861 letter, Spanish and Mexican property claims were not reducible to common property or private property relations.

The letter writers' suggestive claim to private property, by virtue of common property relations, tells a different story of property. It also suggests that liberal notions of property were not exclusive to Anglo property law but were, in fact, familiar to Spanish and later Mexican citizens. The Tierra Amarilla land grant was distributed by Mexico during a period in which Mexican liberalism, particularly regarding property, was influential. Colonization and property were important political topics during the 1820s, and the colonization laws of 1824 and 1828 emerged out of a version of Mexican liberalism consistent with, rather than contradictory to, U.S. property law and focused most of all on resolving the particular challenges of settlement along Mexico's northern border.

Mexican liberalism, like U.S. liberalism, valorized colonization "as a social panacea" in which progress was defined through the elevation of the rights of individual property owners. The development of property laws was understood as essential to "increase and fortify [a] class of small rural property holders."[23] The refusal, for example, of La Corporación de Abiquiú to endorse Manuel Martínez's 1832 appeal for a private land grant was consistent with liberal reforms to colonization and property in Mexico that sought to limit the political and economic influence of the owners of large private holdings. Its recommendation that the grant be distributed to scores of settlers, rather than to Martínez alone, reflected "a general conviction among [Mexican] liberals that it was *small* property that should become the economic base of the new society."[24] Despite the imprint of liberalism on Mexican property law, Spanish and Mexican land grants in New Mexico were, and remain, misunderstood as an unmanaged commons in violation of liberal commitments to private property.

The appeal in the 1861 letter offers a historically contingent and geographically specific articulation of property relations in Tierra Amarilla. The letter writers also suggested that this contingency was at the heart of internal conflicts threatening the property rights of many settlers. The next section examines how the efforts to legitimate land grant property relations to U.S. property adjudicators created internal conflicts among settlers.

Performing Property in Tierra Amarilla

The Treaty of Guadalupe Hidalgo required that the United States "inviolably respect" the preexisting property claims of Mexican citizens. The final version of the treaty, however, lacked specific language regarding precisely how the United States would do this. As a result, the United States established adjudication procedures of its own design. Beginning in 1854 the territorial surveyor general was charged with receiving and investigating claims to property and making recommendations to Congress, the final authority over property adjudication. Among the first land grant claims reviewed by William Pelham, New Mexico's first surveyor general, was a claim filed for the Tierra Amarilla land grant in August 1856 by Francisco Martínez, the son of Manuel Martínez.[25] After a brief review of Martínez's claim, Pelham recommended that Congress confirm Martínez's claim. As with nearly all the earliest claims before the surveyor general, Pelham never visited the grant to verify that any settlement existed. In his brief report he took care to note that Manuel Martínez had requested a private grant but that La Corporación de Abiquiú had recommended against a strictly private claim, and as a result, Mexican authorities made a community grant instead. Congress confirmed the grant in 1860 as part of a bill that included several property claims in New Mexico.[26] In doing so, however, it ignored Pelham's explanation of Tierra Amarilla's common property origins and instead confirmed the grant as a private land claim in the name of Francisco Martínez.

After suddenly becoming one of the largest landowners in the United States, Martínez snubbed the speculators lining up to buy land grant properties in New Mexico and instead conveyed scores of small plots of land to settlers from Abiquiú and villages to the south. Between 1860 and 1865, he made 130 separate conveyances in which he distributed small private plots to settlers in language that described individual rights for the collective use of a shared commons. The number of deeds, and the language in each regarding the distribution of private *and* common rights, suggests that Martínez intended to make common what

Congress had made private. Of these 130 transactions, 113 were notarized and filed with the county clerk and were called *hijuelas*. In each *hijuela* common property existed alongside private property in ways similar to other Spanish and Mexican land grants. On August 24, 1863, a settler named Francisco Montoya filed a *hijuela* with the county clerk in which Martínez

> grants and conveys to the second a piece of land which came to him from his father and sons through a Royal Grant of the Mexican Government and is situate in Tierra Amarilla as it is commonly known; approved by the Congress and registered in the Survey of the Territory of N. Mex. Which he grants and conveys according to the articles of the said Grant, and transfer . . . one hundred varas. Said varas of land have the rights of pastures, waters, wood, lumber, watering-places and roads, free and common.[27]

The wording of the *hijuelas* was consistent with the wording of many common property grants in northern New Mexico during the Spanish and Mexican periods. Like those grants, Martínez vested the ownership of small private homesites in individual settlers only after various conditions were met, such as three years of continuous settlement and various collective performances of common property relations. Although one interpretation of the tactic is that the *hijuelas* were just deeds "for a share in a land grant," such a view ignores the historical specificity of *hijuelas*.[28] *Hijuelas* are commonly found in wills and estates under both Spanish and Mexican law and their use continued even after the arrival of U.S. authority in 1848. Throughout the latter half of the nineteenth century, *hijuelas* were commonly found in estates in which common property was being partitioned.[29] Scholars have described *hijuelas* as documents that stipulate the division of homes among heirs, for example, room by room. Trees were bequeathed to one heir and the land below the trees to another. Vigas, the rough-hewn logs that supported roofs or porches, were distributed to sons, for example, while the walls of a home were bequeathed to daughters, and the land below the home was given to grandchildren. Mattresses were bequeathed in fractional shares. Although *hijuelas* are not found in all wills during the territorial period, when they were used they were documents legally dividing the physically undividable.

Why would Martínez choose this type of legal instrument to convey land grant property? The answer to this question may be that Martínez used *hijuelas* in order to make complex land grant property relations legible to U.S. property adjudicators. Had Martínez and various settlers used standard property documents, such as warranty deeds, the common rights at the heart of the *hijuelas* could have been more difficult to defend. Although Spanish and Mexican law prohibited the partition and privatization of the common lands of a community land grant, an 1876 New Mexico territorial statute provided for a part owner of common property to divide common interests through auction.[30] The possibility of partition was precisely the threat that the *hijuelas* appeared to resolve. In an estate a *hijuela* served as a kind of receipt ensuring that common property rights survived a person's death. By using *hijuelas* Martínez distributed collective resource rights to settlers while still preserving private property claims. The use of *hijuelas* in Tierra Amarilla, it seems, reflects an attempt to identify and adapt a more flexible conveyance form capable of resolving the challenges to common property relations. The *hijuelas* made the Tierra Amarilla land grant common in practice, while it remained private by law.

Although the legal magic act that the *hijuelas* appeared to perform for their holders provided apparent legal protections, *hijuelas* came with inherent risks that gave pause to a number of settlers, particularly it seems to the writers of the 1861 letter. In particular, the writers described rather cryptically the problem of certain "promises that [had] not been honored" by Martínez. Although the language included in the *hijuelas* guaranteed access to the commons, U.S. law considered the commons to be the private property of Francisco Martínez. His continued ownership of the grant, therefore, created an unresolvable tension to the common rights claimed by settlers. What would happen to those common rights, for example, if Martínez decided to sell the land grant, as he eventually did, in its entirety? What legal remedies could *hijuela* holders seek to protect their claims to a commons not recognized by U.S. law?

The settlers who came to Tierra Amarilla with Francisco Martínez in the 1860s had much to worry about despite what their *hijuelas* promised them. Despite the 1860 congressional confirmation, there was significant confusion in New Mexico regarding it. In the years immediately following the confirmation, Martínez's five brothers, two sisters, and their families each claimed one-eighth ownership of the grant, and all eventually sold their claims to various speculators. Whether or not the sales reflected an honest or opportunistic confusion, the land transfers clouded existing property claims in Tierra Amarilla. This confusion began in earnest on June 11, 1864, when a Santa Fe merchant and saloon keeper named Henry Mercure announced the purchase of one-eighth of the grant in an ad he took out in the *Santa Fe Gazette*. The *Gazette*'s editors not only printed his ad but found it important enough to comment on: "Our readers in Rio Arriba County will do well," wrote the *Gazette*'s editor, "to read the advertisement of Mr. Henry Mercure in this day's paper." In the advertisement Mercure offered a warning: "All persons concerned are hereby notified that I am the owner of the undivided one eighth part of the tract of land situated in the county of Rio Arriba, New Mexico, and known as the Tierra Amarilla grant, confirmed by Congress to Manuel Martin of said County, and are warned not to trespass upon said land or purchase or sell any portion thereof without my knowledge for no valid title can be made to said land without my consent."

Mercure had purchased a one-eighth share of the grant from Frederick Muller, a Santa Fe–based investor and banker, who only months earlier had purchased a share in the grant from Francisco Martínez's brother and sister-in-law, Julian and Refugia Martínez, in March 1864.[31] Muller, who was among the first land grant speculators in New Mexico, entered into eight separate transactions involving Tierra Amarilla between 1864 and 1881. Mercure quickly sold his claim for a profit to Santa Fe attorney Elias Brevoort, but before doing so he leased land within the grant to the U.S. Army for the development of Camp Plummer, later called Fort Lowell.

Over the next decade, Brevoort, part of a large network of investors and speculators, bought and sold property in Tierra Amarilla. The patterns of speculation in Tierra Amarilla, the subject of the next chapter, continued throughout the 1870s and 1880s as a small group of attorneys, merchants, and speculators purchased and consolidated interests. By the early 1880s, Thomas Benton Catron, one of the most prominent and powerful politicians in territorial New Mexico, claimed full ownership of the entire grant. The threat posed by speculators and the possibility that Martínez's *hijuelas* would not provide the necessary protections created anxiety among settlers in Tierra Amarilla. And yet there were still other, even more immediate difficulties clouding their claims. Though not mentioned in the 1861 letter, Mexican settlers were also engaged in a violent struggle with various Ute bands for the control of property in Tierra Amarilla. Mexican settlers not only engaged in legal struggles with speculators for control of the grant but also actively participated in the practices and policies of Indian removal throughout the 1860s and 1870s.

Mexican Property Claims and Indian Removal

When settlers and land and mining speculators arrived for good in Tierra Amarilla in the early 1860s, they found semipermanent and permanent Ute and Apache settlements along the Rio de Chama and within the boundaries of what would become the Tierra Amarilla land grant. Though the 1861 letter makes no mention of this presence, efforts to remove the Jicarilla Apaches and the Capote Utes preoccupied land grant settlers and U.S. authorities throughout the 1860s and 1870s. The settlers in particular constantly complained of horse and cattle thefts against which they organized retaliatory militia raids.

Mining speculators, who began flocking to Tierra Amarilla in the late 1860s, clashed with Utes and Jicarilla Apaches in a pattern that produced increased political pressure for Indian removal. The Bureau of Indian Affairs, pushed by local militias from Abiquiú and Tierra Amarilla and sympathetic to mining interests, pursued aggressive policies of administrative and spatial control of nomadic Indians in northern New Mexico. Tierra Amarilla became a key site where federal officials waged various campaigns of Indian removal, campaigns that culminated in the final, violent removal of the Utes in the 1872 "Battle of Tierra," a pitched gun battle between the U.S. military and the Capote Utes that marked the end of a Ute presence in Tierra Amarilla and the beginning of new private property claims on the grant.

The federal officials perhaps most responsible for establishing the policies of Indian removal in Tierra Amarilla were the various Indian agents who worked in the territory. Indian agents shaped the exclusionary policies regarding nomadic Indian tribes in the territory, and none was more influential than William F. M. Arny, a Republican political appointee of President Lincoln during the late 1860s. Arny worked throughout New Mexico but focused his efforts in Tierra Amarilla, where, in the early 1870s, he implemented policies that eventually opened up the region for commercial development and resource extraction.[32] Despite the mountain-man image he cultivated during his years in New Mexico, he was born and raised in Washington, D.C., and his parents moved in prominent social circles. Arny arrived in New Mexico in 1861, when the Office of Indian Affairs appointed him the Ute and Jicarilla Apache Indian agent at Cimarron in northeast New Mexico. His deeply held paternalistic views regarding Indian societies in the West and his belief in religious salvation came to dominate the Indian policies and practices he championed. He held a variety of posts within the Office of Indian Affairs as well as with the New Mexico territorial government, including for a short time, that of acting territorial governor.[33]

In New Mexico, Arny found a territory seized by fears of Indian aggression and organized around a commitment to commercial development predicated on Indian removal. The *Santa Fe New Mexican* and the *Santa Fe Gazette* newspapers aggressively editorialized in favor of the militarization of the Indian frontier. "Does the War Secretary know that ninety thousand Indian, minor children of the great father at Washington, are pressing upon and plundering us at all points?" the *Gazette* editorialized in 1853.[34] Throughout the 1850s and early 1860s, seemingly constant conflicts with Indian nations throughout New Mexico preoccupied policy makers. Many of those conflicts raged in northwest New Mexico. In August 1865 the *Gazette* reported on pitched battles between Abiquiú

William F. M. Arny, ca. 1875, wearing the mountain-man outfit he preferred while serving as Indian agent in New Mexico. (Unknown photographer; courtesy of Palace of the Governors Photo Archives [NMHM/DCA], negative 8789, New Mexico History Museum, Santa Fe.)

residents and Navajos west of Tierra Amarilla. As residents of villages north of Abiquiú organized militias to attack Utes, the *Gazette* celebrated the killing of nine Navajo men by an Abiquiú militia over the course of two July battles.[35] The *Gazette*'s and the *New Mexican*'s rhetoric gave momentum to ongoing efforts to remove nomadic Indian tribes from much of northern New Mexico. "The troubles of the times may impede 'Manifest Destiny' for the present," the *Gazette* admitted, "but those very troubles are forming the elements which will at the end of the troubles give an impetus to our natural inclinations."[36]

Indian policy in northern New Mexico was characterized by three elements, all of which were either fashioned or refashioned by Arny and other Indian agents and reinforced through the work of militias such as those in Tierra Amarilla. First, Indian agents distributed food rations and supplies, referred to as "gifts" by Indian agents and Utes alike, in a pattern that interrupted subsistence patterns, established dependent relations, and served as a primary tactic of social and spatial control of Ute society. Second, Indian agents disciplined Utes in Tierra Amarilla through the use of physical violence in retaliatory militia raids meant to punish Ute attacks on land grant settlements or mining parties. Third, Indian agents served as unofficial boosters of, and often official guides for, increased mineral development in northern New Mexico.

In 1867, after only a short stay at the Cimarron agency in northeast New Mexico, Arny was appointed to the Indian agency in Abiquiú. When he arrived, he found the agency in disarray. The previous year Mexican militias, upset that Utes "were committing depredations upon their herds and turning their horses in upon their crops," attacked Ute encampments along the Rio de Chama.[37] A party of 1,200 Utes attacked Tierra Amarilla in July 1866 in a retaliatory raid. Settlers fled south to Abiquiú. In June 1867, when torrential spring rains finally subsided, Arny traveled north from Abiquiú to examine the aftermath of the skirmish and was astonished by what he found. Large villages of Jicarilla Apaches and Capote Utes crowded the creeks that branched out from the Rio de Chama throughout the grant.

Land grant settlers slowly returned to Tierra Amarilla after Arny's arrival but conflicts erupted again in October 1867, when two Ute men killed two Tierra Amarilla sheepherders.[38] Arny spent much of the summer of 1868 mediating disputes and trying to convince Utes to move north to Colorado. Capote Ute leaders, however, refused to move despite the Ute Treaty of 1868, which forfeited all Ute claims to northern New Mexico.

Arny's 1868 travels through Ute-controlled Tierra Amarilla brought him into contact not only with Utes but also with mining parties scouting the area. The trip convinced him that the region was a critical mineral region. Former and active Indian agents became enthusiastic boosters for mining development in New Mexico, and when Arny left the Indian agency after 1868, he hired himself out to prospecting outfits. He sent much of the fall of 1869 panning for gold along Rio de Chama tributaries near Tierra Amarilla and leading tours of mining prospectors throughout northern New Mexico and southern Colorado. He wrote a series of articles in the *Santa Fe New Mexican* in February 1870 detailing the resource riches and commercial potential of northern New Mexico.[39] In a long letter to President Grant, he laid out his program of policy prescriptions for northern New Mexico. Indians, he argued, should be negotiated with as "wards of the government," not sovereign states.[40] His plan included reservations, Indian education, and assimilation. In March 1870 President Grant appointed Arny as the "Special Agent for the Indians of New Mexico."[41]

Arny's first task as special agent was a comprehensive tour of northern New Mexico. The tour began in May 1870 and occupied him for more than a year. It included visits to nearly every Indian camp, pueblo, reservation, and settlement in northern New Mexico and southern Colorado, where he conducted a census, mediated property conflicts, examined land titles, and recommended Indian policy throughout the territory. Arny left Abiquiú on May 15 with an interpreter, the new Indian agent, J. B. Hanson, Arny's son, and seven Spanish-speaking assistants. Two days out from Abiquiú, the party found fourteen Ute lodges along the Rio de Chama just miles from land grant settlements west of the village of Tierra Amarilla.[42] Hanson noted that Capote Utes controlled the land grant outside the land grant villages and lived within five miles of the village of Tierra Amarilla. Although Arny and Hanson tried to convince the Utes to move to the reservation in southern Colorado, Ute leaders refused to acknowledge any obligation to move and expressed fear that ongoing conflicts with the Weeminuche Utes made relocation dangerous. Hanson noted that the Capote Utes were outfitted with muzzle-loading rifles and Colt pistols. Every member, including children, had a personal horse. "The prevailing vice with the Capotes," noted Hanson, "is horse-stealing." Local residents in Tierra Amarilla were the easy targets of the equestrian Utes.[43]

On the first morning after the party encountered Utes in Tierra Amarilla, twenty Ute men confronted Arny and complained of continued intrusions into Ute lands by mining speculators. Arny made vague promises to resolve the problem but tried to make his help contingent on Capote Ute relocation to southern Colorado. The following day Arny met two groups of miners returning from the San Juan Mountains. Despite treaty language that banned mining activity in much of the San Juan Mountains in southern Colorado, speculators and prospectors had opened more than two hundred mines. Meanwhile, land grant settlers in Tierra Amarilla complained about "the incessant depredations of the Utes" and threatened "a war of extermination" against the Utes unless the government intervened.[44]

During the course of his tour of Ute territory, Arny submitted eight lengthy reports with specific recommendations that argued against a militarized Indian policy in New Mexico. A peaceful resolution to Indian conflict was possible, according to Arny, not through treaties and negotiation but through social engineering. "The wild Indians of New Mexico are now in a condition to be placed upon reservations so as to be civilized, Christianized, and made self-sustaining."[45] Arny's recommendations, however, found little support in the Indian agency or with local interests in Tierra Amarilla. The flood of miners into Colorado and northern New Mexico had changed the politics of Indian removal.

Capote Utes, however, remained intransigent. While the efforts to pacify and resettle Mouache and Weeminuche Ute bands had been successful, all efforts with the Capote Utes had failed. Under the leadership of a chief named Sabota, who rejected the authority of Ute signatories to speak for him, they refused to leave Tierra Amarilla. Despite their small numbers they controlled huge swaths of land outside the small villages of the grant, where they hunted in the surrounding mountains, clashed with mining speculators, and appropriated the stock and horses of land grant settlers. By the time of Arny's 1870s tour, Capote Utes had become a powerful force in Tierra Amarilla.[46]

Arny's hopes for the peaceful removal of Utes from Tierra Amarilla were finally dashed on the morning of May 6, 1872. Abiquiú Indian agent John Armstrong, under enormous pressure from mining and commercial interests and local settlers to put an end to Ute hostilities, invited Sabota to a meeting in the land grant village of Las Nutrias, where he hoped to begin negotiations to remove Utes from Tierra Amarilla. Sabota's willingness to attend the meeting despite his disdain for the Indian agency offered a hint at a profound shift in New Mexican–Ute relations. Years of diplomatic and military coercion by territorial and federal officials had produced "irreversible demographic and subsistence declines" among New Mexican Ute bands.[47] Limited raiding opportunities and uncertain government aid drove most Ute and Apache bands from northern New Mexico. Gold discoveries in the San Juan Mountains in the late 1850s had brought thousands of prospectors into what was nominally Ute territory. Colorado officials and federal negotiators clamored for Ute land concessions in the mineral-rich San Juans even before most Utes had settled the new reservation. The few Capote Utes who remained in New Mexico found limited subsistence prospects and fierce opposition to their presence. Those who remained were forced to seek legal protections for continued settlement in New Mexico.

With the Eighth Cavalry behind him, Armstrong presented Sabota with a series of ultimatums: return all recently stolen horses; end hunting on land grant property; and finally, as per the 1868 treaty obligations, resettle on the Colorado reservation. Armstrong's demands were the basic terms of Indian policy in northern New Mexico, terms accepted by thousands of Utes who had moved north to make the slow transition to sedentary reservation life. The Ute leader Ouray, a key figure in the 1868 treaty, had settled in Colorado to become a sheep rancher complete with a crew of local ranch hands to manage his large flocks.[48] But the Utes under Sabota's command blanched at the idea of abandoning Tierra Amarilla. They interrupted Armstrong's speech with laughter and jeered his description of what he called their "perfidious conduct."[49]

By midday Armstrong had yet to obtain a single concession from Sabota. Frustrated, he ordered the Eighth Cavalry to escort the Ute party from Tierra Amarilla to Santa Fe to meet with military authorities. Sabota refused, telling Armstrong he had said everything he intended to say. A frustrated Armstrong ordered the cavalry to surround the armed Utes and forcibly take them to Santa Fe under guard. As cavalrymen moved into position, the Utes broke through their line and stormed out of the small building. With the cavalry in pursuit, the Utes raced out of Las Nutrias and found cover on a bluff overlooking the Rio de Chama from where they rained bullets and arrows on the advancing Eighth Cavalry. The cavalry scattered among the piñon and juniper trees on the sloping bank and returned fire. The gun battle lasted twenty minutes and left one cavalryman injured and one of Sabota's men dead. Sabota led his band in a fighting retreat into the mountainous terrain above Las Nutrias.

The Battle of Tierra Amarilla, as the skirmish came to be called, marked a dramatic shift in Indian policy in northern New Mexico. While Indian removal was long an official goal, it was generally pursued through the negotiation of treaties rather than forced removal by federal troops. The years after the Battle of Tierra Amarilla, however, were characterized by constant military and militia attacks amid intense diplomatic pressure for Indian removal in a pattern that eventually forced all Ute bands, including the Capote Utes, from New Mexico by 1878.[50]

Capote Utes and Mexican land grant settlers were key players in the property struggles dominating conflicts in northern New Mexico in the 1860s. The Utes, and to a lesser extent the Jicarilla Apaches, fiercely defended their claims to Tierra Amarilla against land grant settlers and mining speculators. Although the 1861 letter hints at other property conflicts in Tierra Amarilla, Ute removal was the necessary condition for all land grant claims. Land grant settlers were squarely at the center of the policies and practices of Ute removal. They lobbied the surveyor general to recognize land grant property claims and joined local militias to drive the Capote Utes from Tierra Amarilla. While land grant settlers were the immediate beneficiaries of Indian removal, they found little to celebrate. The future of Tierra Amarilla anticipated by U.S. officials after the forced removal of Utes was not one that included common property. The Battle of Tierra Amarilla marked the end of the struggle over Ute and Apache claims to Tierra Amarilla and the beginning of a new struggle over Mexican land grant claims.

CHAPTER TWO

"Under the Malign Influence of Land-Stealing Experts"

IN THE SUMMER OF 1866, a twenty-two-year-old Irish immigrant named Thomas Burns rode a mule from Colorado to Abiquiú and then north to Tierra Amarilla. It was the end of a long journey for Burns, who had come to the United States as a child with his family and settled initially in Wisconsin. He left Wisconsin at sixteen and slowly worked his way west to Colorado peddling pamphlets and begging rides; he arrived in 1860 at the beginning of the gold rush. Though the southern San Juan Mountains were in a frenzy of gold fever, Burns was an immediate and total failure as a gold miner, lasting less than a day. One failed scheme followed another, and without the money to return to Wisconsin, Burns spent the early 1860s bouncing around Colorado working in trading houses and mercantile posts, losing what money he had on cattle speculation and failed military contracts. He drifted south and arrived in New Mexico in the mid-1860s as a bankrupt speculator and out-of-work military sutler. When he reached Tierra Amarilla, a group of Capote Utes stole his mule.[1]

Burns's bad luck, however, would soon change. Escalating conflict with the Utes spurred the construction of Camp Plummer on the Tierra Amarilla land grant soon after his arrival. The camp offered commercial opportunities for merchants and military suppliers. Burns seized the opportunity. He brushed up on his Spanish, studied local property relations, organized militias, exaggerated his expertise at military supply, and married Josefa Gallegos, the daughter of a wealthy Abiquiú family. His transformation from migrant to merchant was swift. Tax records from 1872 listed his total commercial wealth at $200,000.[2]

Burns was not alone. A surge of Anglo newcomers descended on Tierra Amarilla in the 1870s looking for easy money through land acquisition and resource extraction. Most failed miserably, some spectacularly. Among them was a man named Thomas Benton Catron. Catron, who eventually partnered with Burns in a shared quest to seize control of the Tierra Amarilla grant, was named after Missouri senator Thomas Hart Benton. The senator was an architect of westward expansion, and his namesake Catron eventually made a name for himself in the newly opened West. By the end of the nineteenth century, Catron was one of the largest landowners in the United States. His rise to political prominence and wealth was as rapid as Burns's. After serving as an officer in the Confederate Army in the 1860s, he migrated west to New Mexico, where he learned Spanish and was accepted to the New Mexico Bar in 1866. By 1867 he was a local district attorney and by 1869 New Mexico's attorney general, a position in which he quickly learned to parlay his political connections into investment opportunities.[3]

Catron was among the most prolific speculators in land grants, claiming at one time to own an interest in the Mora, Beck, Espiritu Santo, Tecolote, Juana Lopez, Piedra Lumbre, Gabaldon, and Baca grants as well as nearly ten thousand acres in patented homestead claims.[4] One historian has concluded that Catron owned all or an interest in thirty-four land grants.[5] But whether it was nine or thirty-four, Catron was to the territory what Burns was to Tierra Amarilla: both maintained huge property holdings, dictated the terms of commercial exchange, and fiercely controlled local politics. Between 1874 and 1893 Catron relied on Burns's political power in Tierra Amarilla to acquire a controlling interest in the Tierra Amarilla land grant. While Catron consolidated titles, Burns tightened his grip on local sheep production. While Catron set up land and cattle corporations, mining companies, and oil businesses, Burns moved into timber production and commercial sheep production on land leased from Catron. Catron relied on the income from leases on the grant to prove claims in the courts and market the property to investors worldwide. By the early 1890s Burns was the most powerful merchant in Tierra Amarilla, and Catron was the largest landowner in New Mexico. Burns owned scores of small property claims throughout the land grant, and his sheep flocks numbered in the tens of thousands. Catron's property claims extended from the vast open plains of east-central New Mexico to the rugged mountains of its far northwest, with holdings in excess of three million acres.

Their land acquisition efforts in Tierra Amarilla were made possible by the cooperation and collusion of the politicians, merchants, judges, territorial bankers, and even three of New Mexico's surveyors general who made up the Santa Fe Ring. The ring saw New Mexico's land grants through a lens that brought the forests into focus as marketable timber, the mountains as mineral lodes, and the vast grasslands as commercial pastures. Through dubious, often extralegal, and sometimes fraudulent means they acquired title to millions of acres of common property Spanish and Mexican land grants in New Mexico.[6] They cultivated contacts with investors from Chicago, Boston, New York, and London to liquidate their holdings.

The focus on land grant acquisition was matched by an organized effort to acquire huge acreages through fraudulent homestead claims. The methods and motivations of ring speculators were diverse, but their efforts mirrored events throughout the intermountain West, where they joined in a land grab of enormous scale.[7] The events in New Mexico, however, became a focus of intense national interest. The *New York Herald* sent undercover reporters to investigate "the New Mexico land thieves."[8] Articles on New Mexico's "swindling cattle kings" prompted the paper to editorialize, "[New Mexico is] surrounded by a gang of swindling herders, all of whom are in collusion with swindling surveyors who have swallowed our Western acres as a gourmand swallows oysters."[9] For nearly half a century they controlled the legal structure for property adjudication in the territory and used that power to dispossess scores of community land grants throughout northern New Mexico.

This chapter examines a period of intense property and resource speculation by newly arrived investors who targeted New Mexico's many Spanish and Mexican land grants. The Homestead Act of 1862, which limited individual property claims to 160 acres, made it nearly impossible for investors to acquire and consolidate huge land holdings in places like New Mexico. Spanish and Mexican land grants thus became a target of investors. Most were thousands of acres in size; a few exceeded half a million acres. Tierra Amarilla, among the largest common property land grants in New Mexico with perhaps the most diverse and valuable collection of resources in the territory, became an early target of speculators. Burns and Catron operated as merchants, sheep barons, and land grant speculators in Tierra Amarilla, and their tactics came to define the practice of land speculation in New Mexico. As leaders of the Santa Fe Ring, they used their wealth to organize the legal, political, and social structure of territorial New Mexico in ways that accommodated the transfer of property from land grant communities to commercial investors.

I begin by first tracing the tactics and practices of land speculation in New Mexico, where speculators and investors manipulated weak adjudication procedures to acquire millions of acres of common property. They were helped by corrupt federal and territorial officials and profited from the arrival of railroads and banks. I then examine the specific ways in which Burns and Catron acquired title to Tierra Amarilla. Burns focused on sheep and mercantile contracts and eventually acquired enormous sheep flocks and thousands of acres of land within the boundary of the grant. Catron spent hundreds of thousands of dollars buying up interests in the Tierra Amarilla land grant from Martínez heirs. By the late 1880s, the pair would own the entire land grant, control the sheep economy, and dominate local politics.

Land Grant Speculation in New Mexico

The pattern of speculation that took hold in New Mexico in the 1870s unleashed an "oligarchy of land sharks," as one reformer described it, who conspired with the most powerful federal officials to acquire the resources held in common by land grant communities.[10] By the turn of the century Burns and Catron claimed to own the entire Tierra Amarilla land grant, while other ring operatives claimed ownership of nearly every land grant in New Mexico, an area in excess of thirty-five million acres that comprised the largest grasslands, mining regions, and forests in New Mexico.[11] The scale, scope, and intensity of speculation overwhelmed land grant communities up and down the Rio Grande and across the mountainous northern half of the territory.[12]

Land grant speculation in New Mexico was not a fixed practice but rather a shifting social struggle in which various actors worked in collaboration and occasionally in open conflict to reshape property relations and property law to their advantage. At the height of speculation, roughly from the early 1870s until the mid-1890s, the property claims of sheepherders and agriculturalists were transformed into securities on international markets. Whole land grants were bought and sold. The territory came to be defined by patterns of political corruption and international capitalist investment that ultimately undermined land grant property claims.

Despite the intensity of late nineteenth-century land speculation in New Mexico, merchants and real estate investors like Burns and Catron were not the first land and real estate speculators. The violent sixteenth century incorporation of Pueblo peoples into a new Spanish order initiated New Mexico's first speculative period in which colonial expansion transformed New Mexican society. The geopolitical promise of a Spanish colonial New Mexico motivated an imperial presence that lasted for more than two centuries. From its precarious beginnings Spanish New Mexico seemed always on the verge of collapse and calamity. Mexican designs on New Mexico, in contrast, lasted less than a generation. From the beginning Mexican interests in New Mexico reflected a measured gamble made by a nearly bankrupt country seeking a unified national presence and a buffer against its jostling territorial competitors to the north.[13] The U.S.-Mexican War and the Treaty of Guadalupe Hidalgo, which ended the Mexican era, marked the beginning of another intense period of political and commercial speculation in New Mexico.

In many ways it was an unlikely fate for New Mexico. Of all the former Mexican territories incorporated after the war, New Mexico seemed to offer the least for developers, speculators, and settlers. Though mineral wealth existed, it paled in comparison to that of Colorado and California. Though irrigable land could be found, it made up only a small fraction of the total area, and every inch was already claimed by Spanish and Mexican land grants. The ponderosa pine forests were largely inaccessible to timber operators and small compared to forests found elsewhere in the West. Opportunities for real estate investment, resource extraction, and Spanish and Mexican land grant investment required conditions not found in the territory: reliable and cheap transportation connections, clear titles, and capital for investment.

Also the hodgepodge of land laws and settlement policies were designed to populate the West with an agrarian yeomanry, but dry-land farming was impossible, and cattle ranching required huge acreages that the Homestead Act made almost unattainable. While cattle barons acquired tens of thousands of acres in southern and western New Mexico through fraudulent homestead claims, the tactic was largely ineffective in northern New Mexico, where the most valuable land was already claimed by large Spanish and Mexican land grants.[14] The Treaty of Guadalupe Hidalgo and the property adjudication procedures set up by the U.S. Congress stood in the way of land speculation. Its dismantling therefore became a focus of the Santa Fe Ring. If the adjudication of property claims could be manipulated for commercial gain, the last barrier to private investment and commercial extraction would be lifted.

Directing and controlling the processes of property adjudication thus became the key political struggle in New Mexico during the last half of the nineteenth century. Although a willful ignorance or outright rejection of existing property claims and land grant communities in New Mexico was a central tenet in the theology of progress shared by all ring members, the ring was not a homogenous political entity. Instead it was a diverse group of political and economic actors all focused on resource development and personal wealth but divided by motives and tactics. Two opposing camps of speculators imagined radically different futures for New Mexico. One camp was populated by men like Catron, often credited (or condemned) for developing the legal tactics and political strategies that undermined Spanish and Mexican property claims. Catron came to dominate New Mexican politics for nearly half a century. He was revered and reviled in equal measure. To some he was a single-minded, land-grabbing businessman disguised as a public servant whose greediness lurked where a conscience should have been.[15] But he thrilled the growing commercial and political class of merchants, timber speculators, and cattle barons who saw in his tactics a way to unlock the vast commercial potential in New Mexico's scores of community land grants.

In the other camp were politicians such as Surveyor General George W. Julian and Territorial Governor L. Bradford Prince, who believed in the promise of progress via the development of small-scale agricultural settlements and intense commercial development of natural resources in New Mexico. Catron's self-interested speculation tactics, they believed, threatened progress in the same way that Spanish and Mexican land grants did. To Julian, Catron was a caricature of Gilded Age greediness, "a politician for revenue only."[16] Governor Prince, who brokered land grant sales and promoted commercial timber extraction and railroad development in the common lands of land grant village after land grant village, often condemned Catron for a brand of speculation that he predicted would ruin New Mexico.

Catron's particular genius lay not in political guile or conscienceless greed, as some would suggest (though he displayed those traits throughout his life), but rather in his ability to marshal the shock troops of speculation. He had a talent for coordinating, controlling, and directing the complicated business of land grant acquisition. Along with Burns he became an expert at acquiring land grants by manipulating adjudication procedures, securing deeds, and controlling information. Catron understood that, despite the faith in westward expansion, progress would not unfold on its own. There were existing property claims to overcome, adjudication procedures to manipulate, and local, territorial, and federal officials to control before common property relations could yield to private rights and corporate control. Acquiring land grants required more than rhetoric; it demanded a diverse set of tactics and skills and an army of agents and attorneys all working in concert.

Land grant speculation was labor intensive. It required a team of lawyers and brokers who understood or could uncover the histories and patterns of Spanish and Mexican land grant making and then use that information to direct adjudication procedures of the General Land Office and the Office of the New Mexico Surveyor General. Catron and other speculators started by placing Spanish-speaking attorneys in the field to acquire titles, locate grant papers, and negotiate legal or purchase agreements with land grant settlers. These brokers were often among New Mexico's Hispanic elite, trusted as locals by land grant settlers. The most successful brokers conspired and colluded behind the backs of land grant settlers and out of view of the courts to hoard land grant property for their investors. They took advantage of language barriers, class divisions, the limited knowledge of Mexican grant making, and legal contradictions in adjudication procedures.

The brokers worked land grant communities like a circuit, searching for the land grant settlers whose names they found on the original Spanish and Mexican grant documents. If they could find them, they negotiated sale agreements for small parcels. Often these agreements were with the heirs of original settlers who had long since sold rights and interests in the grants. Many were happy to accept small payments for deeds they considered worthless, unaware of the legal consequences of these transactions to existing land grant communities. With deeds in hand, the brokers would submit a claim to the surveyor general for the entire grant. These claims were based on the bogus theory that community grants were actually the private property claims of only those settlers named on the original grant papers. This tactic was plausible because New Mexico's surveyors general misunderstood the patterns and practices of Spanish and Mexican land grant making. They were largely unaware of the Spanish and Mexican practice of listing only one or two representatives of a community land grant by name. Brokers capitalized on this ignorance. When it worked, the tactic culminated in a recommendation for confirmation by the surveyor general and a vote by Congress confirming the grant as a private land claim.

This work was made easier by the fact that three of New Mexico's surveyors general were active land speculators and conspired with other investors to profit from their position adjudicating property in the territory. James Proudfit, who resigned in 1876 under pressure from the General Land Office, was a notorious land speculator. Henry Atkinson, who was even worse, replaced him. Atkinson co-owned four companies that invested in land grants while he was in office, and he actively recruited buyers for land grants that were under adjudication by his office. In at least two grants he purchased deeds and allowed staff members to purchase deeds for land grants under consideration.[17] On more than one occasion he served as the representative of the federal government regarding claims to land that he owned or would later acquire. In the early 1880s Atkinson incorporated the New Mexico and Kentucky Land and Stock Company with Max Frost, a man convicted of land fraud, and his former deputy surveyor General William McBroom, also convicted of land fraud. With Catron, Atkinson started the Boston and New Mexico Cattle Company and the American Valley Company, two firms that carpeted the territory with homestead claims and invested widely in Spanish and Mexican land grants. His surveys routinely expanded the size of Spanish and Mexican property claims, particularly when business associates owned those claims.

Once the field attorneys or brokers completed their work and Proudfit or Atkinson recommended approval, lawyers like Catron took over. Catron served as a middleman between on-the-ground brokers and field attorneys and outside financial interests. He and others like him scoured their networks and connections in pursuit of investors to whom they could sell timber rights, mining interests, grazing leases, and eventually an entire land grant. They pursued investors in New York, Boston, Chicago, and Europe with brochures and reports exaggerating the rich resources and prime investment potential available in New Mexico.[18]

An attorney named Samuel Ellison was one of the earliest lawyers-turned-speculators. He was a prodigious land grant attorney in the 1870s and brought more land grants into the adjudication process than any other attorney. He claimed to represent the settlers of twenty-three of the forty-nine total claims that came before Proudfit and thirteen of the thirty-five land claims reviewed by Atkinson.[19]

In 1875 Ellison submitted a claim for a grant adjacent to Tierra Amarilla in which he claimed to represent "the inhabitants of the town of Vallecito in the County of Rio Arriba."[20] In another petition for the Petaca grant, he presented himself as the representative of the "heirs and legal representatives of the parties named as grantees."[21] In both cases Proudfit deposed witnesses provided him by Ellison and wrote recommendations for the grants on the same day that the claims were filed.[22] Though Congress ignored Proudfit's reports in Ellison's cases (in previous cases confirmed claims were later shown to be fraudulent, and Congress looked with increasing scrutiny at recommendations for confirmation), the anonymous claims of Ellison and Proudfit's recommendation stimulated an active market in deeds, which operated without the knowledge of land grant communities.

Other speculators specialized in locating international investors. William Blackmore, a prominent British investor in the U.S. West, pioneered speculative investment in New Mexico's many Spanish and Mexican land grants. As early as 1872 he was soliciting international investors for land grants he claimed to own or could acquire with sufficient capital. In one such solicitation Blackmore offered five grants for investment, including the Maxwell, Mora, Cebolla, and Los Luceros. In his sales pitch he described the unusual investment potential that New Mexico offered London investors:

> An interest in either of these properties can no[w] be acquired for a few shillings an acre, whilst I believe that from the rapid development and opening up of the country by means of Railways now in course of construction, the price now paid will be tripled and quadrupled and in some cases increased tenfold in the course of a few years. As a rule, large tracts of land in a body are only rarely met with in the United States and in almost all cases the title to these large tracts of land is derived from an early French, Spanish or Mexican Grant made prior to the acquisition of these portions of the territory by the United States Government.[23]

As adjudication procedures changed over time so, too, did speculation tactics and investment patterns. Speculation of the kind Ellison practiced became increasingly difficult when the General Land Office tightened procedures and oversight of the Office of Surveyor General. With increased scrutiny of the work of that office came more sophisticated tactics and more emphasis on specialized work. Amado Chavez, a mayor of Santa Fe during the territorial period and the first secretary of education for New Mexico after statehood, was a prolific real estate broker and an expert at Spanish and Mexican land grant speculation. He became a model of the field attorney on whom Catron would eventually rely: a Hispanic elite or local with close connections to Anglo speculators. Chavez understood both the practices of Spanish and Mexican grant making and the politics of property in territorial New Mexico. He was remarkably adept at acquiring titles, negotiating legal contracts between Anglo attorneys and Hispano settlers, and quieting titles to community land grants. Chavez often solicited commissions from wealthy investors from all over the United States and Europe for land grant work, in an elaborate scheme to acquire vast acreages:

> If you will get your friends to employ me with a salary of one hundred and fifty dollars per month and actual traveling expenses I will at once start and secure the interests and get them under contract. I can secure one third of all the interests for proving them up. And will secure contracts to buy the other two thirds very cheap, not to exceed fifty cents per acre. I can in this way secure not less than one hundred thousand acres the work of proving up would be done through Mr. A. B. McMillan as atty. When the work is done I would agree first to have all the money advanced returned to the party who advanced the same and then divide profits as follows. One third to the parties who furnished the money, one third to McMillan for his services in doing the legal work and one third to A C [Amado Chaves] for doing the field word. The parties advancing the money to secure contracts would have to furnish the necessary expenses for getting the witnesses to attend court and for publication. This would be a nominal expense compared with the value of the land to be acquired.[24]

Spanish-speaking attorneys like Chavez made legible the complex legal, cultural, and political matrix of land grant property relations and adjudication procedures in ways that opened the door to more and more speculative investments. In 1899 he solicited then-governor L. Bradford Prince's legal assistance in selling land grants. In a letter Chavez described in detail his method of land grant speculation:

> For some time past I have been trying to interest a gentleman from the east to take an interest in some land grants in this territory but he hesitates because the whole

matter is something new to him and he does not seem to care to put his money in experiments that are not with his line of business, yet he says that he may take interest in some one grant and if it comes out as I represent to him he will then aid me in forming a company with sufficient capital to handle all the good grants that may come within our reach. I have suggested the Jemez grant to him as a starter and he wants to know whether I can get a good attorney to take charge of the suit for partition for a reasonable fee. His idea is this: to pay an attorney a retainer of say $250, and to give him at the end of the suit one eighth of the land that he may acquire or five hundred dollars at his option. He proposes to put in the field a man to secure all the interest he can and to deposit in the bank here subject to your credit some money, say about $750, to be paid by you to his agent on duly certified vouchers for his traveling and other necessary expenses. That is if you accept the proposition and undertake to manage the suit for him. If this experiment is successful he will at once organize a company that will be ready to handle any good grant that may be suggested to him.[25]

For brokers who lacked the expertise of Chavez, other tactics proved equally effective. Several Santa Fe Ring lawyers pursued legal defense contracts with whole land grant communities that were desperate to defend their interests in the courts. George Hill Howard, one of Catron's occasional business partners and a frequent collaborator with Amado Chavez, offered his legal services to cash-poor land grant communities and in return would receive "una tercera parte indivisa de su derecho e interés, en y a la dicha merced o sitio, e recompense a dicho Howard por sus servicios" (one-third part to the rights and interests of the grant of land as compensation to Howard for his services).[26] Under Spanish and Mexican law the common lands of a land grant could not be sold, but an 1876 New Mexico territorial statute allowed the part owner of a common property land grant to petition the territory for the partition of a land grant. Few of the settlers who contracted with Howard understood that winning the case meant losing their land. Howard teamed up with Chavez and entered into contracts with petitioners in 1894 on the Piedra Lumbre land grant. After securing a confirmation on that grant, Hill filed a partition suit in New Mexico district court.[27] In July 1903 Chavez wrote to Howard congratulating him on their success with the Piedra Lumbre partition: "I have copied a few lines from the report of the Commission that made an actual partition of the land. I send you that copy in order that you may see that we got the best part of the grant. The partition was actually made and the grant is not now in common at all."[28]

Within a generation scores of community land grants were stripped of their common property by speculation and dubious adjudication procedures. Nearly every land grant distributed by Spain and Mexico in New Mexico became, at one time or another, the property of a Boston capitalist, a Santa Fe Ring speculator, or a British or Dutch corporation. Yet despite the unremitting land speculation and onerous adjudication procedures that began with the acquisition of New Mexico by the United States, despite the territorial and federal structures and regulatory configurations designed to destroy common property relations in favor of private property, and despite the millions of dollars spent speculating on Spanish and Mexican land grants by investors from as far afield as London, speculation in Spanish and Mexican land grants remained a risky financial investment. Though brokers like Chavez could acquire huge acreages and lawyers like Ellison and Catron could acquire speedy confirmations, there were few affordable ways to get timber, minerals, and cattle out of New Mexico. During the 1870s the speculation on Spanish and Mexican land grants was premised on the anticipated arrival of the railroads, those great "agencies of change in the interior west."[29] When they finally arrived, speculators hoped, they would transform remote land grants into "an investment arena for surplus capital, a source of raw materials for the industrial sectors, and a seemingly vast vacant lot to enter and occupy."[30]

And the railroads did come. By 1885 more than 1,100 miles of track had been constructed in New Mexico.[31] Between 1879 and 1888 four railroads constructed lines through New Mexico and transformed the territory from a commercial backwater into an important node in the circulation of global capital. The Atchison, Topeka, and Santa Fe was the first railroad to arrive, and it eventually constructed more than 690 miles of rail connecting Santa Fe to the Chicago and East Coast lumber markets. The Atlantic and Pacific laid nearly 200 miles of lines in the early 1880s. The 167 miles of the Southern Pacific crossed through New Mexico along the thirty-second parallel and connected southern New Mexico to West Coast markets. By 1883 William Jackson Palmer's Denver and Rio Grande Railroad (D&RG) connected the Tierra Amarilla land grant to the national network of railroad connections.[32] Speculators such as Catron understood that railroad development was the key to commercial development in northern New Mexico. He enticed Palmer to build D&RG main and trunk lines through Tierra Amarilla by giving a right-of-way throughout the grant. Palmer enticed British, Dutch, and East Coast investors in a pattern that defined western development in the late nineteenth century. As Palmer explained it:

> Young men without money can only make a fortune by connecting themselves with capitalists. The heaviest of these reside in the East where they look after their own affairs. But the best place to invest capital is in the West. Eastern capitalists

must therefore have representatives here to attend to their interests if they wish to invest heavily in the West. Such representatives, if able and correct, must acquire great wealth and influence with their distant principles — to a greater extent and more rapidly than if they lived in the East where the capitalist can judge for himself.[33]

The railroad was built with timber purchased from outfits that leased Tierra Amarilla land from Catron. The locomotives ran on coal mined on the grant by Catron's Monero Coal and Coke Company.[34] The railroads promised to turn forests into lumberyards and grasslands into cattle pastures. The network of transportation linkages ratified the highly speculative investments in land grants that had preceded railroad development and intensified new commercial interest in the land grant resources.

With railroads came also financial institutions to pool and distribute capital. There were no banking institutions in New Mexico in 1870, but by 1890 forty-six banks operated in the territory.[35] The scores of financial institutions and banks that opened in New Mexico following the construction of railroads increased the possibility of profitability in land grant speculation. Newly opened territorial banks competed to fund speculative investments in even more rail spurs, larger land purchases, and massive timber and cattle operations. Linked to St. Louis, Chicago, and New York financiers, New Mexico's nineteenth-century banks absorbed huge capital investments from East Coast and European investors who profited from New Mexico's resource bonanza. Catron and his associates established banks, named themselves and their friends directors, and took out loans. The pooling of capital into the hands of bank directors meant that money poured into even more timber, mining, and cattle operations.[36]

With economic and transportation infrastructure constructed and financial service firms established, the ring positioned territorial New Mexico at the center of the feverish investment exuberance that gripped the former Mexican territories in the late nineteenth century. Huge investments in resource extraction and real property by wealthy European speculators and East Coast bankers flooded the territory. Between 1865 and 1900, 1,500 British companies invested enormous sums in resource development throughout the American West.[37]

In addition to railroad and cattle, mining investments contributed to the late nineteenth-century economic transformation in New Mexico and the intermountain West. Territorial officials advertised "mountains of silver" in pamphlets designed to entice European investment.[38] British mining investments in the U.S. West exceeded £77 million, or U.S.$417 million, in the last forty years of the nineteenth century.[39] Twelve British mining companies invested £1.3

million (U.S.$6.3 million) in New Mexico in the last fifteen years of the nineteenth century.[40] The New Mexico Bureau of Immigration advertised New Mexico's resource wealth, relentlessly describing the area around Tierra Amarilla as rich in minerals: "Coal is found everywhere; gold (placer) occurs on the Chama, west of Abiquiú."[41]

By the late 1880s coalfield production exceeded one million tons in New Mexico with values approaching $2 million.[42] Spiking interest rates fueled ever-increasing investment. The most remote mountain villages in northern New Mexico were bundled into real estate investments and peddled by New Mexico–based brokers on international markets. Catron's cartel of politically connected Santa Fe lawyers and business agents circulated growing numbers of investment portfolios among wealthy clients throughout the United States.

The frenzy of speculation in New Mexico drew the attention of the General Land Office, which investigated corruption and land fraud in New Mexico in a four-year probe in the 1880s that included the careful scrutiny of nearly every private land claim in the territory. Its March 1885 report to Congress, which included more than four hundred exhibits and four hundred pages documenting land fraud in New Mexico, implicated commercial cattle ranchers, railroad companies, territorial politicians, and federal officials in a coordinated campaign of wide-ranging land fraud that had resulted in thousands of acres of illegal enclosures.[43]

That same year New Mexico territorial governor Edmund Ross suggested in his annual report to the secretary of the interior that land fraud and bureaucratic incompetence were having deleterious effects on efforts to fairly adjudicate Spanish and Mexican property claims in the territory.[44] Decades after treaty guarantees, scores of Spanish and Mexican land grants and millions of acres of property claims lingered in legal limbo. The majority of these claims, he told the secretary of the interior, were "unimpeachable" and "as perfect and conclusive as can be found anywhere."[45] Ross found it inexcusable (a "serious embarrassment," he called it) that thirty years of federal adjudication had failed to resolve the issue.[46] According to Ross, "public robbers" capitalized on the uncertainty in property claims.[47] Fraudulent homestead, timber culture, and preemption claims "have been thus absorbed into great cattle ranches, merely for the purpose of getting control of water courses and springs, and thus keep out settlers and small herds, and in others the lands have been thus stolen for purely speculative purposes."[48]

The land fraud scandals were impossible to ignore. President Grover Cleveland appointed former Indiana Republican congressman George Julian as the new surveyor general. The seventy-year-old reformer arrived in New

Mexico in July 1885, intent on ridding the territory of a ring that, he wrote, "hovered over the territory like a pestilence."[49] By the time Julian arrived in New Mexico, "speculators owned nearly every Spanish and Mexican land grant."[50] During his tenure as surveyor general, Julian carefully detailed the full extent of land fraud and land grant speculation in New Mexico and condemned the work of the land rings in language forceful and direct. He heaped scorn on the Santa Fe Ring, describing the territory as "under the malign influence of land stealing experts."[51]

His contempt for speculators, however, did not translate into support for the land grant property claims, which he believed hindered the development of a modern New Mexico. He considered it a "systematic robbery of the Government" to conclude that land grant heirs owned the vast common lands.[52] Julian, a true believer in the abstract idea of private property as a necessary condition for progress, was blind to the interdependent relationship between land grant property relations and ecological conditions. Operating under the fantasy that the land grant uplands could be carved into lots and farmed, he argued that the commons should be made available for new settlers to support the inexorable spread of an "intelligent and enterprising population" to replace the "rough and miscellaneous" one found in New Mexico.[53] He imagined a stream of settlers passing through New Mexico for California suddenly "arrested by the new order of things." Captivated by the possibilities, they would pour "into her valleys and plains. Small land-holdings, thrifty tillage, and compact settlements [would] supersede great monopolies, slovenly agriculture, and industrial stagnation."[54]

The land grant settlers in Tierra Amarilla and other land grant communities thus found themselves caught between two forces of dispossession. On one side merchants and speculators like Burns and Catron, who preyed on grant property for financial gain, aggressively pursued land grants. On the other side reformers like Julian, a man who found land grants incompatible with private property and agrarian democracy, developed legal theories he hoped would lead to the legal rejection of common property entirely.

Partido Mercantilism and the Land Speculation in Tierra Amarilla

The land grant speculation that unfolded in Tierra Amarilla in the late nineteenth century began in mercantile stores like those owned by Thomas Burns. After arriving in Tierra Amarilla in the 1860s, Burns opened two mercantile stores, one at Camp Plumber/Fort Lowell and another in the land grant village of Los Ojos. The stores brought him into daily contact with the sheepherders and small farmers who populated the Tierra Amarilla land grant and to whom he sold clothing, sugar, and coffee at exorbitant prices. Tobacco and whiskey were his best-selling items.[55] While the store at the fort proved lucrative, the store on the grant made little money for Burns. Locals, assuming that he could entice them to shop at the store at all, could pay only in *carneros*, or sheep. This was not an ideal arrangement for a mercantile capitalist hoping to develop a cash business. But Burns understood that what the sheepherders, or *carneradas*, lacked in money they made up for in land and labor. Burns thus began to accept sheep as payment for mercantile goods and quickly became the largest sheep owner in Tierra Amarilla.

Sheep raising in New Mexico largely followed a pattern called *partido* production, a practice developed first in Spain in the fourteenth century. A large sheep owner, or *patron*, would rent ewes to local sheepherders. The renter, or *partidario*, would acquire the flock of sheep on credit and split the flock's natural increase with the *patron* during a negotiated time frame, often a period of five years. Throughout the Spanish and Mexican period in New Mexico, large sheep owners south of Santa Fe managed huge flocks that they slowly built through the labor of hundreds of *partido* sheepherders under contract.[56] The terms and conditions of these contracts were traditionally limited to the natural surplus in wool and sheep that *partidarios* managed. In theory *partido* contracts offered small sheepherders the possibility to build their own large herds. But while *partido* production vastly increased the sheep population in New Mexico during the nineteenth century, it was an increase that usually benefited *patrons* at the expense of *partidarios*.[57] As it developed in northern New Mexico in particular, *partido* production became a "system of debt peonage [that] provided economic security at the cost of personal freedom."[58] The contracts offered the tantalizing prospect of economic security because *partidarios* could enter into contracts whenever they wanted and then freely run sheep on the large common lands to which they had access. But there were unavoidable risks. If they were unable to meet the terms of a contract because of sheep mortality due to predation or disease, for example, they were obligated to pay off the debt by entering into new contracts with increasingly more onerous terms.

When Burns arrived in Tierra Amarilla in the mid-1860s, *partido* production was not common in northern New Mexico. The land grant sheepherders who did raise their own sheep did so largely for household consumption. Burns, however, began offering *partido* contracts to local sheepherders in the 1870s as a way to manage his growing flocks. Tierra Amarilla land grant settlers lacked money to purchase ewes for their own flocks but had access to abundant forage on the common lands. The terms of Burns's contracts, however, differed sharply from traditional *partido* arrangements. First, Burns understood quite well that if the goal of sheep production was profit and not subsistence, then the manifold risks and uncertainties of sheep production would have to be shifted from the sheep owner and to the sheepherder. Most contracts developed by Anglo merchants thus passed along all responsibility for the loss of sheep from wolves and weather to the *partidario*.[59] The contracts, therefore, established arms-length rental arrangements between sheep owners and sheepherders that transferred the hazards of sheep production entirely to the *partidarios*.[60] This was a departure from traditional *partido* practices in which risk was shared between *patron* and *partidario*.

Second, Burns's *partido* contracts required that *partidarios* outfit themselves with supplies from his mercantile store. Since few Tierra Amarilla sheepherders had money to purchase supplies, most were forced to buy on credit at rates usually in excess of 10 percent. In order to pay off credit, *partidarios* paid in sheep. The contracts therefore increased Burns's share of any production surplus and gave him the ability to control both local labor and the abundant grazing resources of land grant settlers. *Partido* mercantilism as Burns developed it guaranteed him a return of between 10 and 15 percent.[61]

Third, since many sheepherders secured *partido* contracts and mercantile credit with Burns by mortgaging their *hijuelas*, the contracts became a vehicle for land acquisition by Burns. While the specific terms of *partido* contracts varied over time and space, *partidarios* in general were obligated to return twenty adult male sheep and an amount of wool, often between twenty and forty pounds, for every one hundred adult females rented. If sheepherders were unable to meet the terms of the *partido* contracts, which also included mercantile credit, they would go into default. Nearly a quarter of all *partido* contracts ended in default, an event that announced the start of a debt peonage relation.[62] When a *partidario* lost sheep to wolves, weather, or disease, for example, and could not meet the terms of the contract, Burns foreclosed on land he held as collateral.[63] But this did not always satisfy the debt obligation. *Partidarios* also owed interest on credit purchases at the store. To service this debt *partidarios* were forced to enter into new contracts with terms that now included a rental fee on lands they once owned or had free access to. The *partido* agreements grew Burns's flocks, the credit terms grew his store, and the defaults grew his land holdings.

The *partido* production that developed with the arrival of Anglo merchants in the 1870s and 1880s was not a meeting of equals in exchange, as some historians have contended, but rather a means to capture rural labor and control common land.[64] The terms of the rental contracts trapped land grant settlers in cycles of debt from which few could escape and allowed Burns to acquire thousands of acres of land grant property.⁶⁵ The *partido* mercantilism Burns practiced in Tierra Amarilla altered the terms of a traditional practice in ways that transformed the social and economic lives of land grant settlers. By 1880 the Territory of New Mexico boasted flocks in excess of four million sheep, and *partido* arrangements dominated production throughout eastern and northern New Mexico. As indebtedness increased, the contracts became "mechanisms of control" that changed land grant settlers into sheep "sharecroppers."⁶⁶

Of the forty property transactions Burns filed for small acquisitions on the Tierra Amarilla land grant, thirty-seven were titles acquired directly from sheepherders and holders of *hijuelas*.⁶⁷ Some of the properties were as small as thirty square yards, and none was larger than two hundred varas, the size of a large suburban lot. One *hijuela* holder, Juan Pablo Martin, split his *hijuela* into four smaller sections as he mortgaged parcel after parcel, all of which he eventually lost to Burns. The sheep contracts made Burns enormously wealthy, and the defaults made him a local land baron.

Through the credit terms on his sheep contracts, he transformed land grant settlers into debtors and captured the commons to serve as a factory for meat and wool production. He owned tens of thousands of sheep managed by an army of sheepherders under contracts with terms that few could ever meet and burdened by debt that few could service. His Tierra Amarilla adobe home reflected his enormous wealth. It featured huge, high-ceilinged rooms with velvet carpets and ornate wall hangings. A crowd of servants quartered in small adobes across a watered lawn sustained his opulent lifestyle.⁶⁸

With the sheep industry under his control and his mercantile trade firmly established, Burns turned to lumber. In June 1897 he partnered with Edgar Biggs, a New Mexico and Colorado lumberman who had been cutting timber on the Tierra Amarilla land grant at a rate of more than 500,000 board feet per month since 1891. In the first seven months of their partnership they cut more than 4.2 million board feet from the grant.⁶⁹ In October 1898 they cut more than 1 million board feet of timber from the forests around Tierra Amarilla. Much of the timber was cut on contract with the Denver and Rio Grande Railroad. The contract with the railroad gave Burns and Biggs access to timber along an ever-increasing right-of-way on the grant's timbered slopes.⁷⁰ Biggs and Burns provided ties for new track and trunk lines that opened up new timber stands deeper into the grant. Railroad passengers on the Chama route marveled at the "desolation" of the clear cuts. Along the entire length of the route between Chama and Tierra Amarilla, the D&RG's passengers saw only stumps where a forest once stood.⁷¹

Catron and the Consolidation of Tierra Amarilla

Throughout the late 1870s Burns acted as a seemingly friendly advisor to local *hijuela* holders interested in clearing legal questions to their property claims. In the spring of 1877 he hired the prominent Santa Fe attorney Eugene Fiske to investigate the veracity of settler claims to Tierra Amarilla. The gesture was not altogether altruistic. Burns was collecting *hijuelas* as collateral on sheep contracts, and his business depended on the legitimacy of settler claims. He spent years doing the due diligence necessary to confirm the property claims of his clients and thus his growing real estate portfolio.[72] He also examined birth, death, and baptismal records of Manuel Martínez's many heirs to determine the legitimacy of their claims. He hired a translator and sent deeds and names of heirs to Fiske by the dozen for examination and opinion.[73] Fiske was uniquely qualified for the task. He had been the chief of the Land Claims Division of the General Land Office in Washington, where he used his authority almost exclusively to grow his personal wealth. He solicited bribes and, with the help of Surveyor General Henry Atkinson, sold bogus surveys to speculators. He was forced to resign after a series of questionable transactions finally marked him as a land speculator.[74]

While Fiske did the legal and political work, Burns collected and managed the deeds, commissioned their translations, and slowly constructed an archive that traced the full history of the Tierra Amarilla land grant. As Burns studied the legal and property histories of Tierra Amarilla, a speculator named Wilmot Broad worked on a parallel track. He bought deeds from Martínez heirs and partnered with Santa Fe speculator Elias Brevoort. Broad hired William F. M. Arny to help locate a site for a new village. Arny, the former Indian agent who now worked almost exclusively as a guide to mining speculators and real estate brokers, selected a spot along the Rio de Chama that Brevoort called Parkview, a name designed to resonate with midwestern farmers to whom they hoped to sell property. They advertised in Chicago newspapers for settlers to relocate to the grant, which they described as a place "of green and luxuriant vegetation" where "the scenery... [was] grand and beautiful."[75] Brevoort recruited a miller named Theodore Seth to operate a flour and sawmill in Parkview while Broad made sales trips north looking for midwestern immigrant farmers.[76] According to Broad and various regional newspapers, Chicago settlers began streaming westward into Parkview. Mills and machinery followed, they claimed, but it was all an elaborate fraud. Despite optimistic reports the colony never took hold, and by 1877, when travelers and federal surveyors visited Tierra Amarilla, they found Parkview abandoned. Broad and Brevoort eventually sold out to Catron.

Catron's early reluctance to pursue aggressive speculation stemmed from the fact that the land grant had not been surveyed. In 1875 a Santa Fe speculator named John Isaacs, working in league with Brevoort as one of the many partial owners of the grant, finally pushed their demands through the General Land Office, which resulted in a survey by Henry Atkinson of nearly 600,000 acres.[77]

The careful genealogical research of Burns and Fiske and the survey finally convinced Catron that the time to buy up deeds had finally arrived. Both he and Burns began purchasing deeds in earnest in early 1877. Over the course of the next year a parade of Martínez heirs unloaded their claims, often fractional shares of the entire grant, to Catron, Burns, or associated ring investors. In a financial funnel the deeds all eventually found their way to Catron and Burns. Catron bought out the claims of Frederick Muller and the rights from another heir of one of Manuel Martínez's children. During the first three days of February 1881, Catron finalized his investment; he bought nearly every outstanding deed left on the market and registered some ten land transactions with the county clerk. The transactions consolidated the property claims that had already been slowly combined through investments by nearly a dozen speculators.

Catron's flurry of transactions in 1881 corresponded with the issuance of the congressional patent for the land grant and the sale of the right-of-way to the Denver and Rio Grande Railroad, which included lots for a depot and residences in the lumber town of Chama, a few miles north of Tierra Amarilla and just south of the Colorado line. Less than a year later he mortgaged the grant with the Mercantile Trust Company of New York for two hundred thousand dollars.[78] Over the next two years he worked behind the scenes to quiet his title while also working to stimulate the development and expansion of commercial activity on the grant.

During this period Catron earned royalties from lumber contracts. He also leased grazing land to Burns and to more than a dozen other sheepherders. In August 1883 he drew on the research conducted by Burns and Fiske to file a quiet title suit in district court. The suit was a model of how land grant speculation was done. His complaint alleged that only Manuel Martínez settled the grant, therefore reserving sole ownership for only Manuel Martínez and no others. He made an exception to his claim based on conditional donations, which he estimated accounted for fewer than six thousand acres. "Francisco Martínez... in order to induce people to settle on and cultivate said grant and tract of land made conditional donations of small strips of cultivable land in the valleys of the Nutritas, Chama and Brazos rivers."[79] The language referred to the private home sites of the more than 130 *hijuelas*. But the complaint did not name any settlers in either the notice published in the newspaper or in the handbills posted around Rio Arriba County. Although Burns and Fiske had produced a complete genealogy that served as Catron's road map to property acquisition, he claimed not to know the names of any of the land grant settlers. The complaint was filed against the "unknown heirs of Manuel Martínez, Sesto Martínez and Eusebio Martínez, and all others the unknown claimants of interest."[80] He agreed to a number of exceptions on forty separate former *hijuelas* in an agreement that protected Burns's land acquisitions from Catron's quiet title lawsuit.[81]

With the heirs out of the way, the rights to the commons severed from the sheepherders, the survey and patent finalized, and the transportation infrastructure in place, Catron turned his full attention to finding a buyer for the grant. He was a better speculator than salesman. Although royalty income was substantial, real money would come only from selling the grant outright. Over the next twenty years Catron marketed the grant with a price tag that fluctuated between $500,000 and $4 million. Confident he could sell the grant for as much as $2 million, he started negotiations with interested buyers from New York but quickly drove many away with outrageous terms and financial demands. Early on, he turned down an offer of $1 million for the entire grant and drove interested buyers away one after the other.[82] His efforts continued over the next few years while rental and royalty income and the rumors of million-dollar land sales worked their way down to the settlers living on the grant.

In September 1889 forty-six local residents, led by the Parkview lumber mill operator Theodore Seth, filed suit in district court against Catron. The suit declared that Catron's claim as sole owner of the grant was "scandalous," and it demanded that the court declare the complainants "tenants-in-common" with Catron.[83] The wording of the complaint makes clear that the plaintiffs did not seek to invalidate Catron's claims. Instead they were after a share in the sale of the grant. The complaint asked the court to appoint a committee to partition the grant so that the proceeds from a sale could be split equally. The plaintiffs were apparently convinced that Catron was on the verge of selling the grant for upward of $1.5 million, and they staked a claim to an equal undivided interest in the 595,000-acre grant and the possible windfall the sale could bring. Catron countersued, claiming that the suit clouded his title and ruined a possible land sale he was negotiating. Though the $1.5 million figure was an exaggeration, the suit apparently did cloud the title enough to scuttle a possible sale to a German buyer.[84]

The complainants also sought a share of Catron's rental income from timber harvesting. In the lawsuit he downplayed the importance of timber income. It was true that Catron's $36,000 yearly royalty payments for timber collapsed in the late 1890s when demand in Denver and Pueblo, Colorado, sagged. In truth, however, Catron expected a rebound in demand and wrote to a colleague that he planned to raise his stumpage rates and intensify timber harvesting. Five mills operated on the grant, and each one milled 125,000 board feet of lumber per day. Catron planned to let out contracts to harvest all 500 million board feet of timber that he estimated the grant held. He told the court, however, that the grant was bankrupting him.[85] If anyone was a victim, he told the court, it was he and not those suing him. The complainants were "cunningly contriving" to use the courts to defraud Catron of his rightful property claim and cash in on timber royalties (Seth, he reminded the court, ran a lumber mill and was already milling lumber "illegally" cut by settlers).[86] The Seth suit went away without any record of its adjudication.

With the legal challenge out of the way, Catron intensified his efforts to find a buyer. But failures hounded him. A sale to a London-based buyer collapsed in 1891 at $1.35 million. He circulated a prospectus in 1901 that estimated the value of the grant in excess of $5.2 million, but no investors were interested.[87] He struggled to service debts and pay taxes for the grant, and by the turn of the century he was in arrears on his taxes and awash in debt.[88] He shifted ownership to his son Charles Catron and in 1902 mortgaged the grant a second time for $250,000 with the Continental Trust Company in Denver.[89] In a letter and report he sent to a mortgage company, he blamed the settlers for his failures to sell the grant. It was impossible, he wrote, to sell "lands occupied by squatters."[90] No one, it seemed, wanted Catron's overpriced Mexican land grant.[91] By then he was in debt for nearly $500,000, earning royalties that barely paid the taxes and the interest but still holding out for more than $1 million for the grant. In 1909, with creditors threatening foreclosure, Catron sold the grant in a fire sale for less than $500,000 to the Arlington Land Company, a firm owned by a consortium of Minnesota investors. The amount barely covered his debts.

When Thomas Burns died of pneumonia at the age of seventy-two in March 1916, the local newspaper in Tierra Amarilla called him a "man of unusual business ability."[92] It was an apt description. By the time of his death he had almost single-handedly restructured the regional economy from one organized around household agriculture and sheep production to an economy focused on wool, timber, and mineral exports. Through *partido* contracts he grew flocks of sheep in the tens of thousands. He owned thousands of acres of land in and around Tierra Amarilla and had lease arrangements for even more. In the years before his death, he expanded his mercantile operation to include more stores, more *partido* contracts, and even a mercantile bank in southern Colorado. After his death his son, T. D. Burns Jr., along with a coterie of Anglo ranchers and local merchants, moved quickly to consolidate control of his various enterprises. They expanded sheep contracts, extended more credit to mercantile customers, launched new banking ventures, and opened large commercial timber and mining operations.

The local newspaper, the *New State*, devoted page after page in each issue to legal notices of new incorporations in and around Tierra Amarilla. In each edition local readers found advertisements for new construction companies, mining and timber operations, and new merchants and commercial businesses. Burns Jr. organized the Rio Arriba State Bank in Chama in 1919, and a partner incorporated the eponymous J. H. Sargent Toll Road linking rural villages to the east of Tierra Amarilla with a pay-per-use road. A year later the two men and a number of other investors incorporated the Pound Brothers Lumber Company, a firm whose directors included Burns's brothers-in-law, George Becker and H. L. Hall. The Anglo commercial elite bought the wool and, at times, entire flocks of debt-bound *partidarios* at a discount. They bought the bulk of sheep, and captured much of the profit, from the sheep markets in Chama throughout the first decade of the twentieth century.[93]

Thomas Catron died less than five years after Burns, on May 15, 1921. Though he owned no property in Tierra Amarilla at the time of his death, his legal and speculative interest in it transformed property relations on the grant. By 1920 land grant settlers were increasingly forced off the land when miles of barbed-wire fences erected by new private owners like the Arlington Land Company enclosed their former common pastures. By then most land grant settlers in Tierra Amarilla were awash in a sea of unpayable debt. Without grazing lands many migrated seasonally out of New Mexico to work as contract sheepherders, on railroad construction crews, in mines, or in the Colorado beet fields.[94] For those who stayed, crop failures in parts of northern New Mexico, which reached 59 percent in the 1920s, made land grant living almost impossible.[95] New taxation policies on land also contributed to growing patterns of property loss. The slow erosion in resource access for land grant sheepherders by new corporate owners in Tierra Amarilla produced sharp antagonisms between settlers and Anglo ranchers. Those simmering conflicts boiled over in the summer of 1919, when bands of clandestine night riders burned barns, cut fences, and threatened ranchers who now made private claims to the former commons. The eruption in open and violent conflict is the subject of the next chapter.

CHAPTER THREE

The Night Riders of Tierra Amarilla

IN AUGUST 1919 Tierra Amarilla's Spanish-language newspaper, *El Nuevo Estado*, reported that clandestine bands of night riders had destroyed the fences of two Anglo ranchers on the Tierra Amarilla land grant. The ranchers, according to the report, found threatening notes identifying the fence cutters as La Mano Negra (The Black Hand). The attack marked the beginning of a string of late-night raids on local ranchers. Throughout the summer of 1919 and into the spring of 1920, stories of fence cutting and arson filled newspapers in Tierra Amarilla and Santa Fe. Frightened ranchers, desperate for help, flooded Governor Octaviano Larrazolo with letters that chronicled a summer and fall of threats, arson, and constant harassment. The governor, concerned that the attacks marked the beginning of an organized rural insurgency, sent two undercover police agents to Tierra Amarilla in May 1920 to investigate the reports.[1]

Officer Alcario Montoya and his partner spent a frustrating week in Tierra Amarilla in early May investigating the stories of night riding. They met first with two ranchers, George Becker and H. L. Hall, who told the officers of fences cut, repaired, and cut again. They described days riding their fences and finding wire cut up and posts burned or chopped to pieces. Both men had lost horses in fires that had destroyed their barns and consumed most of their hay. While Becker and Hall, two early targets of the night riders, had plenty to say to Montoya and his partner, few others in the area would talk to the officers. On their last night in Tierra Amarilla, Montoya talked his way into a card game in the home of a land grant sheepherder. Although the talk among the men at the card game was of ongoing injustices in Tierra Amarilla, they were not the injustices that Montoya expected to hear. "They are stealing land from the people through fraud," explained one cardplayer when asked why Becker and Hall were targets. "And they are fencing everything — they have not left a place where one can pasture a goat."[2] Soon after the first attack, according to the cardplayers, Becker threatened his neighbors with promises of swift punishment to anyone who attacked his home or property. He guaranteed a police crackdown unless the fence cutting stopped immediately. Montoya voiced incredulity that the two men would have made such threats. They did, came the reply, "because they are stealing land from the people," and this has made them insecure in the community.[3]

Montoya and the other agent left Tierra Amarilla the following morning with vague reports of shadowy horseman and unsettling local anger. In his final report to the governor, Montoya explained that the fencing that had begun in earnest after Burns's death had ignited intense animosity in Tierra Amarilla toward the new class of commercial ranchers. Becker and Hall, as large landowners, creditors, and sons-in-law of Thomas Burns, were especially despised. Many of the people Montoya encountered, he explained to the governor, considered vigilantism their last and best option to rid the grant of private fences. As one cardplayer explained to him, "[We] are all poor," and justice is only for those who can afford it. It "must be bought."[4]

The failed investigation frightened Becker, who buried the governor in a mountain of panicky letters, pressing him to do more. He even offered to pay the salaries of more undercover agents and new police patrols on the grant.[5] Hall's complaints and lobbying lasted for more than a year, and by May 1921 land grant members began their own campaign with the governor. In letters to the governor they explained why locals considered the fences illegal. Catron, they wrote, had acceded to demands from land grant residents in the late nineteenth century and agreed to respect their claims to the common lands. Catron never fenced the commons because he acknowledged their legitimate claim, they told the governor. Becker and Hall, however, were violating this agreement.[6] The governor contacted Catron. From his sickbed in Santa Fe, Catron refused to acknowledge any agreement with local sheepherders. He died just days later. Without proof of an agreement with Catron, the governor refused to intercede on behalf of local sheepherders in their conflicts over land grant fencing. Just days after Catron's death and Larrazolo's refusal, a huge blaze destroyed Becker's stables and various outbuildings and killed three teams of horses.[7]

Few reports of fence cutting or arson appeared in the local newspapers in the years following the first uprising and the Montoya investigation. But in April 1924 newspapers reported that fence cutting and arson had returned to the grant. Kenneth Heron, a surveyor and rancher in Tierra Amarilla, wrote a letter to the governor claiming, among other things, that the attacks had never ended. Anglo residents and the largest landowners in Tierra Amarilla had been under constant attack, he wrote. From 1919 until the present, ranchers had faced "robbery, murder, fence cutting, hay burning and other outrages in the upper

Chama Valley."⁸ In one attack fence cutters destroyed more than twenty-five miles of fences on private ranches within the borders of the grant. As earlier, ranchers made repairs only to find fences quickly destroyed again. Night riders burned haystacks and barns.

Homes too were bursting into flames. In the rubble of one destroyed home, ominous threats were found in handbills that promised still more violence against wealthy landowners. Just as in 1919 private ranchers pleaded with the governor for protection in letters that described the sporadic attacks of previous years as an organized resistance to fencing and private property. Some fled the region in the face of death threats, while a siege mentality gripped those who remained.⁹

The *Santa Fe New Mexican*, a newspaper long allied with the commercial elite in New Mexico, printed sensationalized stories of rural banditry in Tierra Amarilla. The night riders had unleashed "a reign of terror" in Tierra Amarilla, wrote its editors.¹⁰ The newspaper described the grant as seized by chaos and criminality, yet ignored by a government indifferent to the frantic pleas for help by wealthy landowners. Under pressure from ranchers and constant media scrutiny in Santa Fe, authorities issued sweeping declarations of organized banditry in Tierra Amarilla but could do little to stop it.

A number of local ranchers, however, dismissed the threats and fence cutting as the work of a small cadre of land grant brigands. A ranch manager on the large Juan José Lobato land grant between Abiquiú and Tierra Amarilla claimed to be a victim of threats and, echoing Catron's dismissive language of earlier years, speculated that the night riders were "disgruntled squatters who oppose[d] the fencing of land grants when it interfere[d] with the cattle grazing."¹¹ Yet the scope and scale of the attacks convinced many that a broad-based, organized movement was to blame.

The possibility of a guerilla army patrolling the former common lands in Tierra Amarilla and exacting revenge on ranchers responsible for the enclosures was at the root of the widespread fear among private ranchers. Newspapers agreed and when referring to the Tierra Amarilla night riders deployed a rotating repertoire of names that included "terrorists," "marauders," and "arsonists."¹² In April 1924 Heron wrote to the governor complaining that night riders had destroyed nearly all the fences "of practically all the Americans in the Valley." The fence cutting in April had followed an eventful March in which suspicious fires had consumed most of the hay in the valley.¹³

The attacks so frightened Mary Emma Burns Becker, the daughter of Thomas Burns and wife of George Becker, that she fled Tierra Amarilla, claiming, "[I am] afraid to go back there to live, as you never know what they will do next."¹⁴

Heron criticized local law enforcement in April for its inability or unwillingness to deal with "a band of forty to fifty bandits responsible for these outrages."[15] He had just written the governor days earlier complaining of new "outrages in Rio Arriba County" that included reports of arson, nearly every fence on the grant cut, and poisoned guard dogs on the largest ranches.[16] Newspapers narrated tales of terror in which a secret society of land grant insurgents conspired to murder private ranchers; set homes, barns, and haystacks on fire; and destroyed the fences of large landowners. Public indignation, at least among the targets of the night riders, was "at the boiling point."[17]

As suddenly as the ominous black hands appeared, however, they were gone. In their place a new and curious threat emerged. In the spring of 1924 handbills were found nailed to telephone poles around burned-out homes and businesses.[18] Heron removed one and included it, and a translation of it, in a letter to the governor. Only his English-language translation survives. "Notice to Night and Day Watchers," the proclamation begins,

> Notice is hereby given to all watchers that they must watch their own business and leave the big Whale (T.D.) alone for he is the cause of all this doings.
>
> As the reason was told to the public on the last notice there is no use to be telling the same thing again. Now mind this you watchers for we know who they are and we know every step you make, they blame only the poor Mexicans for all this doings, it is not so, there are members from every nationality, for there are Americans, Mexicans, Spaniards, Indians, and every kind of good citizens that want to defend the justice of the poor people. For we know that now a days there is no justice on the courts for the poor, no matter is they have the justice.
>
> You know who manage the courts, there is no chance for the poor, another think, why is it that this son-of-beaches always employ people from outside this State on their ranches? They must say that this people doesn't know how to work. Yes a good answer for the son of beaches, The truth is because the poor people that comes from outside of the State don't know that they are going to be robbed, and that they only last from twelve to eighteen months, and then what?
>
> T.D. sends them away without any drawers nothing to cover his nuts, he has done plenty of this job-lot, now he is making his retreat away from home but he will be here some day and we are going to stop all his schemes, and you are not going to believe this until you see some of his watchers hanged on the telephone posts, and the whale found drown near Espanola, or El Paso.
>
> We have heard that he is not afraid of this notices, if he is not afraid who is it that he brought that chile Colorado (the sheriff) along to take the notice off, but poor little fish,

Now this notice ought to stay at least 10 days and if it is taken away before that time, then we will be ready for the first opportunity, and we are going to show you that we mean what we say, this is no story-telling either, by and by you will see what is going to happen to this fawners.

We are ready any time no matter if you bring the PACK OF HOUNDS.[19]

At the bottom of the new handbills, Heron included, without comment, the initials he found on the handbill. Instead of the expected La Mano Negra, the letter writers included the initials KKK — the Ku Klux Klan.

Understanding Race and Class in Northern New Mexico

What makes the night riders of Tierra Amarilla in the 1920s so remarkable is not only that the challenge to private property on the grant was so widespread, sustained, and frightening to politicians and private ranchers but also that resistance to the enclosures has confounded historical analyses of land grant unrest in New Mexico. Every historian who has examined this period has arrived at a different explanation for the sudden emergence of rural unrest. But despite the variety of explanations, none has considered how and why local land grant residents would draw on the rhetoric of the Ku Klux Klan in making threats against private ranchers. Under what conditions, after all, could the notorious Klan have found common cause with a Spanish-speaking rural populace? How could the universally Catholic land grant villagers in Tierra Amarilla have forged a shared politics with the racist, anti-Catholic Klan?[20]

One early history of rural protest among land grant communities in New Mexico ignored racial conflict entirely and explained social unrest and rural discontent as various manifestations of internal, primitive cultural characteristics claimed to be unique to rural land grant villages in northern New Mexico. "He did not worry about the future," writes historian Andrew Schlesinger, describing New Mexico's land grant settlers, "as he did not regret the past; it would not change."[21] For Schlesinger land grant protest reflected a fear of progress and change rather than a defense of existing property relations and cultural practices.

The histories that followed Schlesinger have located exogenous factors at the root of land grant protest. Although it is unclear whether local authorities in the 1920s considered the images of black hands painted on destroyed fences important, one historian has argued that La Mano Negra was a reference to a clandestine, anarchist organization active in Spain in the late nineteenth century. The Black Hand channeled the discontent of Spanish peasants and rural farmworkers in Andalusia in a campaign of crop burning, property destruction, and, according to local authorities, murder of landed elites. Spanish newspapers frequently sensationalized violence in Andalusia as the ongoing plotting of rural terrorists. Spanish authorities described Mano Negra as an international network of anarchist revolutionaries. The story made for good copy and filled mainstream Spanish newspapers for years.[22] Hideouts were discovered, police officials declared, where blackened human hands were found hanging from ropes, around which, they surmised, La Mano Negra members took their secret blood oaths.

Revolutionary Spanish anarchists roaming the Tierra Amarilla hills? It seems far-fetched, yet Frances Leon Swadesh, in her influential book *Los Primeros Pobladores*, interprets the threats as proof that Spanish exiles from the struggle in Andalusia came to Tierra Amarilla in a "steady migration of Spanish miners, herders and common laborers" to escape a violent rural crackdown on labor activism and organizing.[23] These radicals landed in Tierra Amarilla, she suggests, and infused the nascent, unorganized anti-enclosure movement among land grant settlers with a revolutionary anarchist consciousness imported directly from Spain. But despite these fantastic claims, there is little evidence of any Spanish anarchist migration or influence in northern New Mexico in the 1920s.[24]

Historians of the Spanish anarchist movement offer more reason to doubt the link. While agricultural workers in Andalusia were overwhelmingly allied with the anarchist labor union Confederación Trabajadores, the sensationalized claims of murder and banditry attributed to La Mano Negra were largely circumstantial and may even have been invented by authorities as a pretext for the expansion of a brutal campaign of rural repression against unionized agricultural workers.[25]

The historian Sarah Deutsch makes no mention of Spanish anarchists in Tierra Amarilla in her book *No Separate Refuge* and instead links the emergence of La Mano Negra in Tierra Amarilla to an anti-enclosure movement in the 1890s led by a group called Las Gorras Blancas (the White Caps) in San Miguel County, New Mexico, in the 1890s.[26] Vicious cycles of credit and debt undermined the land grant economy on the Las Vegas land grant in San Miguel County east of Tierra Amarilla in the late 1880s and created the conditions for a wave of night riding and rural unrest. As in Tierra Amarilla the privatization of land grant common lands in Las Vegas relied on new economic and political arrangements sparked by expanding railroad development and speculative investment. By the late 1880s fences and fraudulent private claims had remade the subsistence geography of the common property grant. Once organized around common property land tenure arrangements, the grant was seized by speculators, who transformed it into a huge commercial landholding reinforced by barbed-wire fences and expanded by homestead, preemption, and timber-culture claims. Land grant settlers found themselves trapped in a sea of commercial cattle and surrounded by fences that blocked their access not only to the pastures and waters on which their livelihoods depended but also to the schools, churches, and neighbors that sustained whole communities and existing cultural traditions. With land grant production largely impossible, many turned to wage labor with the railroad or on the new commercial ranches.

Night riding erupted in Las Vegas in the late 1880s, when a clandestine group of land grant settlers who called themselves Las Gorras Blancas cut hundreds of miles of barbed-wire fences, destroyed miles of railroad track, and threatened to evict wealthy ranchers from the grant in a campaign that lasted eighteen months. Deutsch argues that Las Gorras Blancas resistance declined in the early 1890s but was immediately picked up by La Mano Negra.[27] Her conclusions, however, have been contradicted by extensive research on Las Gorras Blancas that has documented the local roots of the protest movement in Las Vegas and its distinction from related protest or anti-enclosure movements elsewhere in New Mexico.[28]

In Richard Gardner's history of Tierra Amarilla, he describes La Mano Negra as an organized bootlegging enterprise and local criminal network.[29] For Gardner the stories of fence cutting in Tierra Amarilla were part of a long history of rural criminality among land grant residents in Rio Arriba County. Gardner's dismissiveness of La Mano Negra is matched by Tierra Amarilla native and former New Mexico State historian Robert Tórrez's celebration of La Mano Negra. Tórrez has written one of the few histories of La Mano Negra. In it he relies on oral histories of the movement to conclude that "there is a little of the Mano Negra in each of them. . . . They wait, with wire cutters ready, for the mysterious call to gather and take their revenge."[30] For many contemporary heirs to the Tierra Amarilla land grant, La Mano Negra night riders were the heroes of a guerilla struggle against the enclosures that threatened land grant society.

Other than Tórrez's brief mention, however, no histories consider any possible Klan role in the land grant struggle. Given the dearth of historical research and limited documentary evidence on the Klan in Tierra Amarilla, what reasons could there possibly be to focus on the Ku Klux Klan? First, the threat of the Klan in the Heron letter was a threat made by the same Tierra Amarilla residents who actively resisted the privatization of the commons. To declare the Klan–Tierra Amarilla connection a topic unworthy of historical investigation, therefore, would be to reject the premise that motivates this research, namely, that land grant residents were active and sophisticated actors in the struggle for land grant property in northern New Mexico. I focus throughout this book on the way legal knowledge is constituted in a struggle that includes the words and deeds of ordinary land grant residents. For this reason I take seriously the variety of tactics that Tierra Amarilla night riders used in property struggle.

Second, the Klan appears in more than just one threatening handbill. There is ample evidence that the Klan was well known to New Mexicans during the tumultuous period of night riding in Tierra Amarilla. Throughout the early 1920s local newspapers in New Mexico relentlessly covered the rise of the Ku Klux Klan in regional and national politics. At the same time that Tierra Amarilla night riders menaced private ranchers in Tierra Amarilla with Klan threats, the *Santa Fe New Mexican* reported, in article after article, that the rise of the Klan in Colorado, Texas, and national politics frightened local elites in New Mexico.[31] The Klan was well known to Tierra Amarilla residents, in particular as a group that political and economic elites in New Mexico, the very people with whom land grant residents fought over property claims, considered a threat.

Last, I do not argue in this chapter that Tierra Amarilla night riders were organized by Klan promoters or influenced by Klan ideology. Although various Colorado and Texas klaverns (as Klan chapters were called) actively organized in New Mexico during this period, none found success in northern New Mexico. Also I make no claims that Tierra Amarilla night riders were duped by the rhetoric of racist populism reflected in the Klan's version of 1920s nativism. The people populating land grant villages such as Tierra Amarilla were targets, not the possible allies, of a reactionary social movement such as the Klan. As historian Robert Rosenbaum argues, "To nineteenth-century nativist eyes, [land grant settlers] clearly embodied the racial and papist threats, and as time went on they were seen as a political threat as well."[32] Instead I take seriously the threat of the Klan made by the Tierra Amarilla night riders as a way to examine how the rise of nativism in the U.S. Southwest in the 1920s, and the racialized and uneven geographies of property and citizenship that nativism produced in the West, influenced land grant struggle in New Mexico.

The Uneven Geographies of Race and Class in Land Grant Struggle

As I show in this chapter, the Ku Klux Klan, powerful in Texas and Colorado, could not find success in New Mexico. While Anglo elites in Texas and Colorado embraced the Klan, where nativism reinforced patterns of white privilege that served the elite political and economic interests of a settler colonial society, the Klan frightened Anglo and Spanish-speaking elites in New Mexico, where Spanish colonial history had produced a much different racial order. New Mexico's racial order operated as a kind of caste system that valorized not only Anglo settlers but also elites of Spanish descent. The racial order in New Mexico was complicated by a history of colonial conquest that muddied strict racial categories. But as Laura Gomez notes, "it was precisely such ubiquitous and multidimensional racial mixture that spawned a hardening of formal racial categories" in New Mexico.[33] The result was a racial order that reserved the privileges of whiteness not only to an Anglo political or merchant class but also to elite Hispanic society at the expense of what elites considered socially backward land grant communities.[34]

The version of whiteness that had become hegemonic in New Mexico during this period was one that defined whiteness though a conquering culture's rhetoric of Spanish American identity "deployed primarily by and for elite New Mexicans."[35] "'Spanish Americans' began to invoke their European racial identity and long history of conquest and colonization to gain acceptance and recognition of their political rights through statehood."[36] They called themselves Spanish American, a term that relied on a blood-of-the-conquerors rhetoric, to distinguish them from land grant settlers. They were "Known as *los ricos* (the wealthy)," according to the historian Charles Montgomery, and "they accounted for less than 5 percent of the Hispano population. Sending their sons to Midwestern and eastern Catholic academies, they made small fortunes in trade and sheep ranching. . . . At the other end of the Hispano society were the people known as *las mases de los hombre pobres* (the poor masses), or, more simply, as *los pobres* or *los paisanos* (the poor peasants). These farmers, house servants, woodcutters, sheepherders, and day laborers accounted for roughly eight of every ten Spanish-speaking people."[37]

The racial order in New Mexico was unusual compared to the rest of the West, where the racist logic of citizenship came to be reflected in legal codes that reinforced unequal legal and property rights along lines of race and class.[38] "Mexicans who were White were given full legal citizenship, while mestizos, Christianized Indians, and Mexicans of African descent were accorded inferior legal rights."[39] In California and Arizona Spanish-speaking residents "were not eligible to vote, hold public office, or practice law because citizenship was a prerequisite."[40]

These histories suggest that race is at the heart of the politics of citizenship.[41] They also suggest, as legal scholar Cheryl Harris has argued, that whiteness is itself a kind of property claim. As Harris has posited, "the set of assumptions, privileges, and benefits that accompany the status of being white [became] a valuable asset that whites sought to protect."[42] The rise of nativism and the Klan in the 1920s posed a new threat to whiteness and property in New Mexico. "Spanish American became dangerously entangled with Mexicans as older stereotypes combined with the issues of recent United States relations with Mexico, labor unrest in the Southwest, and rising nativism to create a more negative response to both Mexicans and Spanish Americans."[43] Despite the appeals to *limpieza de sangre* (pure blood), Spanish-speaking elites in New Mexico found themselves included in racialized dismissals of all New Mexicans, regardless of class, "as a people not possessing the best blood on the American continent."[44]

For land grant settlers the Klan was an agent of social repression in Colorado. But it was also a group that frightened the Anglo elites in New Mexico, who relied on a close alliance with Spanish-speaking elites. A Klan presence in Tierra Amarilla may have been unlikely, but the threat of the Klan was an effective way to frighten those enclosing the commons. What seems at first contradictory (a Spanish-speaking klavern?) appears instead as part of an evolving tactic designed to interrupt New Mexico's racial-economic order. In the next section I turn to the growth of the Klan in the Southwest and consider the ways in which the rise of nativism intersected with an increasingly racialized land grant struggle in northern New Mexico.

The Ku Klux Klan and the Geographies of Nativism in the U.S. Southwest

Although the Klan glorification depicted in D. W. Griffith's notorious 1915 film *The Birth of a Nation*, particularly the second half of the film, in which Griffith rationalizes racial violence based on the premise that former slaves could never be integrated into white society, received a torrent of critical denunciations, including a call for a ban by the editors of the NAACP's journal *The Crisis*, then edited by W. E. B. Du Bois, it rang true with as many as it repulsed. Among those for whom the movie's racist message resonated was a part-time doctor, occasional preacher, and Spanish-American War veteran from Georgia named William Simmons. Charmed, it seems, by the film's depiction of the Klan, Simmons reconstituted the group in November 1915.

At first Simmons presided over the Klan as a local fraternal organization, but he quickly saw the potential to expand beyond the South. He turned to a team of public relations promoters, who hatched a plan to grow the Klan beyond Georgia by developing it into a kind of pyramid scheme.[45] The public relations team hired an army of promoters and paid them on commission based on the number of local organizers they could recruit. Local organizers were also paid on commission based on how many new chapters and members they could sign up in their territory. No one made any money until new klaverns were up and running with new dues-paying members. In general Klan organizers appealed to a growing nativist and anti-immigrant sentiment, but in practice organizers developed highly localized organizing campaigns designed to produce the most dues-paying members. They found particular success by positioning the Klan as a defender of a populist and racialized version of social justice for poor whites.[46]

Despite intense organizing efforts, the group floundered along until the fall of 1921, when a series of exposés on the return of the Klan ran in nearly twenty major newspapers around the country. Alarmed members of Congress convened investigations and a congressional hearing that attracted national interest and gave Simmons and the Klan a national platform. Just months after the congressional hearings, Klan membership skyrocketed from fewer than two thousand members to nearly one million.[47]

The rapid growth was largely a function of a dramatic demographic shift in new Klan membership. Most new members and new klaverns were organized not in the East but in western and southwestern states. By 1922 nearly a quarter million Texans had joined the Klan and had even elected Earle B. Mayfield, a Klan member, to the U.S. Senate.[48] The Klan in Texas was diverse. Several chapters, Beaumont among the most notorious, were organized around active and violent campaigns of vigilantism in defense of white privilege fueled by anti-immigrant (particularly anti-Mexican) sentiment.[49] Cross burning and tarring and feathering became common practices. Other Texas groups, such as the Sam Houston chapter, successfully recruited bankers, public officials, and law enforcement officers more interested in nonviolent means of social coercion. They tapped telephone conversations, organized spy networks, and opened mail in campaigns of morality policing and social "purification drives."[50]

Less than two years after the first reports of fence cutting in Tierra Amarilla, and during the rapid rise of the Klan in Texas, the group unleashed a massive organizing effort along the length of Colorado's front range under the slogan "Every Man under the Capitol Dome a Klansman."[51] From Grand Junction in the north to Durango in the south, with a stronghold in Denver, the Klan organized dozens of chapters statewide and eventually counted nearly forty thousand Coloradans as members.[52] Under the leadership of John Galen Locke, the Colorado Klan came to completely dominate Denver and statewide politics in the 1920s. Democrat Benjamin Stapleton, Locke's close friend and Colorado Klan member number 1,128, received broad-based support from progressive political elements in the city and organized labor and was elected mayor of

Denver in 1923.⁵³ Stapleton appointed Klan members as city attorney and city clerk. The police roster under Stapleton read like a Klan membership list and operated "like an instrument of the Klan's will."⁵⁴ In the wake of the Klan takeover of city politics, crosses were routinely burned in front of Catholic churches and synagogues and in Denver barrios.⁵⁵

With thousands of members and klaverns established throughout the Front Range, the Colorado Klan announced an ambitious plan in 1924 to capture the state legislature, the governorship, and both U.S. Senate seats. That it nearly succeeded demonstrates the depth of Klan sympathy in the state. Despite a flurry of anti-Klan editorials on the eve of the Republican primary election, Klan candidates swept nearly every statewide election. In the run-up to the general election, surprising alliances emerged. Despite the Klan takeover of the Republican Party, the state's black newspaper, the *Colorado Statesmen*, advised its readers to support the slate of racist candidates rather than abandon the party of Lincoln.⁵⁶ Labor unions took no stance on the Klan issue in the election as increasing numbers of white union members joined the Klan. In November 1924 Colorado voters elected Klan candidates to the offices of governor, lieutenant governor, secretary of state, attorney general, and supreme court justice.

Estimates of national Klan membership during this period vary. One estimate counts more than two million men and women as Klan joiners between the years 1915 and 1944, with Texas and Colorado accounting for the bulk of new members. The experience in New Mexico, however, was dramatically different. There were fewer than one thousand Klan members in New Mexico, the lowest membership total of any state in the U.S.⁵⁷ Although the membership numbers were low, organizing efforts were aggressive. In the early 1920s Klan recruiting in New Mexico centered in Las Cruces, in southern New Mexico, where organizers targeted members of fraternal organizations, particularly the Masons. The Klan chapter in El Paso, Texas, became a base of operations where organizers staged constant recruitment sorties into New Mexico and found success in New Mexico's few Anglo-dominated towns such as Hatch and Deming.⁵⁸

In central New Mexico, Klan organizers focused their efforts just south of Albuquerque in campaigns that alarmed New Mexico governors throughout the 1920s. In August 1922 New Mexico governor Merritt Mechem offered to help Valencia County fight Klan influence in local politics. "I have heard with a great deal of concern" he wrote, "of the activities of the Ku Klux Klan.... I think that we should not fail to take any possible steps to fight such influence."⁵⁹ In 1923 Governor Hinkle continued Mechem's Klan monitoring. Klan influence waned, however, until the late 1920s, when Governor Dillon received new reports of Klan organizing in the state.⁶⁰

The Klan found organizing in New Mexico, particularly northern New Mexico, impossible. In 1925 the Klan chapter from Roswell, in southeastern New Mexico, entered a float in a northern New Mexico civic parade and was roundly jeered by the largely Catholic, Spanish-speaking crowd.[61] The Klan failed to find purchase among even the powerful Anglo political and commercial elite. The more powerful the Klan became in Texas and Colorado, the more it became a threat to a racial order in New Mexico dominated by a close political and economic alliance among Anglo and Spanish-speaking elites.

The differences in Klan organizing success created uneven geographies of race that land grant settlers experienced firsthand. The fences that enclosed the commons in the 1920s produced fierce resistance but also forced thousands of land grant settlers off the land and into racialized wage relations. The New Mexico–Colorado border became a racial boundary, particularly for land grant settlers, navigated by thousands of "Hispano families in northern New Mexico's upper Rio Grande Valley [who] sent seven to ten thousand individuals north for work each year," where they labored in Colorado's beet fields and sheep camps.[62]

New Mexicans found brutal working conditions in Colorado, where migrants from Tierra Amarilla and other land grant villages, and more than a million Mexican migrants, suffered "harrowing living conditions, chronic ill health, and eternal poverty."[63] In Colorado the backbreaking harvest required a labor force of twenty thousand workers trapped in labor contracts structured by onerous terms and conditions. "Embracing the labor of all family members able to work, the contract obligated the beet worker to both spring and fall work seasons but did not guarantee payment upon completion of the job."[64] The wage structure required workers to rely on credit during much of the year in patterns that trapped whole families in cycles of debt. The only way workers could make money to pay off debt, given the wage/credit pattern, was to place whole families in the fields. Children as young as nine crawled through the fields blocking, thinning, and harvesting beets during workdays that lasted from sunup to sundown. In 1928 five thousand Mexican children worked the Great Western Sugar Company's 110,000-acre beet field.[65] Denver barrios, populated by New Mexican and Mexican migrants, increased fourfold to nearly ten thousand inhabitants.

The arrival of night riding and the appearance of references to the Ku Klux Klan in Tierra Amarilla corresponded to an upsurge in racist antilabor practices throughout the Southwest. By the 1920s "the ways in which capital structured workplaces and labor markets contributed to the idea that competition should be both cutthroat and racialized."[66] In Arizona in 1917 sheriff's deputies deported more than a thousand striking miners from Bisbee, Arizona, abandoning the mostly Spanish-speaking labor force in the middle of the southern New Mexico desert.[67] Bisbee marked the beginning of labor crackdowns focused on Spanish-speaking workers. Less than a month after Bisbee, violent labor clashes engulfed Gallup, New Mexico, when local and state police brutally put down the largely Spanish-speaking workforce.

The difference between New Mexico and Colorado was made most obvious in the mid-1930s, when the governor of Colorado declared martial law and sealed the border to all but English-language speakers. The blockade effectively shut down migratory patterns of farmworkers moving north from Tierra Amarilla.[68] The embargo against Spanish-speaking New Mexicans reinforced what migrants from New Mexico already knew, that citizenship was defined along strictly racial lines and produced distinctly different spaces of exclusion. Race and class worked differently in Colorado than it did in New Mexico.

It was at the beginning of this period of increasingly racialized violence in Colorado and Texas that reports of apparent Klan influence in Tierra Amarilla first surfaced. A May 1924 article in the *Albuquerque Journal* under a headline that read, "Houses Burned, Threats Posted by Terrorists," reported that fires had consumed haystacks on land owned by T. D. Burns Jr., and letters were found that threatened the life of other Anglo ranchers. The article described a new round of "incendiary fires, cutting of fences and posting of warning signs, presumably by a gang of night riders."[69] Rumors swirled that the letter included the initials "K.K.K." Less than a week later the *Santa Fe New Mexican* reported that the Ku Klux Klan had acquired a majority of delegates at the Republican conventions in Indiana.[70] In June, after the Republican National Convention had all but capitulated to Klan demands, the Democratic National Convention geared up for a fight with the Klan over control of its platform. But "mainstream political actors in both the Republican and Democratic Parties were willing to openly embrace the Klan," and Democratic Convention delegates refused to pass a resolution that condemned the Klan by name.[71] The *Santa Fe New Mexican* described the "Democratic Convention in [a] Wild Riot of the Ku Klux Klan."[72]

The Klan of the 1920s found success by serving "different purposes in different communities" where it often "represented mainstream social and political concerns, not those of a disaffected fringe group."[73] In Indiana, where it eventually found broad appeal, a quarter million members advanced an anti-Catholic, white-supremacy nativism. In the West, however, the organizing tactics, public message, and local appeal varied according to local issues, conditions, and social tensions. The Klan often packaged its reactionary politics and anti-immigration racism in terms acceptable to progressive politics and the populist movement. The "coercive moralism" of Progressive Era racism offered a broad political constituency to the Klan.

In New Mexico, however, the rhetoric of race and the legacy of Spanish colonialism contributed to a much different experience for land grant settlers. Although the particular patterns of enclosure, racialized wage labor, and citizenship valorized whiteness as the organizing category for the expression of national belonging, the complicated politics of identity in New Mexico undermined simple racial distinctions through which citizenship could be expressed. To claim whiteness in New Mexico, one had to claim a colonial legacy in both historical and spatial terms. The Klan, at least in New Mexico, served as a means for land grant settlers to interrupt these patterns in ways that defended their claims to property.

I take the Klan seriously in the land grant struggle, not to argue that Tierra Amarilla land grant claimants shared the Klan's nativist fears. Indeed, the letter that Heron forwarded to the governor is interesting not only because it was signed "K.K.K.," but also because of the ways that the letter writers chose to define the racial and national identities of those lodging specific complaints, and the way these complaints were rooted in a defense of the poor: "Now mind this you watchers for we know who they are and we know every step you make, they blame only the poor Mexicans for all this doings, it is not so, there are members from every nationality, for there are Americans, Mexicans, Spaniards, Indians, and every kind of good citizens that want to defend the justice of the poor people. For we know that now a days there is no justice on the courts for the poor."

While the language of the letter drew on elements characteristic of the Klan lexicon, the use of the threat of the Klan was, I have argued, a rhetorical tactic that interrupted the particular spatial construction of whiteness and the property claims based on claims to whiteness that increasingly threatened land grant claims.[74]

In the four decades that followed the first reports of night riding in Tierra Amarilla, resistance to the enclosures took a legal turn. During this period Tierra Amarilla land grant settlers sustained a pattern of collective social struggle that relied on, and continually reproduced, land grant identities based on collective claims to common property. In the next chapter I examine how Tierra Amarilla land grant residents transformed these patterns of resistance from fence cutting and night riding into a sustained and sophisticated legal challenge to private property that moved the struggle into the courts.

CHAPTER FOUR

An Unquiet Title

MEDARDO ABEYTA MUST HAVE BEEN a strange sight to his neighbors in the spring and summer of 1937. Nearly every day he could be seen walking the rutted, dusty roads on the Tierra Amarilla land grant in a stiff black suit, carrying an overstuffed briefcase. Each morning the fifty-year-old tenant farmer left his small adobe home in the village of Los Ojos and walked northeast past small corrals and planted fields into the village of Brazos, or sometimes south along walking paths that skirted tributaries of the Rio de Chama that led into the small settlement of La Puente. He stopped at every small adobe house he found to sit at kitchen tables or under shady *portales* and talk to his neighbors about the land grant. They were familiar stories, but to most of his neighbors they must have sounded like fairy tales. By the 1930s few land grant residents believed the stories of Tierra Amarilla's common pastures. The fences on the grant told only a story of private property.

Day after day Abeyta patiently explained that the fences encroached on *their land*. The private ranchers claimed to own the land that Thomas Catron stole from their grandparents. Catron had convinced the courts, he told his neighbors, that common property was a legal fiction, and now everyone believed it. The sheepherders and small farmers of the valley, however, were collective legal owners of the entire 600,000-acre land grant, not the Anglo ranchers, those "usurpers and encroachers of property."[1]

When he wasn't canvassing his neighbors, he was writing articles about the land grant for *La Opinión de Río Arriba*, a Tierra Amarilla newspaper. In one of his first articles he explained how speculators had "stolen the land and sold it piece by piece."[2] He used a familiar *dicho*, or saying, to suggest that speculators stole the land because the U.S. Congress and U.S. courts misconstrued common property as land owned by no one: "Con lo que no cuesta se hace fiesta!" he wrote. When it is free, they feast!

The land grant, according to Abeyta, was not empty land available for private ranchers to acquire but rather the collective property of all the small farmers who had *hijuelas* stored in shoeboxes under beds or in the back of closets. Abeyta argued for a new strategy to win back the land. The tactics of intimidation, in his mind, no longer worked. Instead of fence cutting, violence, and incendiarism, Abeyta advocated a legal approach. He educated his neighbors about the international treaties that he believed protected their Mexican property rights. He pulled documents out of his briefcase that, he promised, would someday confirm their property claims, and he explained that because the law robbed them of their collective rights, it must be through the law that they recover them.

Abeyta's organizing attracted a small cadre of supporters.[3] Together they made the three-hour drive to the offices of the State Corporation Commission in Santa Fe in mid-September 1937 and filed paperwork to establish what they called La Corporación de Abiquiú, Merced de Tierra Amarilla (the Abiquiú Corporation, Tierra Amarilla Land Grant), an organization described in the incorporation papers as "a unified effort toward peace, equity and justice . . . to protect the membership which comprise said Corporación from the injustices of selfishness of tyrants and despots, of usurpers and encroachers of property; law and justice; to file suits in matters of litigation; to acquire, to hold, to possess, to distribute through the proper legal channels, the rights, interest, privileges, parcels, timbers, waters and mineral rights that were prescribed and inherited from our forefathers, heirs and assigns of the Tierra Amarilla Grant."[4]

During the fall of 1937 La Corporación convened a series of weekly meetings in a small village on the land grant. Articles about those meetings, many written anonymously by La Corporación members, appeared in *La Opinión*. The meetings and the articles chronicled the struggle for land grant property claims in Tierra Amarilla. The meetings drew heirs and former residents from as far away as Denver and southern Colorado's San Luis Valley. The surge in interest in the land grant convinced Abeyta to formally announce the formation of La Corporación in a late-December newspaper advertisement. The new organization, the notice declared, represented the interests of all member-heirs of the grant. Hopeful members were directed to present legal evidence of their individual claims at the weekly meetings in order to obtain official grant membership.[5] At a mid-January meeting more than five hundred heirs thronged a small meetinghouse in Los Ojos. Clutching letters, deeds, *hijuelas*, and wills, they joined Abeyta's campaign to "remove [private ranchers] from this property which ha[d] been fraudulently appropriated."[6]

With money from member dues, some as little as ten cents a month, Abeyta sent emissaries to Washington, D.C., to show land grant documents to various federal officials. He established contacts with New Mexico politicians, including New Mexico senator Dennis Chavez, who advised the group on possible political solutions to land issues in Tierra Amarilla.[7] Despite the growth of La

Corporación, many of the member-heirs were pessimistic about their chances against the "millionaires" and "capitalists" arrayed against them. Our "hopes have become as distant as the heavens are to the earth," wrote one member.[8]

This chapter examines a period of intense legal struggle in Tierra Amarilla that began with Medardo Abeyta's organizing in the late 1930s and continued through the 1960s. Despite the influence and importance of Abeyta and La Corporación, historians have ignored both him and the organization. Only Richard Gardner, in his study of social conflict in northern New Mexico in the 1960s, has examined the rise of La Corporación.[9] In his hands, however, Abeyta is just another opportunistic, criminal leader in the long history of the Hispanic land grant struggle in New Mexico, and La Corporación appears as merely one of many "fiercely nativistic, secretive and rebellious organizations" that, according to Gardner, "throng the folk memory of Rio Arriba."[10] Gardner's patronizing (and completely uncited) history of the Tierra Amarilla land grant settlers depicts Abeyta as the boss of a criminal operation that "elect[ed] state senators by day and burn[ed] haystacks by night" and presents land grant communities in Tierra Amarilla as the violent and angry victims of law's authority.[11]

Gardner could not be more wrong. As this chapter demonstrates, the group was not the criminal enterprise that Gardner describes but rather operated as a broad-based membership organization that pursued spectacular and provocative tactics to rid the grant of private ranchers and proposed creative and fascinating legal remedies for land grant loss. I examine those efforts by focusing on a series of four lawsuits involving La Corporación that began in 1938 and lasted until the 1950s.[12] These quiet title and ejectment lawsuits offer a remarkable view into the legal logic and inner workings of the group and its sophisticated legal strategy. La Corporación developed a nuanced legal theory of property that its lawyers argued in court in efforts to establish legitimate claims to common property on the grant.

Perhaps most interesting was that the approach was not limited to legal theories argued in courtrooms. La Corporación members recognized that in order to make property claims compelling to the courts, they needed to perform their property claims in the forests and fields of the grant. So they mailed eviction notices and rental bills to private ranchers. They wrote new deeds to land they claimed as their own and filed them with the county clerk. They cut private fences and erected their own in the same place. As I argue in this chapter, these were tactics designed to bring common property relations to life in ways that would become legible and persuasive to the courts.

Their efforts illustrate the idea that property, as the legal scholar Carol Rose has argued, is always about persuasion. The ways in which La Corporación sought to persuade the courts of its property claims are interesting for a number of reasons. First, as Rose contends, one of the myths of property is that the law is an objective arbiter of legitimate origins of first possession. She argues instead that law is a struggle in which claimants compete over who can make the most persuasive claim to first possession. This is so, she argues, because the common law doctrines of possession in U.S. property law require a story of property's origins. Acts of possession, posits Rose, are a kind of text, "and common law rewards the author of that text."[13] In quiet title or ejectment lawsuits, such as in the ones examined here, the law is preoccupied with how claimants prove, or demonstrate, possession. Making improvements such as building fences, enforcing exclusive use by erecting "no trespassing" signs, and demonstrating a long history of use through grazing animals, for example, are all different kinds of "acts" that the law searches for when adjudicating competing claims to property. When these performances are not found, neither is property.

Second, while law requires that property be performed, it also valorizes the written word over performance and takes into account only those "acts of possession" that arise out of documentary evidence. In common law doctrine this is referred to as "color of title," a condition in which claimants can explain their behavior by reference to a written instrument that tells the story of the transfer of ownership of real property to them. Anyone can behave like a property owner, but if that behavior is not rooted in a deed, he or she is a trespasser in the eyes of the law.

Each of the four court cases examined here demonstrates that La Corporación offered nuanced legal arguments that combined "color of title" with "acts of possession" in a compelling meld of theory and practice. But despite playing property's language game the tactics of La Corporación befuddled judges, infuriated ranchers, and ultimately failed to establish legal claims to the commons. While the four court cases chronicled here tell a story of a creative and sophisticated campaign in defense of common property, it is ultimately a story about how the law constructed private property in Tierra Amarilla. The courts rejected a history of common property on the grant and constructed in its place a history of private property telescoped into the past. La Corporación members may have behaved like property owners under "color of title," but the courts rejected this claim repeatedly.

Although most histories of the land grant struggle in New Mexico locate land grant dispossession in the tactics of land speculators in the nineteenth century, a review of the four court cases here reveals that despite the efforts of speculators in the nineteenth century and the fences of private ranchers in the early twentieth century, common use of the land grant continued well into the middle of the twentieth century. Dispossession, therefore, was not a historical event but rather has been an ongoing struggle that eventually found its way into the courts.

HND Land Co. v. Suazo

As word spread about Abeyta and La Corporación, the small Sunday meetings became large gatherings, and each issue of the local paper carried a new article by or about the group and its claims. At a late-January meeting in Los Ojos in 1938, Abeyta stood before the newly organized member-heirs in Tierra Amarilla and declared that together they would "never lose heart." La Corporación, he promised, would "recover their legacy."[14] An opportunity to claim that legacy came quickly. Running alongside the article about Abeyta's January meeting in *La Opinión* was a legal notice about a quiet title lawsuit filed by a small ranching operation called HND Land Company. On January 13, 1938, HND filed suit in district court against several defunct corporations and absentee landowners in order to quiet title to a ranch known as El Rancho del Poso, a property claimed by HND but considered part of the common lands by La Corporación.[15] Upon seeing the ad, Abeyta declared a *grito de alarma* (call to arms), believing that the case provided a perfect opportunity for La Corporación to assert its legal claims to common lands.[16] Writing in Spanish proverbs thick with religious imagery, Abeyta implored La Corporación members to pursue the issue with the courts. He appealed to the members to remain faithful and explained that only through a legal struggle in the courts could La Corporación ratify its legal claims.[17]

Over the course of the next year, Abeyta brought a parade of lawyers and land grant heirs to Los Ojos, where they briefed members on law and legal strategy. In May he invited an heir of the Chilili land grant near Albuquerque to the weekly Sunday meeting. In a short speech he described how the attorney for their grant "successfully [argued] that the alleged owners who presently lived on the Chilili land grant had no legal right to sell the whole or even part of the grant. The attorney was able to restore the land to the proper land grant holders."[18]

As La Corporación prepared to intervene in HND's quiet title suit, it settled on a legal strategy similar to the one the Chilili heir described. Instead of making an adverse claim for possession of El Rancho del Poso — a claim that would have been based on historical and contemporary use of the land — it would argue instead that HND had no legal claim to the land. The strategy was a simple one. Despite what its deed might say, HND could not own the land that it claimed to own because El Rancho del Poso was part of the inalienable com-

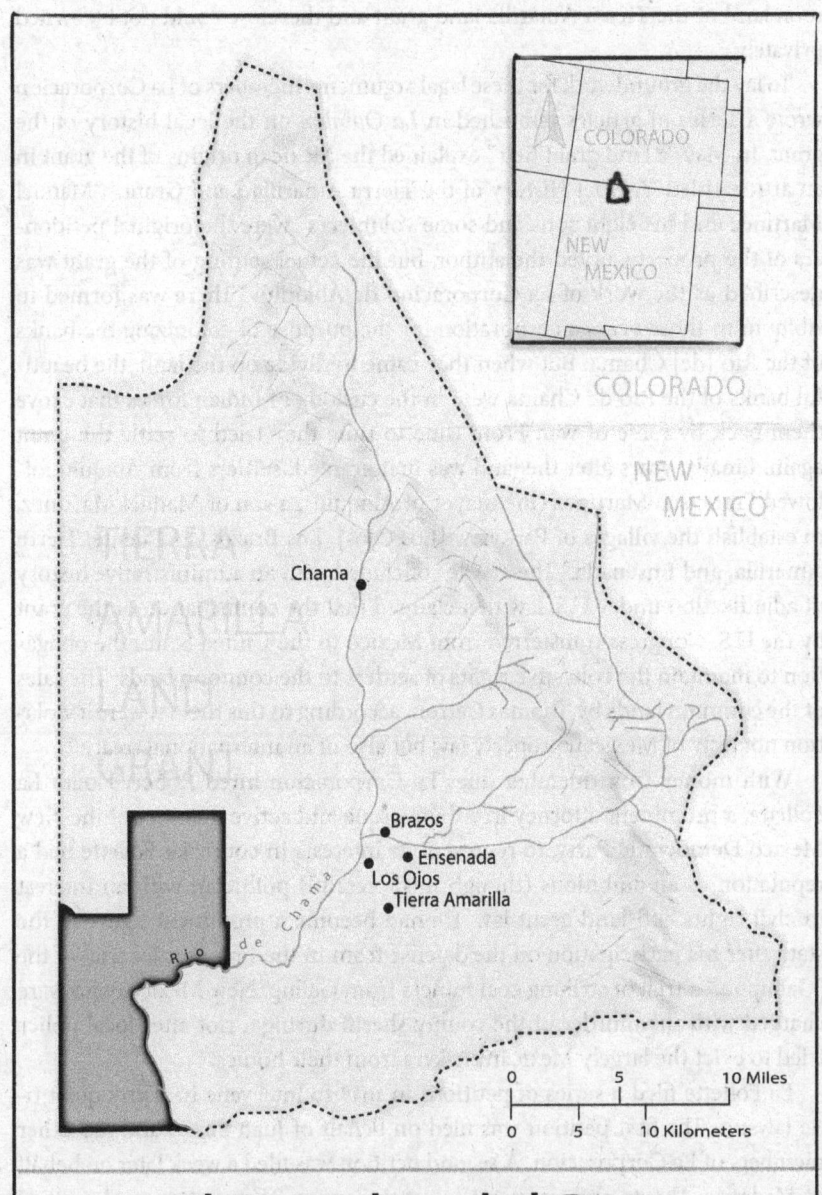

El Rancho del Poso

Property in Dispute in the Lawsuit *HND Land Co. v. Suazo*,
44 N.M. 547, 105 P .2d 744 (1940)

mon land of the Tierra Amarilla land grant and therefore could not be owned privately.

To lay the groundwork for these legal arguments members of La Corporación wrote a series of articles published in *La Opinión* on the legal history of the grant. In May "a land grant heir" explained the Mexican origins of the grant in an article titled "A Brief History of the Tierra Amarilla Land Grant." "Manuel Martínez and his eight sons and some volunteers" were the original petitioners of the property, noted the author, but the actual settling of the grant was described as the work of La Corporación de Abiquiú: "There was formed in Abiquiú in those years a corporation for the purpose of colonizing the banks of the Rio [de] Chama. But when they came to divide up the land, the beautiful banks of the Rio de Chama were in the custody of Indian forces that drove them back by force of war. From time to time they tried to settle the grant again. Finally, years after the land was first granted, settlers from Abiquiú followed Francisco Martínez (the mayor of Abiquiú), a son of Manuel Martínez, to establish the villages of Parkview [Los Ojos], Los Brazos, La Puente, Tierra Amarilla, and Ensenada." The article concluded with an administrative history of adjudication under U.S. law that claimed that the confirmation of the grant by the U.S. Congress transferred from Mexico to the United States the obligation to maintain the collective rights of settlers to the common lands. The sales of the common lands by Thomas Catron, according to this theory, were a violation not only of Mexican property law but also of an international treaty.[19]

With money from member dues La Corporación hired Robert Hoath La Follette, a prominent attorney in Albuquerque and active member of the New Mexico Democratic Party, to represent its interests in court. La Follette had a reputation as an ambitious (though unsuccessful) politician with an interest in civil rights and land grant law. He had become a prominent figure in the state after his participation on the defense team in the 1935 murder trial of the "Gallup 14," a trial of striking coal miners from Gallup, New Mexico, who were charged with the murder of the county sheriff during a riot after local police tried to evict the largely Mexican strikers from their homes.

La Follette filed a series of petitions in 1938 to intervene in HND's quiet title lawsuit. The first petition was filed on behalf of Juan Suazo and 180 other members of La Corporación. A second petition was filed a week later on behalf of Medardo Abeyta and 111 members of the group. The petitioners described themselves as "persons having a direct and substantial interest in the matter in litigation against the success of the plaintiff corporation and against the success of the defendants specifically made parties by name in the complaint of plaintiff filed herein."[20]

As part of the legal strategy, none of the nearly three hundred land grant heirs in either of the two petitions claimed adverse possession for the property. Adverse possession is a legal term that describes a process in which a person can acquire title to another's real property without compensation if that person has used it unmolested for a period of time. La Corporación decided against arguing adverse possession because to do so required admitting that HND had a legitimate private property claim in the first place. Instead La Follette simply denied "that the plaintiff [HND] [was] the owner in fee simple of the real estate described in the complaint."[21] In an April 1939 reply HND's lawyers counterargued that the question of private property had been resolved in 1860 when the U.S. Congress confirmed Francisco Martínez's private claim to the Tierra Amarilla land grant. In addition, they noted that for more than ten years HND Land Company had been in "open, notorious, actual, exclusive, hostile and adverse possession of said land and real estate under claim of right and of fee simple title thereto, against all the world."[22]

The parties traded briefs throughout the summer of 1939; the exchange culminated in the fall with a "Stipulation and Agreement as to Facts of the Case" in which HND agreed that its deed was based originally on the Mexican property claim of Manuel Martínez. The stipulation was important to La Follette's argument because if HND's property claims were traced back to Manuel Martínez, then according to his theory, its claims should be adjudged by the standards of Mexican common property, standards that precluded private claims for the commons.

To develop this theory La Follette carefully detailed in the stipulation agreement the procedures of the Mexican confirmation with language that included the text of the Mexican colonization laws governing the distribution of land grants, the 1860 act of Congress confirming the claim of Francisco Martínez, and a comprehensive list of all the *hijuelas* filed in Rio Arriba County. In return for this stipulation, La Follette filed an "Admission of Facts upon Issues of Adverse Possession" in which he stipulated "that for more than ten years preceding the commencement of this suit, the plaintiff, together with its predecessors in title, ha[d] done every act and thing, which, if it were not the legal effect of the facts involving the title and possession of all of the land described in plaintiff's complaint as a part and portion of what is known as the Tierra Amarilla Grant . . . would amount to a holding and claiming of all of said lands and real estate described in the complaint."[23]

La Follette's admission of HND's adverse possession dealt a death blow to his case and, even worse, would haunt the legal efforts of La Corporación for the next quarter century. At the time he was convinced that the court could not find for HND and the stipulation would not matter. According to La Follette's theory, the unalloted common lands of the grant could not, under any circumstances, be claimed as private property any more than a city park could be claimed by a family of picnickers or a public street claimed by someone driving along it. The naked title to the common lands of Tierra Amarilla, according to La Follette, was held in trust by Mexico for the use and benefit of the grantees. Since HND's property claims were based on the Mexican grant, the commons could not be owned privately. Instead common lands had been transferred to the United States after the U.S.-Mexican War and the signing of the Treaty of Guadalupe Hidalgo. This requirement to hold the common lands in trust, according to La Follette, was not extinguished by the 1860 confirmation of Tierra Amarilla as a private land claim to Francisco Martínez. Instead, the confirmation merely transferred the obligation to administer the lands in trust to Martínez. This was the crux of the argument La Follette advanced in court: first Mexico, then the United States, and finally Francisco Martínez owned the land grant and managed the property *in trust* on behalf of the grant settlers. The Mexican colonization laws required that pastures, watering places, and roads remain in common *in perpetuity.*

He based his theory on the obscure legal term *manos muertas* or *mortmain*, translated literally as "dead hands," in order to argue that Mexico intended to "prohibit any corporation or person other than a bona fide colonist from acquiring lands within said grant."[24] The theory equated the Tierra Amarilla land grant to a church or religious order, the usual context of a prohibition of *manos muertas*, in that the grant should be recognized as a legal entity separate from the individuals who administered the land. Just as the religious leader of a church did not own, and could not claim, the church's land and therefore could not alienate the church's property, so too were members of the Tierra Amarilla land grant prohibited from selling the common portions of the land grant. If the court accepted this theory, as La Follette expected, HND could claim neither ownership of the common lands nor title by adverse possession because the grant was similar to public property.

"It would be as impossible," argued La Follette, "to the plaintiff corporation to acquire title by adverse possession to said lands as it would for them to have acquired the title by adverse possession if said lands had remained merely a part of the public domain."[25] In effect La Follette was asking the court to take into account the intention of the Mexican government in granting the property to Manuel Martínez and reinterpret HND's title in this light.

Without explanation district court judge Irwin Moise rejected the theory of *manos muertas*, dismissed La Follette's cross complaints, and quieted title for the ranch in the name of HND Land Company.²⁶ La Follette appealed the decision to the New Mexico Supreme Court. In his appeal he clarified his argument. He was not asking the court to go behind Congress; rather he was asking that the court recognize that the congressional confirmation *included* the encumbrances placed on the common lands by Mexico. These encumbrances, he argued, were not extinguished by the 1860 confirmation.

Chief Justice Thomas Mabry, writing for the court in September 1940, found La Follette's *manos muertas* theory "intriguing in its ramifications and by its vigorous challenge to appellee's title."²⁷ Despite La Follette's careful argument about encumbrances, Mabry construed it as, in fact, asking the court to "inquire into the nature of this original grant by the Republic of Mexico, [thus] going behind the acts of congress which provided a method of establishing and settling title to such grants." Mabry cited a U.S. Supreme Court case from 1876 known as the *Tameling* case, in which the court examined the confirmation of the Sangre de Cristo land grant, a property claim included along with the Tierra Amarilla land grant in the 1860 act of Congress.²⁸ In it the court concluded that Congress acted in its sovereign capacity and the 1860 act amounted to a de novo grant to the confirmees. Regardless of Mexico's intention with regard to the common lands, the 1860 act of Congress established, in effect, a new grant of land. In the aftermath of the 1860 act the intent of Mexico was no longer a question that the courts could consider. After *Tameling*, according to Mabry, the courts were "without jurisdiction to consider such a case" and therefore could not "pass on the meaning, effect or validity of the grant itself" but instead were "limited to a determination simply of the meaning of the act of congress confirming the grant."²⁹

As soon as Mabry finished explaining why he couldn't go behind an act of Congress, he did just that and launched into an investigation of the intent of Mexico in making community land grants in the first place. "Can title by adverse possession be acquired as to common lands of a community grant?" he wrote. "We hold that it can." Citing a recent case covering the Tecolote land grant Mabry noted that the Supreme Court had previously ruled that "a land grant is not a municipal corporation in the sense that it constitutes an instrumentality or agency of the state." Rejecting La Follette's argument that the land grant commons was legally the same as a public park, Mabry wrote, "These common and unallotted lands may be so acquired.... Therefore, even if this could be considered as originally a community grant in spite of the declaration and determination of Congress to the contrary, nevertheless appellee has established his title by adverse possession." In other words, La Follette's argument regarding adverse possession was not persuasive because the courts had already interpreted Mexico's intent and found that it was not equivalent to public property. For this reason, Mabry explained, the court could not consider La Follette's theory because he "admitted by stipulation that appellee together with its predecessors in title, for the requisite period preceding the commencement of the suit, had done every act and thing involving the title and possession of the land described in the complaint, to constitute adverse possession under either of [the] statutes."[30]

Flores v. Brusselbach

Despite the disappointment in the *HND* case, Abeyta reemphasized the importance of pursuing legal remedies for land loss to the membership. In his view the law, not violent or intimidating tactics or political solutions, would return land to the heirs. In March 1943 Abeyta appointed a commission of three La Corporación officers to serve on a property committee. He charged them with finding ways to stop "any person or persons, who [was] not a member of La Corporación... from grazing stock, build[ing] any improvements, cultivat[ing] any land without the consent or permission from La Corporación de Abiquiú, Merced de Tierra Amarilla."[31] The committee was authorized "to deliver to the heirs certain number of varas of land... in the Chama Valley." The tactics were an extension of efforts that preceded HND. If La Corporación claimed to own land collectively, then, according to Abeyta, it should act like an owner. Since landowners file their deeds with the county clerk, pay taxes, fence property, and erect "no trespassing" signs, then La Corporación would do these things.

In April La Corporación began publishing weekly warnings in the local newspaper directed at private ranchers. The notices included a short statement signed by Abeyta: "You are respectfully notified to remove all improvements installed and used in said premises and restrain and not make any further improvements of any kind whatsoever, to be accomplished and complete by November 30 1943."[32] The property committee also compiled a list of private ranchers who grazed livestock on the grant. In March 1944, with the list complete, the committee flooded the valley with a deluge of eviction letters and rental bills mailed or, in some cases, personally delivered to private ranchers. Each letter demanded rental income of ten cents per head for all livestock on land grant property. Abeyta threatened to evict Ed Sargent, one of the most prominent ranchers in Tierra Amarilla, from his huge ranch on the grant if rent was not paid. "If this rent is not received by or before April 5th A.D. 1944, we will enter, and re-possess, and occupy it, rent it, and lease it to other parties."[33]

Despite the threatening language, most ranchers were confused by the letters and ignored the bills, seemingly convinced that the threats of eviction and repossession were a provocative but empty threat. By the following month, however, it became clear that La Corporación had more in mind than threats and intimidation. In the third week of May a rancher from Española named Herquilano Herrera drove a herd of cattle northwest along the Rio de Chama to graze pastures he had rented on the Tierra Amarilla land grant. Herrera, like many small ranchers in northern New Mexico, relied on public lands to graze stock. In the early 1940s the U.S. Forest Service began a series of grazing reductions on public lands based on claims of overgrazing by small Hispanic ranchers.[34] Without land to graze animals, hundreds of small-scale ranchers were forced to sell the few sheep and cattle they had. Many more, Herrera among them, rented private ranches. Herrera rented pasturage in Tierra Amarilla from a Colorado man named Karl Brusselbach. The land had been previously owned by the Arlington Land Company. After acquiring the property from Catron in 1909, Arlington sold it to a rancher named Antonio Valdez shortly afterward. He in turn sold it to a Colorado rancher named William Kinderman in the 1920s. Kinderman, who had been a business associate of Burns, owned scattered property throughout the Tierra Amarilla grant. After Kinderman's death in 1941, Brusselbach, his nephew and the executor of his estate, managed the property.[35] Herrera rented the pasture from Brusselbach sight unseen and, in order to afford the rental fees, split the pastures with other small ranchers from Española.

When Herrera drove his herd onto the ranch for the first time, however, he found pastures newly fenced, fields recently plowed and planted, and horses and cattle grazing the property. A confused Herrera found a local man named Roque Flores on the property. "I told him I had the place leased," Herrera explained, but "he told me I was losing my money."[36] Flores and his son, Rafael, operated a small coal mine on land adjacent to the ranch and frequently crossed the property to transport coal and timber. In the spring of 1943 Roque and his son petitioned La Corporación for a permit to plant crops and graze a herd of cattle on the "unalloted" common lands adjacent to his property. The property committee of La Corporación agreed and gave the father and son a deed for the property. The two plowed a small pasture and planted beans, corn, wheat, and potatoes. Roque Flores improved a dirt road and erected a barbed-wire fence in order to graze a herd of cattle and some horses. By May 1944 they had completed two wells and built a small bridge over the creek that bisected the land.

Herrera drove his herd back to Española and contacted Brusselbach, who quickly dispatched his attorney and a local property manager from Chama to

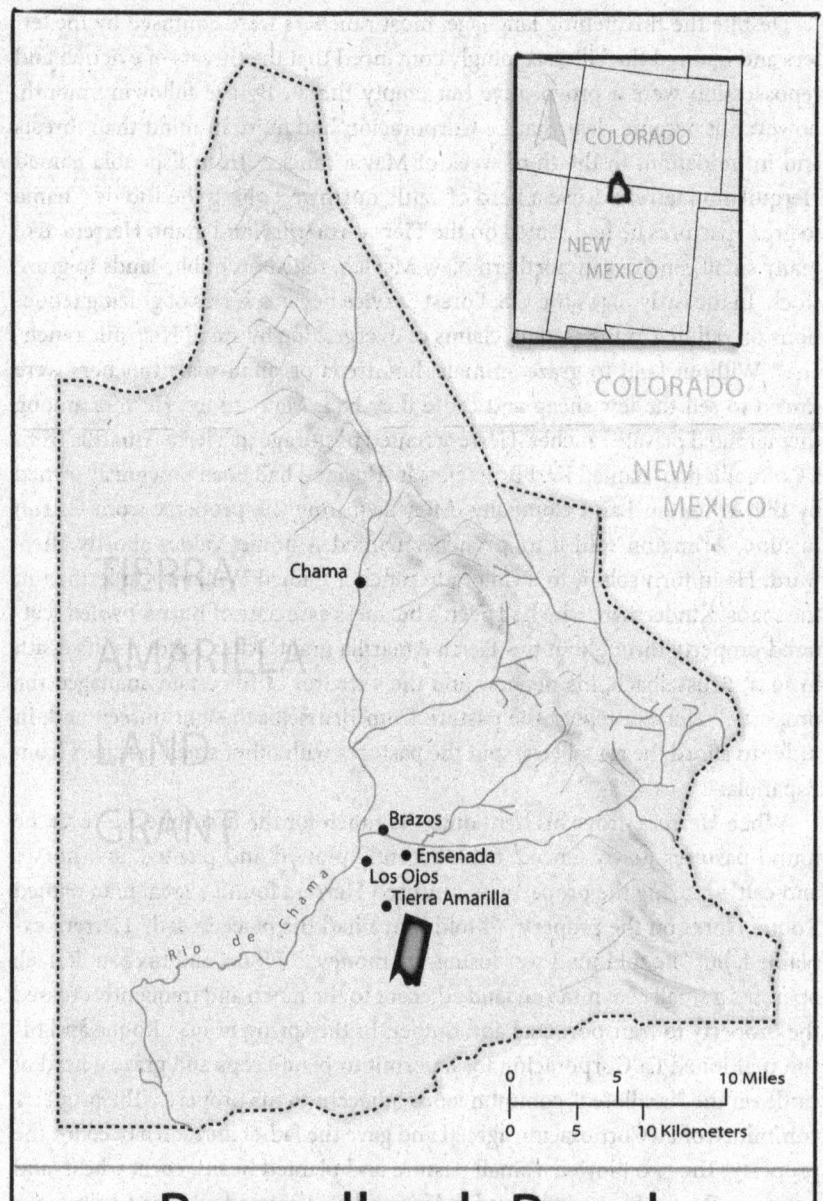

Brusselbach Ranch

Property in Dispute in the Lawsuit *Flores v. Brusselbach*,
149 F .2d 616 (3rd Cir.,1945)

confirm Herrera's story. When they arrived at the property, they found a sign posted on a new fence in front of a small building that read: "I, the undersigned, by this notice say that I do not wish anyone to trespass or use in any manner this, my property, and in case of any person or persons shall be handled in conformity of the law. Signed this 29th day of May, 1944, Roque Flores." Brusselbach quickly filed an ejectment suit against Flores in June 1944 in U.S. District Court. The complaint named Flores along with Medardo Abeyta and six other officers of what it called the "pretended corporation which they call the Corporación de Abiquiú Merced de Tierra Amarilla."[37] In its answer, La Corporación, now represented by Charles Allen of Colorado and a Santa Fe attorney named M. C. Pacheco, claimed to be in "control and authority over the lands" in question.[38]

The court convened in Santa Fe in late June to consider a temporary injunction against the defendants. Brusselbach testified in the hearing that he was intimately familiar with the property. He traveled there at least four times a year, he said, and had helped his uncle run sheep each year beginning in 1929. His claims seemed suspect under cross-examination, however, when he was unable to remember whether the ranch had ever been fenced, and he even admitted that they had made no improvements on the land. Neither he nor his uncle had ever dug wells, erected buildings, lived on the ranch, or irrigated the land. He was unsure if there was any water on the property and was even unaware of the coal mine on adjacent lands. When asked under cross-examination whether land grant residents used the land he admitted, "I am not familiar with the country."[39]

Unlike Brusselbach, Flores testified to a long history of use of the ranch. He, like other land grant residents, had grazed cattle for more than five years and knew of other grant members who had grazed cattle there for at least the past fifty years.[40] In addition to grazing cattle, he had collected wood from the ranch for as long as he could remember. "Who has been on there in possession of it during that time?" asked his attorney. "Just the community of the people that claim to be the heirs of the grant," Flores answered.[41] Medardo Abeyta followed Flores on the stand. Like Flores he claimed not to know anyone named Kinderman who owned land on the grant. As in the *HND* case, Abeyta testified that La Corporación claimed property by virtue of the provisions of the original Mexican land grant. According to Abeyta, despite the ruling in *HND*, when the U.S. Congress confirmed Tierra Amarilla it confirmed the property claims of La Corporación. In cross-examination Abeyta made an argument for adverse possession based on the Mexican patent and the U.S. confirmation as "color of title."[42]

Q: You claim that this corporation, and the heirs of Francisco Martínez, have a right to graze or take timber or water any place on the grant?

ABEYTA: Yes, sir.

Q: And, you gave Roque Flores a permit on that basis?

ABEYTA: Yes, sir.

Q: You, and the officers of your corporation issued these notices posted, Exhibits 6,7,8, [rental notices] on the same theory?

ABEYTA: Yes, sir, we served them a notice by means of the paper, and also a notice by registered mail, all claiming title by adverse possession.

Q: [In *HND Land Company v. Suazo*] you claimed to issue a permit to Pricilliano Martínez under this corporation, didn't you? You claimed there that the Martínez heirs owned the grant, didn't you, that is a fact, and the Court decided against you, isn't that a fact?

ABEYTA: Yes, they decided.

Q: Notwithstanding that decision you kept on issuing these notices and kept on trying to collect rent, and you have undertaken to issue a permit to Mr. Flores, is that right?

ABEYTA: Yes, I issued a permit to Mr. Flores.

Q: What are you going to do, give him a deed to it?

ABEYTA: Yes, we only give a deed according to the regulations of the patent, according to Francisco Martínez, laws and the patent.

Q: You mean, according to what you claim is the laws of Mexico?

ABEYTA: Yes, the laws that the patent contains from the United States.

Q: Well, the patent covered a lease to Martínez, didn't it?

ABEYTA: Yes, sir, giving the land to Manuel Martínez, they had two patents.

Q: You mean the grant?

ABEYTA: Yes, sir, there were two patents. You see one patent was issued by the Government of Mexico, and one by the United States, which is a quit claim patent.

Q: You are claiming under the grant, the patent, from the Mexican Government, is that what you mean, to Manuel Martínez?

ABEYTA: I claim by both patents.

Q: You claim the right to control this whole Tierra Amarilla grant except the little irregular pieces?

ABEYTA: Yes, sir, according to the laws of the patent.

Q: That is what you are proceeding under, and intend to proceed under?

ABEYTA: Well, as long as the people, the heirs sustain the corporation.

According to a brief filed on behalf of La Corporación, the U.S. Congress had confirmed the grant "in favor of Francisco Martínez, by the Act of Congress, approved June 21, 1860, and which Tierra Amarilla Grant was patented by the United States to Francisco Martínez, his heirs and assigns, on February 21, 1881, pursuant to the aforesaid Act of Congress, and [La Corporación] claims title under said patent."[43] The brief further elaborated the theory Abeyta advanced in his testimony that the 1860 act of Congress transferred the obligation to manage the commons for land grant settlers from Mexico to Francisco Martínez.

This recalibration of the legal strategy in *HND* was an effort to confront the *HND v. Suazo* decision. There the court concluded that the 1860 act of Congress was equivalent to a new grant of land. But Judge Colin Neblett, who referred to the defendants as "these individual trespassers," was unimpressed with this argument and issued a temporary injunction against Flores, Abeyta, and La Corporación and ordered the parties to court for the trial portion.[44]

During the trial, attorneys for Flores, unlike in the *HND* case, claimed "adverse possession for the twenty year period, and ask[ed], of course, that the title be quieted in the corporation as trustee for the heirs of Martínez and the members of the corporation."[45] Several members of La Corporación testified to a long history of use in a strategy designed to establish a legal claim of adverse possession.[46] José M. Trujillo, an officer of the group, testified that his father had pastured horses on the property for more than thirty-five years.[47] Another officer, Juan Martínez y Lopez, testified that the lands "had been used for grazing by the community" as part of a network of common lands relied on by heirs from the villages of "Tierra Amarilla, Park View, La Puenta, Encinada."[48] Roque's son, Rafael Flores, testified that he had built the road and bridge on the property claimed by Brusselbach. He denied ever seeing cattle or sheep other than those of local heirs or La Corporación members. Abeyta also testified and described the pattern of resource use on the grant. When asked how long he had used the ranch, he replied, "Since I was born, ever since I remember, that has been the practice."[49] Concerning the use of other land grant members, he explained, "As a rule you know, the people always turn their stock, you know, that is, during certain seasons of the year, you know. They would be on there during the grazing season more often than at any other times." Three hundred families lived in the neighboring village of Parkview. "How many of these 300 families get their wood on this land?" asked the attorney for La Corporación. "Most of them get their wood from that particular place," Abeyta explained.[50]

Brusselbach's attorneys responded that although La Corporación claimed a long history of use, it could not claim adverse possession because it could not show a proper color of title. The attorney for La Corporación argued, as Abeyta had done in his testimony, that the patent provided "sufficient color of title upon which to base a claim in adverse possession."[51] Brusselbach's attorneys aggressively pursued the question of whether the patent could provide color of title under cross-examination of Abeyta.[52]

Q: You said there was an old corporation prior to the one you formed, what do you mean by that?

ABEYTA: Yes, sir, there was a Corporación made by Manuel Martínez since May 25th, 1832, 1833.

Q: How did any title come into the new corporation?

ABEYTA: Because it belonged to the heirs.

Q: Have the heirs transferred to the new corporation or executed any deed?

ABEYTA: Yes, sir, Francisco Martínez gave deeds to most of the settlers in Tierra Amarilla.

Q: Those deeds were executed fifty years before the Corporación that now exists was formed, is that right?

ABEYTA: Yes, but they are just the same.

In his testimony Abeyta hoped to convince the court that Francisco Martínez distributed *hijuelas* to settlers after the 1860 act of Congress because he was bound by legal obligations defined by the original La Corporación de Abiquiú in 1832 and that these obligations were reinforced by Congress in 1860. Judge Neblett disagreed. Reading his decision from the bench in late June, he began by noting that Brusselbach's abstract showed "a complete chain of title from the patent to the plaintiffs." He then described what he called "serious defects" in Flores's claim of adverse possession. Neblett determined that no evidence had been offered by the defendants for adverse possession other than testimony that "they had been in possession for years."

More damaging to the defendants, however, was his conclusion regarding color of tile. According to Neblett the defense could not claim color of title because La Corporación could not produce a conveyance from Francisco Martínez to La Corporación other than the articles of incorporation, which were dated from 1938, not 1860 or earlier. Neblett found for the plaintiff, quieted title to the property, and "perpetually enjoined each and all of the defendants, including the Corporación . . . from interfering with the plaintiff's use of the Tierra Amarilla grant lands."[53]

In its appeal to the Tenth Circuit Court, the attorneys for La Corporación argued that the district court had erred by not taking into account Brusselbach's failure to make tax payments for the property, that he had made no improvements, and that he could not demonstrate open, notorious, continuous, peaceful, and uninterrupted possession adverse to the defendants. Further, despite Neblett's decision, the defendants had in fact demonstrated adverse possession under color of title. They had clarified the color of title claim by claiming that La Corporación was the official organization of those who held *hijuelas* and therefore acted as a trustee of the claims of Francisco Martínez. The court, however, found no conveyance from Francisco Martínez to La Corporación. Lacking it, the Tenth Circuit Court rejected the claims of color of title and enjoined Roque Flores, Medardo Abeyta, and La Corporación from claiming lands owned in fee simple by Brusselbach. In a pattern that would repeat itself, Roque Flores defied the court order and continued using the property. He quickly drew the ire of Kenneth Heron, who published a series of public warnings in the local newspaper threatening land grant members with legal action if they ever bought coal from Flores.[54]

Martínez v. Rivera

The legal setbacks in *HND* and *Flores* eroded confidence in Abeyta's leadership among La Corporación members. He was increasingly seen as a partisan political actor unable to unite the various factions that made up the disparate heirs living in and around Tierra Amarilla. Rumors of his supposed duplicity — according to one rumor, he sold the hundreds of deeds and documents he had collected in his role as president of La Corporación to various ranchers — all but ended his active role in the organization and in the land grant struggle more generally.

Without Abeyta the group lacked its primary organizer, recruiter, fundraiser, and legal tactician. La Corporación went inactive until the spring of 1951, when a local land grant heir named Fred Sierra led a group of former members to a March meeting of the Rio Arriba County Commission. At the meeting Sierra presented a petition to the Board of Commissioners "to call an election to be held on Monday, April 2, 1951, within said Tierra Amarilla Land Grant, located in Rio Arriba County, State of New Mexico, for the purpose of electing five (5) members of a Board of Trustees of said Grant."[55]

In both *HND* and *Flores* the courts had found that *La Corporación* had no color of title to make a claim for the Tierra Amarilla land grant. The petition Sierra delivered to the county commission offered a new strategy to establish a legal color of title. According to the New Mexico code, a community land grant interested in managing grant resources collectively could elect a land grant board and vest it with the authority to manage common property on the grant. The law merely required that the local county administer the election of the board. After noting that the petition included signatures from the necessary number of qualified voters and appeared to conform with the law, the Rio Arriba County Commission voted unanimously to set the date of the election as requested by the petitioners and to reconvene the week following the election to canvass the votes.

In the weeks after the meeting election precincts were set up and notices were posted throughout the grant publicizing the election. But just days before the election twenty-five ranchers, all absentee landowners from Colorado or Texas, including Brusselbach and the relatives of various associates of Thomas Burns, filed a lawsuit with the U.S. District Court to stop the election. The plaintiffs, a group that collectively claimed to own more than one hundred thousand acres of private land within the boundaries of the Tierra Amarilla grant, argued in their complaint that the commission knew that the Tierra Amarilla land grant was a private grant and intended to use the election to "cast doubt upon the titles of the plaintiff."[56] The complaint charged that the county, by administering the election, was in effect giving land grant settlers a color of title by licensing La Corporación to "unlawfully and illegally issue deeds, permits and make contracts purporting to authorize persons to go upon and trespass upon plaintiffs' lands and to record the same and to confuse and cloud the record of title of the plaintiffs."[57]

The county hired Harry Bigbee, a well-known Albuquerque attorney, to defend it against the lawsuit. Bigbee had served briefly as a district court judge and like La Follette was active in Democratic Party politics in New Mexico. U.S. District Court judge Carl Hatch ordered the parties to court on the same day that the county had planned to hold the land grant board election. At the hearing Hatch quickly agreed with the plaintiffs; he wrote in a temporary injunction that "a serious and substantial cloud and doubt may be placed upon the titles to the lands claimed by plaintiffs" if the election were allowed to proceed.[58] He allowed the commission to hold the election but enjoined it from issuing a certificate of election that would make the election official and ordered the parties back to court for a hearing in late June.

In the pretrial conference Hatch explained to the parties that the legal question confronting the court was whether the grant was a community grant or a private grant. In order to invalidate the elections, the plaintiffs, according to Hatch, needed to prove that the commons were not common at all but instead were owned by private individuals. They had "to prove the titling, the origin and how it reached [the] present plaintiffs."[59] If the land grant was private, as the plaintiffs contended, the state law covering land grant board elections would not apply. This was precisely the question Bigbee wanted to force the court to consider. Bigbee explained in his answer to the temporary injunction that the case was about the character of the grant and the disposition of the common lands. "We have a grant," he wrote, "that was made to an individual for the purpose of forming a colony or community.... There was authority in the original patent from Martínez and probably others to grant parcels of land to groups under certain restrictions.... They certainly had the right to grant small parcels to various individuals for the purpose of farming. However, we question the jurisdiction to grant the common lands themselves for grazing purposes."[60]

Because the question of the election required an examination of the character of the original Mexican land grant, the case had far reaching implications beyond merely the question of the election of a land grant board. As Bigbee pointed out in a pretrial conference, the plaintiff's titles "would not be good if the original grant was a community grant or grant of an individual for the purpose of forming a community."[61] In other words, the court could allow the county to proceed with the election only if it found that the land grant was a community land grant. And if it did that, the plaintiffs could not claim to own private lands within the grant. Recognizing the significance of the case, Bigbee was concerned that the court would focus on the title rather than the question of the character of the grant. "We don't want to try the title," Bigbee reminded the court. "We want to try the nature of the grant alone."[62]

To make the argument about the nature of the grant, Bigbee first refused to agree that the plaintiff's chain of title was derived through Francisco Martínez.

Unlike La Follette, Bigbee understood that admitting to a complete chain of title "would throw [his clients] out of Court."[63] Second, he introduced as exhibits a series of certified copies of *hijuelas* from Francisco Martínez to various residents that, he contended, demonstrated the grant was a community land grant. Between 1860 and 1871 Martínez made 130 conveyances, and each was "executed prior to the instruments under which the plaintiffs base[d] their claim from Francisco Martínez."[64] As a result, Bigbee offered evidence that established an alternative chain of title based on the *hijuelas* that preceded the Catron deed on which all the plaintiffs based their claims.

Because Hatch limited the legal questions to those related to the nature of the grant — whether it was a community land grant or a private land grant — Bigbee did not offer any testimony or evidence regarding the patterns of land use on the grant. How the grant was used and who used it were questions aside from the nature of the grant. Bigbee expected that the court's attention, therefore, would be focused squarely on the chain of title. If the court found the *hijuelas* convincing, the election would be allowed and the titles of the private ranchers would be thrown into doubt.

On June 22, 1951, after a short hearing to consider the arguments, Hatch read his opinion from the bench. His decision surprised Bigbee. Instead of focusing on the nature of the grant, as he had said he would in the pretrial conference, he focused on the patterns of land use. "Throughout all these years," he read aloud in court, "70 years practically, since this grant was confirmed and the patent issued it has been operated as a private land grant; and now, after the passage of the Act providing for the board of trustees, from 1907 down to this time, no step has ever been taken by anyone until this proceeding or this election was called to have the control and management by a board of trustees."[65] Though Hatch claimed he knew "something, of course, about the Tierra Amarilla [L]and Grant and its former history," his claim that "no step ha[d] ever been taken by anyone" to make a common property claim to the grant revealed a surprising ignorance of recent case law on the grant.[66] Indeed, the one thing the courts had admitted in *HDN* and *Flores* was that there had been a long history of use by land grant members. Hatch now denied this history in his decision.

A shocked Bigbee interrupted Judge Hatch in the middle of reading his opinion. "While we did admit in argument there had never been a board elected under this particular statute, there was no inquiry that I understood went to the question whether the citizens or committees representing the citizens had at all material times purportedly operated and attempted to manage the grant, or portions thereof, as a community grant."[67] Hatch responded: "What I said was based upon the statement of counsel that there had been at no time elections under this particular statute."[68]

In other words, according to Hatch's tortured logic, a land grant board could not be established for Tierra Amarilla because there had never before been an election of a board of trustees for the grant, and this proved that the grant was a private grant. The loss in *Martínez v. Rivera* must have been particularly frustrating to land grant claimants. In *Flores* the court had rejected the claim of adverse possession because, despite testimony of common property use, it declared a lack of color of title. In *Martínez* Hatch found exactly the opposite. Despite proof of color of title, he found no history of use.

Martínez v. Mundy

The possibility that an election for a Tierra Amarilla land grant board would cloud the titles of private ranchers on the grant had an immediate meaning for Karl Brusselbach. While the lawsuit was working its way through the courts, Brusselbach was negotiating a sale of eleven thousand acres to a southern New Mexico rancher named Bill Mundy. Mundy's attorneys warned their client that the history of constant legal conflict on the grant could create legal problems, but this did not dissuade Mundy. He was captivated by the high-country ranch and enticed by Brusselbach's low asking price. After initial negotiations, and despite the lawsuit, the slender rancher traveled to Tierra Amarilla in May 1951 to examine the property more closely.

Mundy considered himself uniquely prepared to take on the challenge. His father had been a dirt farmer in Texas and came to southern New Mexico at the turn of the twentieth century to finally buy his own ranch. But life as a landowner was short lived. The Mundys lost the ranch during the Depression and were forced back into sharecropping. As a teenager Mundy left home to work as a mule guide in the Grand Canyon and later as a ranch hand in Las Cruces. By the time he found the ranch in Tierra Amarilla, he was in his early thirties, tired of ranching other people's land, and willing to take on the risks of running a private ranch in Tierra Amarilla. "It was what I had wanted all my life," he would say later.[69]

Mundy spent three weeks examining the ranch with a local friend and guide. Every morning they saddled horses and rode along timbered ridges and through wide pastures. The high country on the land is among the most rugged on the grant with an elevation at Brusselbach's northern boundary above ten thousand feet where the land plunges into the Cañones Creek gorge a thousand feet below. From its highest elevation the land slopes slowly to the south for miles, finally emptying into Chavez Creek to the southeast and Brazos Creek to the southwest. The canyons and high elevation limited grazing to only the summer months.

The long days on horseback introduced Mundy to obvious patterns of common property use. On his first day he found signs that the southern pastures were not, as Brusselbach had said, seldom used but were instead a heavily used grazing pasture for cattle herds, sometimes larger than fifty, belonging to land grant members. In early June he found a flock of eight hundred breeding ewes grazing a high mountain pasture. Daily he rode up to bands of horses grazing everywhere on the ranch.[70]

In addition to current uses there were signs of a long history of land use. In the high country, where Ponderosa pine and aspen were thickest, Mundy found mill sites, sheep camps, and evidence of timber harvesting and firewood cutting. An old irrigation ditch ran three miles from Cañones Creek south to the largest field on the property.[71] Logging roads and hunting trails skirted high ground in the central and northern portion of the property.[72] A wide, well-used road bisected the property and served as a main thoroughfare between the small village of Ensenada to the south and Chama to the north. Though the property was unfenced when Mundy first rode it, he found evidence that previous owners had fenced portions of the ranch. Along the ranch's boundary lines and around various pastures, he found old fence lines and "posts that were broken off" lying alongside rusting sections of barbed wire "in small pieces, showing signs of having been cut."[73]

Despite signs that the ranch was and remained a commons and "people in that country at times made claim to the entire Grant," Mundy bought the ranch on June 7, 1951.[74] His attorneys assured him that previous court cases had settled the question of the land grant and despite the evidence he found on his three-week tour "there isn't a bit of evidence that there is a bit of common land there."[75]

Mundy used his life savings to buy the ranch, so he lived his first year on the ranch in a canvas tent in a wide pasture, where he spent his days erecting barbed wire fences, poisoning prairie dogs, and evicting cows and sheep.[76] He rented a few of his pastures to local ranchers and in July planted a wheat crop in an old sheep pasture rich with nitrogen. As the wheat came in, he turned his attention to a wide southern pasture long favored by land grant members. The sloping pasture abutted Brazos Creek and ran up against a small plot of land owned by a sheepherder named José María Martínez.

Martínez was nearly fifty when Mundy moved next door. Born in Abiquiú at the turn of the century, Martínez had been raised in a small adobe house

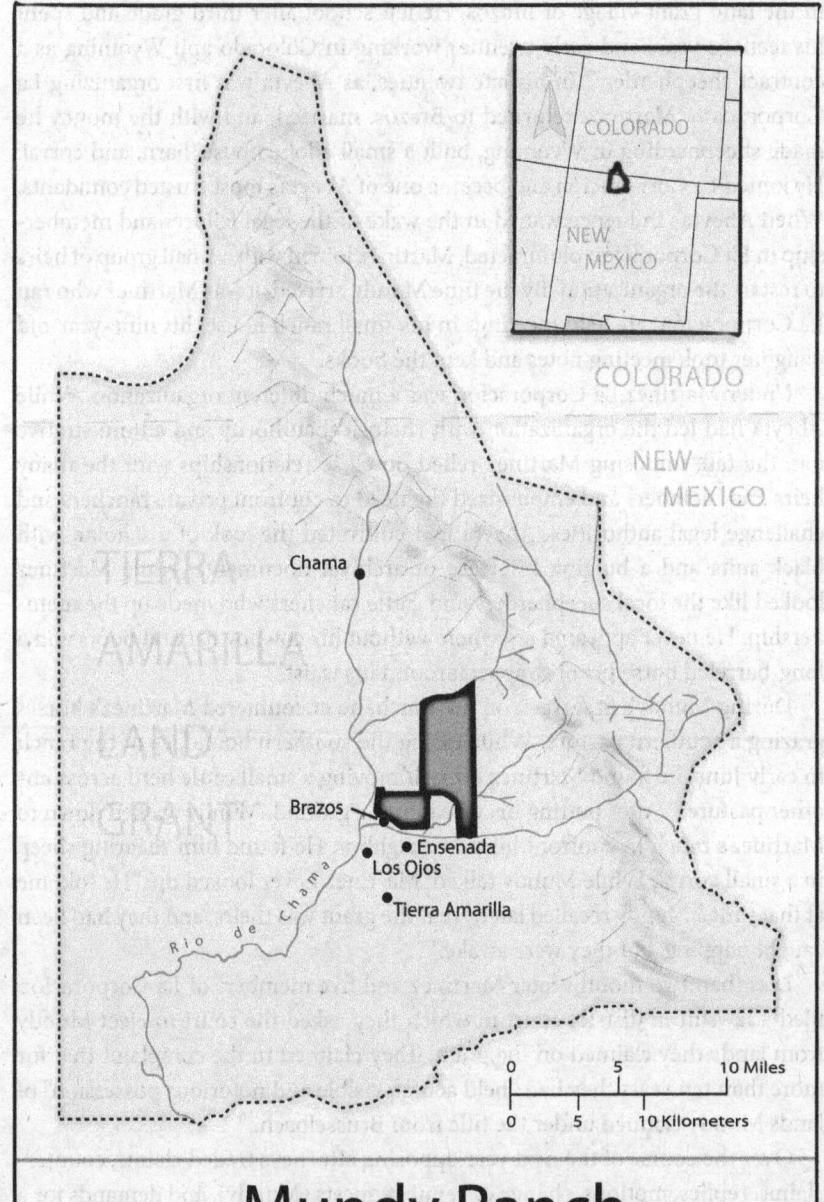

Mundy Ranch

Property in Dispute in the Lawsuit *Martínez v. Mundy*,
61 N.M. 87, 295 P.2d 209 (1956)

in the land grant village of Brazos. He left school after third grade and spent his teenage years and early twenties working in Colorado and Wyoming as a contract sheepherder.[77] In his late twenties, as Abeyta was first organizing La Corporación, Martínez returned to Brazos, married, and with the money he made sheepherding in Wyoming, built a small adobe house, barn, and corral. He joined La Corporación and became one of Abeyta's most trusted confidants. When Abeyta's influence waned in the wake of the legal failures and membership in La Corporación plummeted, Martínez joined with a small group of heirs to restart the organization. By the time Mundy arrived, it was Martínez who ran La Corporación. He held meetings in his small ranch house; his nine-year-old daughter took meeting notes and kept the books.

Under Martínez La Corporación was a much different organization. While Abeyta had led the organization with rhetorical authority and administrative fiat, the tall, imposing Martínez relied on close relationships with the many heirs and members and emphasized the need to confront private ranchers and challenge legal authorities. Abeyta had cultivated the look of a scholar, with black suits and a bulging briefcase of archival documents, while Martínez looked like the local sheepherders and cattle ranchers who made up the membership. He never appeared anywhere without his cowboy hat and boots and a long-barreled horse pistol strapped around his waist.

During Mundy's first week on the ranch, he encountered Martínez's horses grazing a southern pasture. While riding the southern boundary of the ranch in early June, he found Martínez himself moving a small cattle herd across another pasture.[78] After putting his wheat in the ground, Mundy walked down to Martínez's ranch to confront his new neighbor. He found him shearing sheep in a small corral. While Mundy talked, Martínez never looked up. "He told me at that time," Mundy recalled later, "that the grant was theirs, and they had been caught napping, but they were awake."[79]

Less than two months later Martínez and five members of La Corporación filed a lawsuit in district court in which they asked the court to eject Mundy from lands they claimed on the grant. They claimed in the complaint that for more than ten years they had "held actual, visible and notorious possession" of lands Mundy claimed under the title from Brusselbach.[80]

Over the course of the next year opposing attorneys traded claims, counterclaims, replies, motions, change of venue requests (Mundy), and demands for a jury trial (Martínez). The case became a cause célèbre among local media and ignited a renewed interest among land grant heirs in the long struggle for the grant. By August 1952 district court judge David Carmody had concluded that "by reason of public excitement and local prejudice in the County of Rio Arriba

"... an impartial jury could not be obtained in the said County of Rio Arriba."[81] Carmody moved the case to Santa Fe.

Next was the question of a jury trial. In a memorandum filed in July 1953 Carmody indicated his reluctance to reject a request for a jury. "The Court is always extremely reluctant," wrote Carmody, "to take any action which might seem, or appear to, in effect, take away from such part the right to a trial by jury. In these cases particularly, because of the interest aroused among a large group of people, the Court is even more reluctant to do so, than the Court would be if it were merely an ordinary suit between two parties, where the issues were simple, and racial and historical differences had not been magnified."[82] The compromise that Carmody crafted called for splitting the case in two. He decided to allow a jury trial for the ejectment suit but only after first setting a hearing for Mundy's quiet title counterclaim. The decision dealt a major blow to Martínez's case. Instead of plaintiffs in a jury trial in an ejectment suit, Martínez and his co-filers were now, once again, defendants in a quiet title suit.[83]

As the *Santa Fe New Mexican* noted in an article covering the case, Carmody's decision came in the wake of renewed fighting on the grant. Constant "night rider incidents, fence cuttings, burnings and shots in the night" served as the context of the case.[84] To Carmody the violence was a function of the "racial and historical differences" clouding the legal questions in the case. In late June fire destroyed a sawmill owned by out-of-state timber operators who had leased land from a private rancher. Angry sawmill workers set up roadblocks around the destroyed mill and harassed and searched land grant residents. "We understand the sawmill people were stopping the land granters," said an investigator, "and searching them for weapons when they started trying to drive their cattle up to the high pastures. The loggers were looking for the men who burned down their mill."[85] The harassment infuriated local sheepherders, and in late June a group of fifty armed men attacked the timber crew. Twenty armed sawmill workers took cover in the woods on both sides of the road during a firefight that lasted hours. The sawmill workers eventually retreated from the woods to the burned-out sawmill, where they dug in against the assault. State police spent much of that evening talking armed land grant members out of the woods and, according to an officer quoted in the *New Mexican*, "just barely stopped what could have been a bloody new outbreak of the historic Tierra Amarilla land grant feud."[86] In the aftermath of the shootout, state police increased their presence in Tierra Amarilla, surprised to find that "just about everybody seem[ed] to be carrying a gun."[87]

Meanwhile, José María Martínez hired Bigbee to represent the interests of La Corporación in the quiet title lawsuit. In preparing his case Bigbee could not make an argument based on the original Mexican grant because the courts had decided that the 1860 act of Congress produced a new grant of land. Only Congress, and not the courts, could go behind a congressional act. The efforts in *Martínez v. Rivera* also had been unsuccessful. So Bigbee looked for a different way to establish color of title and claim adverse possession. He chose to focus his efforts on the *hijuelas*. He argued in court that the conveyances his clients held from Francisco Martínez provided color of title for their claims.

The *hijuelas*, according to Bigbee, had a very specific legal effect. Each *hijuela* provided private and common property rights and therefore reconverted the grant back to a community land grant. Any conveyance of the entire land grant from Martínez to any other party would not have extinguished these common rights. Moreover, according to Bigbee, the record revealed that even Mundy's abstract was based on a *hijuela*. In 1871 Francisco Martínez sold land in the grant to Francisco Manzanares. Manzanares later sold his rights to Catron. According to Bigbee the deed from Martínez to Manzanares did not convey the entire grant but rather, since it was similar to the other *hijuelas*, conveyed only a small plot of land.

The courts had heard this testimony before. La Follette had originally introduced the Manzanares *hijuela* into evidence in *HND*, but the courts could not see its significance.[88] Bigbee, however, emphasized the importance of the Manzanares deed. If Catron's claim to the Tierra Amarilla land grant is traced through his purchase of the Manzanares deed, and this document did not convey the entire grant to Manzanares after all, *all* private claims to the land grant were thrown into doubt. As Bigbee argued, the Martínez-to-Manzanares *hijuela* was not a conveyance of the entire grant but instead conveyed only 150 varas, a small plot of land for a home and garden.

It would be an injustice, he argued, to believe that Martínez conveyed the entire six-hundred-thousand-acre property to Francisco Manzanares in 1871 for four hundred dollars, which came to less than a half cent per acre; instead it was obvious, according to Bigbee, that the *hijuela* described the conveyance of a small homesite.[89] If it were otherwise, Bigbee asked the court, would Manzanares turn around seven years later and sell the entire grant to Thomas Catron for three hundred dollars *less* than what he had bought it for?[90] The answer he suggested was that the deed was only for a small tract of land and not for the entire grant. To define it as a conveyance of the entire grant was to show "complete contempt for the ability of our judicial processes to ascertain the truth from complete absurdity in even making contentions based on such absurd contentions."[91]

Although the Martínez-to-Manzanares *hijuela* threw Mundy's deed into question, it still remained for La Corporación to establish color of title. In previous cases the courts had found that La Corporación could not demonstrate color of title for its claims because there existed no conveyance from Martínez to La Corporación. To overcome this problem Bigbee focused on the individual heirs instead of La Corporación and showed that a chain of title could be traced through the *hijuelas* to each individual plaintiff. It was an argument requiring a delicate hand because in previous cases the courts had made it clear that in order to claim property by adverse possession, someone, or some entity with color of title, had to *possess* the property in question. But Bigbee could not make a private claim to the common lands without undermining the collective claims of his clients. He therefore argued that the individual *hijuelas* put his clients in collective possession of the property. Any entity they collectively established to manage those common rights was thus the de facto entity in possession of the property.

To advance this theory he offered testimony that described a long history of shared use and, most importantly, an equally long history of collective management of the common lands on the grant. The individual use established adverse possession, and the collective management via the *hijuelas* provided color of title. Local land grant residents used the property individually. They pastured their own sheep and cattle. They cut their own timber and firewood. But they managed this individual use by creating and empowering a group that governed their individual use of common property: La Corporación de Abiquiú.

Mundy's attorney's stuck to a familiar defense. Although Mundy admitted in court that he found evidence of historic and current uses and even "found evidence of fence cutting on all the existing fences, and even evidence in the skeletons of fences that didn't remain usable at the time," his attorneys argued that

> none of the appellants claimed any alleged right to be there exclusively, but only in common with all the people on the Grant who could trace their ancestry to the original settlers or who had a so-called hijuela in their possession. . . . Much the same sort of evidence appears with regard to the appellants' gathering of wood and poles. None claimed to have been engaged in any commercial wood taking from the Mundy place or anywhere else on the Grant. [On the ranch] taking was sporadic, perhaps once every year of so, whenever they felt the need and then wherever on the Grant might be convenient.[92]

For this reason, Mundy's attorneys argued, the use of the land by land grant residents did not rise to adverse possession because "none of the plaintiffs ever lived on the property, herded sheep there, fenced it, or leased it, and they testif[ied] to no other person in privy with them who did so."⁹³

Bigbee, meanwhile, continued to walk a legal tightrope. His arguments tried to prove adverse possession without falling into the trap of translating the common property claims of the land grant into the language of private property valorized by the courts. So he overwhelmed the court with evidence of a long tradition of customary and collective use by land grant members contrasted with a history of irregular and discontinuous use by the many private ranchers who populated Mundy's abstract. While it was easy to overwhelm the court with evidence of intensive use of the land, the strategy hinged on the *hijuelas* in general and the Martínez-to-Manzanares conveyance in particular. Bigbee had to convince the court that the *hijuelas* conveyed certain common rights, served as color of title for a collective claim of adverse possession, and undermined Mundy's claim to the property.

It was a difficult argument to sustain because the Manzanares conveyance was at best an ambiguous legal document open to interpretation, and the courts had a history of interpreting everything as a demonstration of private property. Filed and recorded in Rio Arriba County, the conveyance reads as follows:⁹⁴

> This indenture entered into this 1st day of June, 1871 between Francisco Martínez and wife, María Encarnación García, of the County of RA and Terr of NM, of the first part, and Francisco A. Manzanares of the County of Greenwood and Territory of Colorado, of the second part, and in good faith, party of the first part testifies as follows:
>
> For and in consideration of the sum of Four Hundred Dollars, legal money of the US, to us in hand paid by the said party of the second part before these presents were signed, sealed and delivered, the receipt of which sum is by these presents firmly acknowledged and we have given, granted, sold, conveyed, quitclaimed and confirmed, and by these presents give, grant, sell, convey, quitclaim and confirm to the said party of the second part and his heirs, successors and assigns forever, all of the rights, title and interest which we inherited and originally bought and which belongs or may belong at any time and for any heirs of the line of any other claimants of the property and possession of the grant commonly known as the Tierra Amarilla Grant in the County of RA and Territory of NM, which grant and conveyance was made by the Governor of Mexico on April 29, 1832 to their father, Don Manuel Martínez and eight sons, heirs of our father and grantees of this grant, we make by these presents a quitclaim deed and conveyance, and we advise that the said party of the second part shall take possession of one hundred fifty varas of cultivated land, situate in the place of the springs within

the limits of the grant, justly with all and singular the lands, privileges and appurnances [sic] in the premises and the reversions, rents, uses and products of the same, and also all the dominion rights, titles, interests, properties and possession; I claim to be of certain rights as the same as of the parties of the first part, and as well as to the above-mentioned to all parts or portions thereof of the same, with all its appurentances [sic].

Witnessed by Antonio Jose Martínez and Juan Andres Quintana, certified by Justice of the Peace, Juan Trujillo.

The document begins with language that appears to convey the entire land grant to Manzanares but then explicitly limits the transfer to a small 150-vara plot of land within the grant. In order to convince the court to reject the initial wording and accept the language limiting the conveyance, Bigbee argued that the court must consider the circumstances and context of the conveyance itself. The price of the sale, for example, and the similarity of the document to other *hijuelas* should lead the court, he argued, to conclude that the deed was intended only as a conveyance of a small plot of land. The ambiguity of the language is understandable, according to Bigbee, written as it was "by a person not learned in legal phraseology."[95]

Mundy's attorneys, however, directed the court's attention to the granting clause. The court was not permitted to consider the clause Bigbee highlighted or the circumstances of the conveyance. It had to focus its interpretation instead on the granting clause, which was "the main source for determining the estate or interest conveyed. Although resort may be had to other parts to ascertain its meaning or to supply information lacking therein, the omission of anything on the subject elsewhere in the deed [was] immaterial."[96]

While the suit dragged on, conflict erupted frequently outside the courtroom. Mundy often confronted members of La Corporación who continued to run cattle on the ranch. He ejected sheep and cattle and occasionally attempted to build fences around various pastures. His efforts inflamed La Corporación members, who were convinced that Mundy was trying to establish favorable conditions for a future claim of adverse possession. When Mundy tried to build a fence around a pasture commonly used by members of La Corporación, Martínez, who said later he "felt like they were being invaded" by Mundy, led a party of armed land grant heirs to the Brazos Creek, where they fired shots across the creek at the work party.[97]

It was a pattern that would repeat itself with regularity. Mundy would build fences and then find his fences cut. He would bale hay and then watch as they were set on fire. Even the massive ranch house and barn that he eventually built on his property became the target of local incendiaries and was burned to the ground in 1964. His daily rides throughout the grant became armed patrols.

The court finally convened in August 1953, two years after the original complaint, to hear testimony. Bigbee called all the defendants as witnesses. As in all the other lawsuits, each testified in Spanish and used a local court interpreter. One after the other they described using the property intensively over the course of decades. Under cross-examination José María Martínez refused to use the words "the Mundy tract" when describing the property and maintained that he sued to stop Mundy from "fencing [his] pastures."[98] "I have cut timber," he explained. "I have grazed cattle, I have used the water, and I have used all the elements that are on that land."[99]

José Remigio Martínez, a forty-two-year-old sheepherder and coplaintiff in the case, testified that he also had used the land his entire life and had never heard of anyone named Kinderman or Brusselbach. When asked who used the grant, he replied, "All the people that live in that little town of Brazos, Tierra Amarilla, and all that is enclosed by the grant.... There was no English people in that land."[100] Manuel Gallegos, another sheepherder and defendant in the case, testified, "[I have used] the pasture to graze my stock, I have used the wood for fuel, warming us in our house stoves and fireplaces."[101] Lionel Martínez, a thirty-eight-year-old defendant and descendent of Francisco Martínez, testified that the original Mexican grant placed the pastures, watering places, and roads in common.

Bigbee explained to the court that the point of the testimony was to establish a long record of traditional uses. The customs of resource use and management by the plaintiffs were important because, Bigbee argued, "It goes to the possession and use during the entire period of time, which is material on the issues ... that they have acquired title by adverse possession." José María Martínez explained to the court how the individual use of the common lands was part of an interconnected set of social and ecological relations.[102]

> The customs, generally, it was our custom to turn the livestock loose to whatever area, on whatever side he means, whatever direction the people of those of us that own sheep, which do not own very large flocks, it's customary to have them down in the meadows until the rest of the pasture is in condition. When the pasture around that meadow is in proper shape, has enough pasture in it, then we turn them loose over that area. Those are the customs from which I can testify as to the pasture. Now, as to the lumber, as far as getting wood out, whether it's for fuel or lumber, we take it out from whatever area it's available, also as to firewood, we make similar use of the water, without having any disturbance from either side,

from one side or from the other. It happens sometimes that some of us one year have about 20 cattle, and maybe next year we have only 5, the same thing holds true as to sheep, also as to horses, also as to burros or mules, also goats, also chickens and hens, also hogs. We have lived under those conditions for the last 500 years over that area. All the livestock is pastured together, and we don't define the lines of pasture.[103]

Mundy's attorneys called a series of witnesses that included the plaintiff, local surveyors, and private ranchers. Brusselbach testified, almost comically, that as far as he knew the defendants, all of whom were cattle or sheep ranchers, did not own cattle or sheep. Mundy admitted, however, that local land grant members maintained large herds of cattle, huge flocks of sheep, and numerous bands of horses nearly everywhere on the ranch.[104] Joe Turner, a local ranch hand, testified that two previous owners, Charley Daggett and Welch Nossaman, ran cattle on the ranch and farmed hay on a large pasture near the ranch house. During the decade he worked for Nossaman in the 1920s, Turner claimed he never saw cattle or sheep on the ranch other than those that belonged to Nossaman. When the boundaries of the tract were described to Turner under cross-examination, however, he admitted that much of the property was considered common land that everybody used "more or less, if they could get in there."[105]

Finally, Bigbee called to the stand Brother Rowland, the chair of the Latin American Department at Santa Fe's St. Michael's College. Rowland testified that the *hijuelas* in this particular case differed from the documents that the court considered to be ancient Spanish documents usually found in wills. They were not identified as *hijuelas* at all, in fact, but instead were called *El Traspaso y Reconocimiento*, which Rowland translated for the court as legal documents of "transfer and acknowledgment." Furthermore, the language of the deed related to the common lands. The wording in the *hijuelas*, "las cuales varas de tierra quedan con el derecho," should be translated, according to Rowland, as "which varas of land remain with right to pasture and so on."[106]

Mundy's attorneys pounced on the verb *quedar*. If *quedan con* meant "remain" or "retain," as Rowland testified, then the documents did not *convey* anything. "Those words imply, do they not," argued Mundy's attorney, "something already in existence, and not something being conveyed or brought into being." Rowland disagreed, noting that the verb *quedar* was commonly mistranslated and usually misunderstood when translated into English. "As I see it," Rowland testified "he is giving over this land, together with the rights to water, woods and so on."[107] Mundy's attorneys pressed Rowland on the wording. Retaining land, they noted, is not the same thing as conveying land. Rowland explained that *quedan con* referred not to the 150 varas of land but rather to the rights to pasture and waters, something that "existed before, and [Martínez] want[ed] the land to retain the same rights."[108]

With testimony complete, both parties traded "requested findings of fact" with the court in December. Bigbee argued that Mundy was neither the fee simple owner of the property nor was he in possession of it. Instead, the plaintiffs claimed the property by virtue of the deeds they had received from Francisco Martínez, deeds that gave them common rights to lands in the grant "for pasturing and watering livestock, for gathering wood for use as fuel, fence posts and vigas, and [they had] used the roads and trails thereon, such uses having been open, notorious, uninterrupted, under claim of right, adverse and peaceable for a period of more than ten years."[109] Mundy denied that the *hijuelas*, or *Trespasos y Reconocimientos*, conveyed any rights to the plaintiffs whatsoever.

Carmody issued the Court's findings of fact and conclusions of law two weeks later. Once again he recognized the long-standing claims for the commons and noted that many heirs "periodically used the lands described in the counterclaim for pasturing and watering livestock and in cutting wood for many years preceding the filing of the complaint."[110] Despite this history he was unconvinced by Bigbee's theory or Brother Rowland's testimony and concluded that the *hijuelas* extended no rights to land and therefore did not provide a color of title for a claim of adverse possession. The *hijuelas* didn't "grant or convey any of the land and real estate herein involved or any right, title or interest therein or thereto or any encumbrances thereupon." Despite determining that the language in the *hijuelas* did not convey property, he concluded that the Martínez-to-Manzanares *hijuela*, unlike the others, was a legal conveyance for the entire land grant. Although he admitted that the ranch was unfenced at the time of the suit and that the defendants "used the lands . . . for pasturing and watering livestock and in cutting wood for many years preceding the institution of this action," he concluded, without reference to any testimony or evidence, that the plaintiff had "been in actual and exclusive possession of the land and real estate herein." Martínez and the other defendants therefore would not receive a jury trial in the ejectment suit because they "did not have at the time of the filing of this cause and [did] not [then] have any right, title or interest [in the ranch] nor any right to graze livestock, cut wood, or use water thereon."[111]

In his final decree, issued on New Year's Eve 1953, Carmody declared Mundy the owner "in fee-simple, free and clear of all liens and encumbrances whatsoever." José María Martínez and the other defendants were "barred and forever estopped from having or claiming any right, title or interest" to the property. The case was eventually appealed to the New Mexico Supreme Court and heard in March 1956. In the opinion, authored by Justice John McManus, the court agreed with Carmody that the *hijuelas* did not provide a color of title to the defendants, did not make Mundy's title defective, and did not reconvert the grant to a community land grant. McManus refused to "speculate as to the reference to the 150 varas" in the Martínez-to-Manzanares conveyance. As a result the court was "convinced that the deed from Martínez to Manzanares conveyed the entire grant by such conveyance."[112] It followed, continued McManus, that the Manzanares-to-Catron deed also conveyed the entire grant.

Many of the members of La Corporación, Martínez included, blamed Bigbee, who withdrew prior to the hearing before the state supreme court, for what many considered a devastating legal setback. The *Santa Fe New Mexican* assumed that the opinion of the supreme court put the issue to rest and speculated that it marked the "last legal round in the long and bitter fight over ownership" of the Tierra Amarilla land grant.[113]

In the four lawsuits examined in this chapter, La Corporación de Abiquiú argued for a view of the law as a set of social relations rooted in particular local histories and demonstrated by embodied performances or practices of property. Its members' tactics of writing deeds, paying taxes, evicting private ranchers, erecting fences and bridges, building roads, and digging ditches illustrate that they understood property as a site of social struggle where they asserted claims and performed their rights. La Corporación performed these claims through various "acts of possession" and asserted the claims in court. Its strategy was to establish open, notorious, and adverse possession under a color of title that would be a persuasive demonstration of first possession recognizable to the courts.

The results, however, were not what Medardo Abeyta promised when he founded La Corporación. Instead of restoring the property claims of land grant members, the courts erased the history of common property in Tierra Amarilla and replaced it with a history of private property. It was all the more amazing that the courts did this despite acknowledging that land grant claimants used the property as a commons. In each of the cases the courts construed property as a discrete object in relation to particular individuals. In doing so the courts reduced the complicated histories of resource use and collective management of the land grant into a series of isolated, abstract legal questions that ignored the complex social relations and local histories of land use in Tierra Amarilla. This preoccupation with property as a spatial abstraction constructed property as something "disembodied rather than formed in material and historical conditions."[114] Property as only an object rather than also a set of relations.

Through his *manos muertas* theory, La Follette tried to overcome this narrow view by placing property in a particular historical context. He presented La Corporación as legally equivalent to an individual, with rights including that of owning private property. The strategy translated the common property relations of land grant claimants into a kind of private property claim that the courts could recognize. Attorneys in *Flores* advanced a similar argument. They claimed that individual land grant heirs had reanimated La Corporación de Abiquiú as a corporate trustee and vested it with the authority to manage private lands on the grant. But attorneys for La Corporación were unable to overcome the preconception of various judges that property was always and only an object. The courts were uninterested in testimony regarding traditional custom and use and more concerned with defining the boundaries of property claims and examining the sequence of historical transfers of title to that property. Since the courts saw property as an object rather than a relation, the job of mediating a property dispute was limited to defining a legal definition of real property, locating that object in space, and then examining how and to whom that object circulated in a sequence of market exchanges.

In *Martínez v. Mundy* the court, particularly Judge McManus, constructed a view of property based solely on metes and bounds rather than histories of use. Property was an object located on maps created by surveyors. Technical experts, such as surveyors, played "an important role in the inauguration of a particular view of space as detached and alienable and thus deeply implicated in the ideological creation of property."[115] The production of property became in the view of the court something revealed by surveyors and cartographers and interpreted by judges. McManus relied on the notion of property as an object when he rejected the theory that the *hijuelas* provided common property rights. La Corporación tried to interrupt this view by defining property rights in ways much different from those of the surveyor's grid. What was conveyed was not an exclusive right to a particular piece of property that could be located on a map but instead a set of social relations to property defined in relation to the rights of others.

José María Martínez explained this different view of property in his testimony in *Martínez v. Mundy*. The shifting needs of local land grant members and the changing ecological conditions meant that strict spatial coordinates could not serve the complicated matrix of land grant agricultural production. Pastures were good in some years, but in other years they were not. Some years certain land grant residents had large herds, and some years they did not. Land grant property, therefore, could be understood not as an object in space but rather as a relation among various people based on variable ecological conditions and changing individual needs.

This view of property, however, made no sense to judges obsessed with verbs and granting clauses and ignorant of ecological conditions and household production patterns. To the judges who adjudicated the claims described in this chapter, the *hijuelas* did not convey property because they lacked spatial coordinates and the correct language that *conveyed* common rights. What Martínez described in his testimony were unmappable rights that could not be made legible within the courts' view of property as a relation between a person and a particular parcel of land mapped by grid onto the landscape. Since the *hijuelas* did not provide a spatial description for various common rights to pasture and water or impose a set of coordinates onto the land, judges found nothing that looked to them like property. Moreover, the kinds of social relations that Martínez described not only failed to rise to the standard of property that the courts required but also served in the minds of judges as proof of the lack of property entirely. McManus in particular concluded that the shifting and variable uses that plaintiffs such as Martínez described meant that land grant settlers only used the grant "spasmodically."

Land grant use was seasonal and variable; therefore to McManus it was "permissive" rather than "adverse." It was permissive, he concluded, because the appellants accessed the land "through unfenced portions or through fenced portions at times when the fences were down or in a state of neglect."[116] For McManus this was proof that the patterns of use by Martínez and other members of La Corporación were "similar to that of the general public" and therefore "the appellants certainly could not acquire a private easement unto themselves."[117] The practice of collective resource use, in other words, demonstrated for McManus a lack of private property. This last rejection was the final way in which the courts construed common property use, a use defined outside the law. McManus was in effect admitting that members of La Corporación had long used the land as a commons but that their particular practices and historical patterns of resource use could not rise to the level of property. For McManus and the other judges in the various cases, the history of common uses of the grant actually reinforced private claims for it. Though the legal struggle for the grant failed to accomplish what Abeyta promised when it began, it served as the context for what newspapers would later call "The New Mexico Land Grant War" that followed it.

CHAPTER FIVE

The New Mexico Land Grant War

PAYNE LAND AND LIVESTOCK COMPANY filed a lawsuit in federal court in June 1958 to quiet the title to its seven-thousand-acre ranch on the Tierra Amarilla grant.[1] Among scholars of New Mexico land grant legal history, *Payne* is generally considered the last of five significant legal conflicts over Tierra Amarilla common property.[2] The case is often described as the exclamation point at the end of a long legal transformation in which the courts finally and "unjustly deprived [land grant heirs] of their common ownership of the Grant's common, unallotted lands."[3] At the heart of the dispute was a counterclaim by scores of land grant residents, all of whom irrigated small farms with water drawn from the Brazos and Nutrias Creeks, that they owned seventy of the seven thousand acres for which Payne sought a quiet title. "I was born here and lived all my life here," wrote Bernardo Rivera in an affidavit in which he claimed four acres inherited from his grandfather.[4] Rivera and the other defendants all based their claims on *hijuelas*.

Payne invoked Catron's 1883 quiet title lawsuit's argument that the acreages claimed by defendants were in fact lands quieted in Catron's name in the nineteenth century. At the time of the 1883 lawsuit, however, Catron excepted a number of small properties that he acknowledged were conveyed by Francisco Martínez to various settlers from Abiquiú. The question the court confronted in *Payne* was whether the seventy acres claimed by the defendants were included in these exceptions.

La Corporación de Abiquiú, as in the other cases, was named as a defendant. But unlike in the previous cases La Corporación offered no new legal challenge to private property on the grant, nor did it try to counter the legal logic of previous decisions. None of the defendants, in fact, made a legal challenge to the private property claims of Payne. Rather they merely sought to have the court confirm their private rights to the small plots of land within the boundaries of Payne's seven-thousand-acre claim. Similarly, the opinion of the U.S. District Court, written by Judge Waldo Rogers and delivered on February 1, 1960, added nothing new to the legal construction of private property rights on the grant. Rogers merely recycled familiar legal theories from previous cases in order to reject the claims. He cited the *Tameling* case in order to reject claims by defendants that the Treaty of Guadalupe Hidalgo protected Mexican property rights, and he borrowed familiar keywords found in previous legal opinions in order to reject the defendants' adverse possession claims. Sounding vaguely like every other opinion in the legal conflict over Tierra Amarilla, Rogers wrote, of people who had lived on the land in question all their life, that the use of the property by the defendants "consisted, for the most part, of occasional, sporadic and isolated instances of trespass on the land in question."[5]

As the final quiet title suit regarding the Tierra Amarilla land grant, *Payne* was more epilogue than exclamation point.[6] Although there was nothing very interesting or significant about the legal questions considered in *Payne*, it remains important as the moment when legal interpretation over property claims gave way to a violent struggle over the enforcement of those private claims. The ability of the state to replace diverse systems of local common property land tenure with property as a universal, standardized object represented on the surveyor's map as *things* or *commodities* is always a contested process.[7] While the law may inaugurate new property relations, "a shadow land-tenure system [lurks] beside and beneath the official account in the land-records office."[8]

The legal struggle over *Payne* seemed to finally resolve questions of property in court, but its real significance was the way in which *Payne* inaugurated a new period of violent struggle over the grant. The production of private property detailed in the preceding chapter is a story of how judges interpreted the law; this chapter is a story of the violent enforcement of these new private property relations. The years after the *Payne* decision were ones in which the state and various agencies of social coercion worked to impose private property in Tierra Amarilla and erase common property practices.

This chapter focuses on the efforts of various law enforcement agencies, including the New Mexico State Police (NMSP) and the Federal Bureau of Investigation (FBI), to enforce newly constructed private property relations on the grant. As I show in this chapter, the agents of social and spatial control began wide-ranging programs in Tierra Amarilla that for the first time enforced newly constructed private rights to property. The history of NMSP and FBI violence at the heart of the construction of private property in New Mexico is not well known. If violence is at all part of the story of land grant struggle, it is often depicted as the violence of land grant claimants and not the racialized violence of the state in imposing private property relations. This is not unique to New Mexico. As the political theorist Timothy Mitchell explains in his study of property relations in Egypt in the twentieth century, "the ad hoc, violent, and exceptional character of the law of property was entirely hidden by the presentation of law as something abstract, as a universal rule, with its origins elsewhere, applied to particular circumstances."[9] Mitchell is interested in the logic and irony of the state's use of violence against its citizens as a tactic against the use of violence by its citizens. For Mitchell this violence is central to the relationship of law and property.

State-sponsored violence has a long history in the United States as a means to establish spatial control of particular social groups. As the economist Mary King has argued, "State-sponsored violence has kept people 'in their place.' The U.S. government has made use of violence — or the threat of state violence — to enforce the legal apparatus of slavery, the exclusive access to higher education of white men, and the disenfranchisement of women and people of color."[10] As the previous chapter shows, the construction of private property required the intellectual labor of judges and lawyers to produce private property. As this chapter demonstrates, legal interpretation always gives way to its violent enforcement. Law, in other words, plays out in "a field of pain and death" in which law's enforcers such as the police violently impose new private property relations.[11]

Enforcing Property

When La Corporación filed its countersuit in *Payne*, it hired a young Albuquerque attorney named Alfonso Sanchez. Though not yet well known in legal circles or local politics, Sanchez, who had just graduated from the University of New Mexico Law School, was familiar to members of La Corporación. In addition to being an heir to an Albuquerque-area land grant, Sanchez was a legal advisor to the New Mexico chapter of the GI Forum, a national Hispanic veterans association. It was through forum meetings that officers of La Corporación first met Sanchez and solicited his legal help. Sanchez had fought in World War II and the Korean War before putting himself through law school as an adobe brick maker for Albuquerque contractors. When he graduated in the spring of 1957, the politically ambitious Sanchez took a job in the district attorney's office in Santa Fe, where he brought a religious zeal to the law, a knack for self-promotion, and a fatherly demeanor to his clients. He was prone to delivering long sermons from behind his desk in which he frequently referred to himself in the third person, reminding whomever he was talking to that he was "your pal Al," a phrase that would later become his slogan in campaigns for the state legislature and district attorney.[12]

Sanchez worked for La Corporación outside of his duties for the district attorney's office, devoting nights and weekends to the case. He dug through archives, studied the legal history of the land grant, and discovered a complicated history of strange deed transfers and ambiguous property conveyances. "These people," he concluded, "were screwed."[13] But the law was the law, and according to Sanchez, it was not up to him to interpret it nor should La Corporación oppose it. Instead, it was his job to "educate the people on how the law works."[14] The heirs, however, were less interested in being educated than in getting the land back.

Client meetings became increasingly contentious. Members rejected his frequent requests for more money to conduct additional research or to pay for better title abstracts.[15] They bristled at Sanchez's suggestions that they should pursue a financial settlement for the land. "They wanted the land, not the value of the land," he recalled.[16] At a meeting in late 1958 La Corporación members "threatened to use force to retake the land immediately," a threat that Sanchez took so seriously he withdrew as counsel. He would later explain that his decision was based on a concern that the struggle could turn violent. The "volatile angry feelings," he wrote, "signaled to me ... how easily they could be motivated to violence."[17]

The same year Sanchez agreed to represent defendants in the *Payne* lawsuit, a thirty-year-old Pentecostal preacher named Reies Lopez Tijerina arrived in Tierra Amarilla with a caravan of bearded and robed followers who locals called Los Barbudos, or the bearded ones. With jet-black hair and intense green eyes, Tijerina preached in what appeared to be a kind of trancelike state, yelling in Spanish and gesturing wildly with his arms. He could keep it up for hours, and according to those who saw him preach, he often did. Speaking in private homes and rented halls, he attracted growing crowds from throughout the Tierra Amarilla valley.[18] Soon after arriving in Tierra Amarilla, he met José María Martínez and other leaders of La Corporación, who explained to the new preacher the turbulent history of the land grant. "I felt in my heart a stab," Tijerina would later write. "These ancient humble people had a just and sacred cause. I felt in my body and my soul and my spirit that these people were worthy of justice."[19] He decided to stay in Tierra Amarilla, and he moved in with Juan Martínez, José María's nephew and one of the defendants in *Payne*. With Martínez he attended land grant meetings and studied the documents people brought to him. The stories convinced Tijerina that a colonial history of legal deception and suspicious speculation, reinforced by a climate of racism against Spanish-speaking New Mexicans, had robbed local land grant heirs of their common property.[20] He later recalled, "I noticed that they were conditioned by the education of the Anglos, and they were fearful. My first job would be to remove that fear."²¹

The same month that Rogers delivered his opinion in *Payne*, Tijerina left Tierra Amarilla to visit archives in Mexico City. Over the next few years he traveled back and forth between Mexico and Tierra Amarilla. In Mexico he visited archives, met with scholars, and solicited government officials and prominent lawyers for help in the land grant struggle. In Tierra Amarilla he worked with Amarante Serrano, the new president of La Corporación, and others to organize the various land grant struggles into one large movement. In 1962, with the help of his brothers Cristobal and Anselmo, he started La Alianza Federal de Mercedes, a land grant organization based in Albuquerque. The brothers hoped Alianza would finally unify the scores of Spanish and Mexican land grants in New Mexico and create popular support for a broad struggle to return common property to the many community land grants in New Mexico. Alianza was incorporated on February 2, 1963, the 115th anniversary of the signing of the Treaty of Guadalupe Hidalgo. By 1967 it claimed a membership of between five thousand and ten thousand land grant heirs statewide.

The creation of Alianza in the years immediately following *Payne* coincided with renewed fence cutting and arson on the grant. Three suspicious fires in January and February 1962 destroyed barns on large ranches on the grant.²² With the spring thaw came a flurry of fence cutting and hay fires throughout the valley. Private ranchers blamed La Corporación for the unrest. The arson and fence cutting continued into 1964, when, in July, men calling themselves trustees of La Corporación de Abiquiú confronted a ranch manager for the Chama Land and Cattle Company while he was repairing a barbed-wire fence. The land was theirs, they told him, and they would not allow more fences.²³ The ranch manager ignored the men and continued mending the fence. Less than two weeks later fire destroyed the barn at the Chama Land and Cattle ranch.²⁴ Private ranchers and local sawmill operators soon added armed guards to their payroll.

Rio Arriba County authorities doubted that La Corporación was responsible for the unrest, convinced instead that Tijerina, a figure they considered an outside agitator, was responsible. By the summer of 1964, the NMSP had a long case file on Tijerina, much of it collected by an undercover agent placed within Alianza's ranks. Sanchez, who had just been elected district attorney, initially was unable to get information from state police and so began his own separate investigation of Tijerina's local activities. While Sanchez investigated Tijerina, Serrano and Tijerina traveled to Washington, D.C., and managed to get an interview with Robert Kennedy.²⁵ But Kennedy refused to make any promises.

Disappointed, Tijerina returned to Mexico City to plan a caravan from that city to Tierra Amarilla as a way to publicize the cause of land grant loss, while Serrano returned to Tierra Amarilla and began mailing eviction notices to nonheirs on the grant. Two versions of Serrano's eviction notices circulated among private ranchers. The first was a one-page form letter that was mailed out by the dozens. It ordered nonheirs off the grant by October 20. Another, more dramatic version of the eviction notice circulated with the first. It began:

> In the name of Almighty God and by virtue of the legal land title given to Manuel Martínez, By the Mexican authorities in the year of our Lord on the 20th day of July, 1832, we, the heirs of Manuel Martínez, acting under the *POWER* vested in us by the above-mentioned Land Title, do hereby *SERVE NOTICE* to ALL those *NONE-HEIRS* [sic] now *POSSESSING* either *SMALL* or *LARGE TRACTS* of land with the Boundaries of the Tierra Amarilla land Grant, that on the 20th day of October 1964, we are *DETERMINED* with *FIRM* and *RESOLUTE ACTION* to take *POSSESSION* of these tracts of land that are now being *OCCUPIED* by *NONE-HEIRS*.
>
> WE also want to make it *CLEAR* to *ALL NONE-HEIRS*, that there is no authority on *EARTH* to whom they could *APPEAL* for the simple reason that the tracts of land that they now possess are within the boundaries of the Tierra Amarilla Land Grant, and we are certainly *SURE* that this Grant is covered by an *INTERNATIONAL TREATY*.[26]

The eviction order directed an entity called the "Board of Treaties Patrol" to "carry out this evacuation order to a successful finish." The order asked state and federal authorities to refrain from intervening. Serrano mailed eviction notices to private ranchers and government agencies. The Bureau of Reclamation was ordered to abandon the construction of Heron Dam west of Tierra Amarilla. La Corporación claimed authority over the grant by virtue of the Treaty of Guadalupe Hidalgo and suggested, "This action of ours is sanctioned by hundreds of thousands of workers and peasants in the whole of Latin America." In early August Serrano told the press that La Corporación, a group he claimed at that time included more than 1,500 members, was nearly done mailing eviction notices. "The law says we only have to allow three days," Serrano told the local press, "but we're giving them from 20 to 30 days to get off."[27]

The notices were then followed by a series of additional confrontational tactics. In legal notices published in the newspaper, the group declared its intent to seize authority from the New Mexico Department of Game and Fish over all natural resources on the grant. La Corporación de Abiquiú would now administer fishing and hunting licenses. As this was happening, targeted attacks against ranchers and industrial facilities continued. Local business owners received anonymous telephone threats, while large landowners found the tires on their trucks slashed. Cattle were found shot, while others were impounded by La Corporación, a tactic borrowed from the Forest Service, an agency that regularly impounded the wayward cattle of land grant ranchers. In early August someone wrapped ten pounds of oil-soaked cotton blankets around pipes and under loading docks at a Conoco bulk fuel plant located just outside of Chama. The subsequent blaze engulfed a series of buildings and threatened the entire town when it spread dangerously close to a tank farm that stored huge quantities of gasoline and other fuels. Firefighters barely kept the blaze contained.[28] Much of the fence cutting and incendiarism was directed at Bill Mundy and local authorities, particularly Sanchez, were convinced that a war between La Corporación and Mundy was unavoidable unless something was done.[29]

Sanchez took the threats by La Corporación seriously and worked furiously to stop its plans to evict ranchers. He hosted almost daily meetings with officers of La Corporación and even brought Harry Bigbee back to Tierra Amarilla to speak with land grant heirs. Bigbee attended a land grant meeting and advised the group to respect the courts. "Previous court decisions must be recognized," he declared, "and there must not be further actions such as there have been in the past."[30] Serrano, however, was unswayed. "We're going to keep on with our work" he explained, "until this land is all ours, or until it's taken away—until they drive us out of our own land."[31]

By this time Sanchez was convinced that Tijerina was behind the arson and the provocative tactics of La Corporación.[32] The two men met briefly in 1963, and Sanchez left that encounter convinced that the charismatic leader of Alianza was, in his words, "a communist and a rabble-rouser."[33] Sanchez wrote police departments in Arizona, Texas, and Michigan, where Tijerina and his brothers had previously lived, and found a long criminal record. Anselmo had been arrested in multiple states where he had been accused of assault and battery. Reies had been arrested in Arizona for grand theft. Alarmed, Sanchez wrote FBI director J. Edgar Hoover and requested information from the agency on Tijerina, a man he described to Hoover as "allegedly involved in communistic activities and inciting some of the Northern local residents on land grant matters."[34] Though the FBI ignored Sanchez's request, Sanchez had a bulging case file on Tijerina by then that included NMSP reports, criminal records, and interviews with informants. The file was largely speculative and circumstantial. It relied heavily on a report by a New Mexico lawyer based on supposition: "Rumor has it [Tijerina] is a cult leader. . . . The original rumor is [that] he and

A New Mexico state police officer (*left*) and the Rio Arriba County jailer Eulogio Salazar (*right*) hold up a "no trespassing" sign that was erected by La Corporación de Abiquiú. District Attorney Alfonso Sanchez removed and photographed the sign, 1964. (Courtesy of Alfonso Sanchez.)

another man were up here at the instance of the Communist Party. . . . Locals say Reyes is always there when the trouble starts."³⁵

Sanchez continued monitoring the situation until mid-September, when Serrano announced the formation of his "Border of Treaties Patrol," a unit of armed border patrol guards. On September 25, an anxious Sanchez raced to Tierra Amarilla, where he found newly erected "no trespassing" signs all along the border of the grant. At a meeting of more than thirty La Corporación members, Sanchez angrily told them that they didn't "have the authority to do this." "[This] land," Serrano shot back, "isn't under the jurisdiction of the state."³⁶ Sanchez was convinced that La Corporación was serious and certain that Bill Mundy would shoot any armed land grant activists who entered his property. Serrano claimed that the border patrol was necessary to protect what was left of the grant. "Pretty soon," he told the press, "we won't have anything."³⁷ Sanchez ordered the NMSP to arrest armed members of La Corporación on sight.

Late in September Sanchez announced his intention to sue La Corporación in civil court. He had no evidence of wrongdoing and nothing that tied La Corporación or its members to the arson or the fence cutting that had plagued the grant over the past few years. With nothing to take to criminal court, Sanchez opted instead for a civil complaint. In response Serrano wrote a furious letter to the New Mexico attorney general reiterating his position that New Mexico had no authority over the grant or any right to stop the actions of La Corporación. "We shall," he wrote, "continue to carry out our work as stipulated in our eviction notice."[38]

Sanchez made good on his promise on October 9, when he filed a petition in district court complaining that the eviction notices and threats of armed patrols had created "a potential tinderbox which if not enjoined [would] be a constant threat to the peace and dignity of the State."[39] The court agreed and issued a temporary injunction against La Corporación on the same day. Summonses went out by the dozens as the court ordered a long list of La Corporación defendants to an October 15 hearing. Many of the defendants, however, did not receive notice of the hearing until the day before the court date, and as a result none had legal representation. Men in work clothes and women in simple dresses packed the small courthouse for the hearing, while their children played quietly on the floor and in the aisles.[40] Sanchez dominated the proceedings for more than five hours, reading from previous court decisions and entering document after document into evidence. He argued that La Corporación de Abiquiú was not a valid corporation in New Mexico and that the grant "just [didn't] exist anymore." He called to the stand only Serrano, who admitted under questioning that the armed sentries "had gone onto private property and asked the property owners to leave."[41]

A confused silence fell over the courtroom when Judge Paul Tackett abruptly ended the proceedings a little after 1:00 p.m. and slowly read a prepared statement making the temporary restraining order permanent. Unsure of what the ruling meant, one man walked up to the bench while Tackett was reading and interrupted to ask "if this meant he couldn't go home since his property [was] within the grant."[42] Others, less calm, yelled at Tackett as he read. One man heckled the judge that he must have written the decision "before [he] left Santa Fe." José María Martínez stood up and shouted, "If you want peace, you will have to respect the rights of the people. We will come back and claim our land."[43]

COINTELPRO in New Mexico

While Sanchez and the NMSP were investigating Tijerina and La Corporación, agents from the FBI, under the direction of Hoover, were beginning a wide-ranging investigation of Tijerina and Alianza. Less than a year before Tackett's permanent injunction, in January 1964 a memo from the FBI special agent in charge (SAC) of the San Diego field office crossed the desk of FBI director

J. Edgar Hoover. It reported that agents in Southern California had linked an organization called the Comite Pro-Mercedes por la Corona Español to the Communist Party of Mexico. Hoover directed agents in Chicago, Phoenix, Albuquerque, and San Diego to investigate the organization and its possible communist ties.[44] Agents found nothing of interest related to the Comite Pro-Mercedes, but in the process they stumbled upon Alianza and noted in memos to Hoover that Tijerina, its leader, was moving back and forth across the border.

At the time Hoover was running a covert program against dissent in the United States that he had begun in 1956. Under the code name COINTELPRO, Hoover's agents had been conducting sweeping counterintelligence programs against social movement organizations in the United States for more than eight years. According to congressional investigators who would eventually reveal the full extent of the illegal program during a U.S. Senate investigation in the mid-1970s, COINTELPRO "was designed to 'disrupt' groups and 'neutralize' individuals deemed to be threats to domestic security." The FBI used counterintelligence tactics because Hoover believed "existing law could not control the activities of certain dissident groups."[45] Organizations such as the Communist Party USA, New Left groups such as Students for a Democratic Society, and a variety of civil rights organizations came under intense FBI scrutiny.[46] Civil rights organizations in particular became a focus of FBI interest.

COINTELPRO was not only a counterintelligence program; Hoover also required that agents develop plans to disrupt targeted groups including covert plans to provoke violence. In September 1969, for example, the San Diego SAC reported, "Shootings, beatings and a high degree of unrest continues to prevail in the ghetto area of Southeast San Diego. Although no specific counterintelligence action can be credited with contributing to this overall situation, it is felt that a substantial amount of the unrest is directly attributable to [COINTELPRO]."[47]

FBI agents selected targets according to a set of procedures that were developed first with an interest in identifying communists and organizations influenced by communist ideology. Later guidelines, however, expanded to include race as a factor in determining subversiveness. By the 1960s race had become "a highly salient proxy for subversion" in the FBI and the central criterion in selecting targets.[48] It was in this context that Tijerina, known only to the FBI at that time as "Latin American," was, according to Hoover, a threat to national security.

Tijerina's elevation as an FBI target arrived just as Hoover had become obsessed with the link between race and subversion. Hoover institutionalized this obsession though a program called COMINFIL (Communist Infiltration of the Civil Rights Movement), a special program in the Domestic Intelligence Division charged with identifying communist influences on racial issues. Agents were ordered to intensify the collection of intelligence on civil rights leaders considered "vociferous rabble-rousers." Hoover directed that "an index be compiled of racial agitators and individuals who ha[d] demonstrated a potential for fomenting racial discord. It [was] desired that only individuals of prominence who [were] of national interest be included in this index."[49] Surveillance and counterintelligence activities directed at Tijerina fell under COMINFIL and what later became known as the Rabble Rouser Index.

The Rabble Rouser Index was of central importance in COMINFIL and COINTELPRO, and its use by the FBI in its secret programs against Alianza demonstrate the extent to which law enforcement officials understood the land grant conflict in racialized terms. Rabble Rouser status was designed to coordinate counterintelligence actions against prime targets: "to disrupt groups and discredit individuals."[50] The index intensified surveillance and required field agents to suggest ways in which the Bureau could undermine targeted subjects. Elevation to the index meant that individuals became subjects of active covert campaigns designed not just to investigate but also to discredit and destroy. Hoover, in fact, directed field offices to develop wide-ranging and detailed plans of action against Rabble Rouser targets. Common tactics identified in FBI memos were, for example, to "instigate personal conflicts or animosities" within organizations; create "impressions that certain leaders [were] informants for the Bureau or other law enforcement agencies"; and establish intense surveillance programs designed to harass leaders with constant arrests on trumped-up charges and minor infractions.[51] Eventually fifty-five domestic targets were indexed in the FBI's various Key Activist Programs, including Tijerina.[52]

After agents brought Alianza to Hoover's attention during the investigation of the Comite Pro-Mercedes, he directed the Albuquerque SAC to begin a "wide-ranging investigation seeking information to determine whether to recommend an ongoing surveillance investigation [against Alianza]."[53] FBI agents in Albuquerque told Hoover that they already had a confidential informant placed within Alianza.[54] Despite the secrecy Tijerina was aware of the FBI's interest in Alianza. In July his brother Cristobal walked into the Albuquerque field office and invited FBI agents to attend that summer's first annual Alianza convention in Albuquerque. Surprised agents, already planning to secretly record the event, told Cristobal they could not attend the convention.[55]

The federal investigation of Alianza expanded throughout 1964. Hoping to prove that Alianza was a Mexican front and thus in violation of the Foreign Agents Registration Act, Hoover directed local agents in April to "determine if Alianza is controlled by Frente Internacional de Humanos Derechos (International Front for Human Rights)."⁵⁶ In May he ordered agents to "determine if [Alianza] ha[d] any connection with the Movement for the Territorial Reintegration of Mexico (MTRM) or [was] being controlled by the MTRM." Hoover's memo stipulated, "This matter should be pressed vigorously to develop fully activities of subject group as well as activities of Lopez [Tijerina] and any other affiliated organizations to determine if subject's activities are in violation of Registration Act or other U.S. statutes within the Bureau's jurisdiction."⁵⁷ The program against Tijerina was fueled by Hoover's obsession that the civil rights movement was not reformist but revolutionary. "There are clear and unmistakable signs," he wrote in an August memo, "that we are in the midst of a social revolution with the racial movement at its core. The Bureau, in meeting its responsibilities in this area, is an integral part of this revolution."⁵⁸

Alianza's challenge to racial inequality and economic injustice was the very thing that marked the group as a subversive threat. In October 1964, however, during the same week that La Corporación members fought Sanchez's permanent injunction in court, Hoover's field agents concluded that Alianza could not be linked to any Mexican organization or communist ties.⁵⁹ Hoover ignored the memos and briefed the Central Intelligence Agency, military intelligence, and the Department of Justice on communist influences in Alianza.⁶⁰

The Plan to Take Tierra Amarilla

Unlike Alianza, La Corporación escaped careful scrutiny by the FBI and the NMSP until 1965, when it defied Sanchez's permanent injunction. In a March meeting of the membership, La Corporación changed its name to Colonia Mejicana.⁶¹ In August Colonia notified the district court by letter of its intention to seize the Tierra Amarilla land grant. The threat was forwarded to Judge Tackett, who reminded Colonia of the permanent injunction and threatened to declare in contempt of court any who violated the order. Colonia wrote in response, "[Judge Tackett] is ignorant of the law and wants to use methods of intimidation in order to deter us from claiming our rights and inheritance." The handwritten letter, sent to the district attorney's office, insisted that the heirs had no interest in using violence in their struggle for the grant, but included the warning: "If we had to do so, in the future, it would be at the provocation of the authorities of the State. From today on we will not respect the decision of no District Judge till he will show us what jurisdiction he had to do away with the Treaty of Guadalupe Hidalgo."⁶² In December a legal notice appeared in the local newspaper and officially announced the establishment of Colonia

Colonia Mejicana, formerly La Corporación de Abiquiú, ran this ad in a local newspaper in December 1964. (From Exhibit A of December 31, 1965, Petition for Contempt by Alfonso Sanchez, Transcript of Record, Court of Appeals, p. 42, *State of New Mexico, et al. v. Corporación de Abiquiú*, no. 10939.)

> **"To Whom It May Concern"**
>
> Let it be known that starting with the New Year 1966, Colonia Mexicana Merced de Tierra Amarilla will be issuing Grazing Permits to All Heirs and Non-heirs to Graze Livestock, within the boundaries of the Tierra Amarilla Land Grant which comprises 600,000 acres more or less within the boundaries of the State of New Mexico and Colorado.
>
> Also let it be known that the Board of Director of Colonia Mexicana — Merced de Tierra Amarilla, during the 1966 Hunting and Fishing Season — will be ready to issue hunting and fishing permits.
>
> Issued by the Board of Directors.
>
> President Juan Martinez   Member Juan T. Valdez
> Secretary Gilbert Marcuse   Member Emilio Lobato
>   Member Nicolas Lopez
> Treasurer J. M. Martinez   Member Cruz Aguilar

Mejicana, Merced de Tierra Amarilla. The new organization, according to the notice, would begin "issuing Grazing Permits to All Heirs and Non-Heirs to Graze Livestock within the boundaries of the Tierra Amarilla Land Grant" on January 1, 1966. "Hunting and fishing" permits would be issued as well.[63]

As Colonia Mejicana readied plans to seize the grant, Alianza began a series of marches and public protests. In July 1966 Tijerina led hundreds of Alianza members in a protest march from Albuquerque to Santa Fe. The march, called the "Spanish American March for a Redress of Grievances," was designed to embarrass Governor Jack Campbell, who had refused to meet with Tijerina. In response the governor's office released an opinion on Alianza's claims of land loss authored by New Mexico state historian Myra Jenkins. It was a scathing rebuke. According to Jenkins the documents on which land grant activists relied to make their claims were "outright forgeries," and most Aliancistas, according to her, were not land grant descendants at all. "To be blunt," she wrote, "I think that it is a con game."[64] Undeterred, Tijerina announced that Alianza would follow up the march by taking part in the occupation of federal land south of Tierra Amarilla. "This summer the people will take over San Joaquin del Rio [de] Chama once and for all," he wrote in a letter to Denver-based Chicano activist Corky Gonzalez. "The people of New Mexico have moved together in a miraculous manner which causes joy in the soul of the natives but far greater fear and terror in the strangers who arrived in New Mexico but yesterday."[65]

As with most other Spanish or Mexican land grants, U.S authorities rejected San Joaquin del Rio de Chama as a legitimate property claim during adjudication in the late nineteenth century. It subsequently became part of the massive Santa Fe National Forest in northern New Mexico. In the twentieth century the Forest Service established a campground on the former grant along the road between Abiquiú and Tierra Amarilla at a place known as Echo Amphitheater, a huge natural amphitheater carved out of sandstone rock in the middle of a landscape made famous by the dramatic paintings of artists such as Georgia O'Keefe. Tijerina borrowed a tactic from La Corporación and mailed an eviction notice to the Forest Service ahead of the takeover. In it he ordered the Forest Service off the land and charged the U.S. government with violations of international law.

The "Sons of San Joaquin," as Tijerina called the group, occupied the campground on two weekends in October. State police described the two-day "sit-in" as a peaceful protest. Less than two weeks later, however, Tijerina returned with four hundred Aliancistas and land grant supporters, including members of Colonia Mejicana, in a huge caravan of more than one hundred cars and trucks. They paraded into the campground past Forest Service rangers and uniformed and undercover police agents who scribbled furious notes, snapped photographs, and collected license plate numbers. Sanchez, FBI agents, and NMSP officials closely monitored the four-day occupation. After the U.S. marshal delivered restraining orders against Tijerina and others, the "Sons of San Joaquin" dispersed.[66]

Though dramatic, the takeover was planned not as a violent confrontation or a permanent occupation but rather as a publicity stunt that Tijerina hoped would embarrass state and federal officials and force federal charges against him, thus putting the question of title to Spanish and Mexican land grants into federal court. No federal charges, however, were filed. Instead, Tijerina and the "Sons of San Joaquin" were enjoined from entering public land in northern New Mexico, just as members of La Corporación were enjoined from private land in Tierra Amarilla.

Despite the lack of charges, Tijerina relentlessly publicized the takeover. He sent a telegram to Secretary of State Dean Rusk requesting a meeting in order to present his credentials "as Proctor of the Mission of the Pueblo Republica de San Joaquin del Rio de Chama." A State Department lawyer refused a meeting on the grounds that "the United States [did] not recognize the Pueblo Republica."[67] In January the president of the "sovereign city-state" of the Pueblo Republic of San Joaquin, Victorino Chavez, complained in a letter to President Lyndon Johnson of the "various subterfuges instigated by the officers and agents of the government of the United States of America, to subvert the rights, privileges and immunities of the Pueblo Republic."[68] Each of these correspondences found its way into the burgeoning FBI file on Tijerina and finally into the hands of Sanchez, who was convinced that the letters were a prelude to something much bigger.

The possibility of an Alianza takeover of public lands in northern New Mexico preoccupied law enforcement officials in the first months of 1967. A raft of forest fires swept through northern New Mexico in May and stoked new fears that another confrontation loomed. During the first week of May, three small fires converged into a larger six-hundred-acre blaze east of Tierra Amarilla and burned for more than a week. Three other fires charred canyons north of Taos. A week later firefighters converged on a blaze near Los Alamos National Laboratory, the U.S. Department of Energy facility where the first atomic bomb was developed, and found two fires burning in the steep canyons around the Atomic City, as Los Alamos is known. The public lands fires were accompanied by a new outbreak of arson on private lands. Eight haystacks on private ranches went up in flames during the month, and Bill Mundy lost a barn to a massive and suspicious fire.[69] The sheriff reassured a local reporter that "the worst was over because there was so little left to burn."[70]

With a new wave of unrest in Tierra Amarilla, the NMSP intensified its surveillance of Alianza and Tijerina and even sent undercover officers into Mexico in a covert investigation of Tijerina's activities there.[71] Activity in Tierra Amarilla seemed to increase by the day, with reports of truckloads of armed Aliancistas patrolling Forest Service roads. In mid-May hundreds of land grant activists descended on Tierra Amarilla for a meeting convened by Tijerina to elect a new government for the land grant. The meeting was scheduled in the judge's chambers at the courthouse, but the small office could not accommodate the four hundred to five hundred people who showed up. The meeting was moved to the local high school gymnasium, where Juan Martínez was elected the new mayor of the grant and José María Martínez the new judge.[72] Tijerina declared that the duties of the new government would "include such things as taxing residents and establishing a port of entry."[73]

Sanchez sent two NMSP officers to Tierra Amarilla to investigate the meeting. They went door-to-door canvassing Tierra Amarilla residents, but "none of them would tell us anything for sure," they wrote in a confidential report. "They claimed they didn't remember anything."[74] Rumors swirled that the election in Tierra Amarilla was a prelude to an Alianza meeting planned for June 3 in Coyote, a small village fifty miles south of Tierra Amarilla. Tijerina confirmed the meeting but claimed that it had been called not by Alianza but instead by the new Confederación de Pueblos Libres (Confederation of Free City-States).

The new group was a way for Tijerina to avoid the U.S. District Court's order for Alianza to turn its membership list over to the U.S. attorney. When a U.S. marshal tried to serve the court order, Tijerina refused, saying that no such organization existed. He had resigned as president of Alianza. The membership had voted to disband and reform as the Confederación de Pueblos Libres. "Now," he said, "we have no responsibility to hand over the list."[75]

Sanchez considered the election meeting at the high school "an unlawful assembly" and feared that the Coyote meeting would explode into armed conflict.[76] "Clearly," he wrote in his unpublished memoir, "the people are being mislead [sic] to slaughter. What happens after the revolution? Do the people really know what Tijerina is planning? And if they know, do they know the consequences of their acts. And if we know how foolish this is, what must we do to convince the people and even Tijerina that they must stop?"[77] He put his staff to work looking for an excuse to arrest Tijerina. He instructed aides to study the law of unlawful assembly, obstruction of justice, damage to property, resisting arrest, and even vagrancy. He learned from the NMSP that "armed pistoleros were continually patrolling" a building described as Alianza's barracks and headquarters.[78] Felix Martínez, the son of Juan Martínez, was allegedly buying thousands of rounds of ammunition, carbines, and gas masks. Informants claimed that Alianza was raising an army, drawing up battle plans, and preparing to forcibly retake, and permanently hold, the Tierra Amarilla land grant.

Meanwhile, the newly elected Republican governor of New Mexico, David Cargo, sought to diffuse the potential conflict without arrests, injunctions, or roadblocks, all tactics that Sanchez advocated. Sanchez believed that Cargo was treating Alianza with kid gloves because the group was a large part of the governor's unusual political constituency (it would in fact be revealed later that the governor's wife was herself a member of Alianza, though in arrears on her dues). Cargo had played on rural discontent over the Democratic patronage machine in New Mexico during his 1966 campaign in order to build a coalition of dissident Democrats and progressive Republicans. He won a narrow victory by aggressively mocking the Democratic Party in northern New Mexico. The incumbent governor, Jack Campbell, had spent thirty thousand dollars renovating the bathroom in the governor's mansion during his tenure. Cargo told supporters, "That's too much Jack for a john and too much john for Jack. If you come to Santa Fe and your kids need to go to the restroom, stop by the mansion and I'll put you up."[79]

After the election rumors circulated that Alianza votes had been "delivered" to him by a local Republican operative.[80] The conflict between Alianza and the state completely dominated Cargo's administration from his first day on the job. He frequently met with Alianza members in the governor's mansion, a fact that infuriated Sanchez. Cargo worked frantically throughout May to convince Tijerina to cancel the Coyote meeting, concerned that Sanchez's response to such a meeting would provoke a violent confrontation. The FBI monitored the growing dispute between Cargo and Sanchez and concluded that Sanchez was using Cargo's hands-off approach with Alianza against him. The "news media and other data furnished by your office," wrote Hoover to Albuquerque field agents, "indicate the possibility current activities of [Alianza] may be used by Sanchez in a political dispute with the governor of New Mexico criticizing prior handling of [Alianza]."[81]

In late May Tijerina confirmed publicly for the first time that a "national convention" of La Confederación was scheduled for June 3 in Coyote, at which time the group would discuss plans for the Tierra Amarilla land grant.[82] In an interview with the Associated Press, Tijerina predicted, "The elders of the land grant will vote to set up ports of entry on primary highways through the region and issue visas." He called the meeting a "showdown day" and suggested that the group was preparing for a conflict: "If you have to go to Vietnam and you have these rights at home which have been stolen from you by the federal government you might as well fight for them here."[83] The following day an Albuquerque FBI agent filed a report in which he claimed an airport mechanic in Albuquerque had informed the police that an Alianza member had approached him for help in smuggling machine guns, antipersonnel mines, and hand grenades into New Mexico through the airport. He was told that Alianza needed them by June 3.[84]

The Courthouse Raid

By May 1967, just as the conflict between Alianza and law enforcement intensified, Sanchez finally began receiving selected FBI reports. When he saw an FBI memo on gun smuggling at the airport, he sent police officers to Tierra Amarilla to investigate possible connections to Tijerina. The Alianza leader, however, was nowhere to be found. Instead agents found an armed Anselmo Tijerina in the village of Hernandez, south of Tierra Amarilla. "We will discuss [in Coyote] whether to resort to violence," he told the agents, "and close all the grant, elect our officials and form our own pueblo in order to force a showdown and ascertain true ownership of the land."[85] The same day a former client of Sanchez's who lived in Coyote called to discuss the impending Coyote meeting.

She told Sanchez that she was present when the meeting was being discussed. "They expect 5,000 people at the old school house. After the meeting they will divide posts at La Gallina, Echo Amphitheater, and Ghost Ranch," she said. She confirmed it would be a takeover of the entire Tierra Amarilla grant.

Sanchez decided to preemptively arrest Alianza leaders and base the arrests on unlawful assembly charges related to the October 1966 Echo Amphitheater occupation. First District Court judge Paul Scarborough signed twelve arrest warrants for Reies Tijerina, his brothers Cristobal and Anselmo, and nine other members of Alianza. The list included Juan Martínez, José María Martínez, and the rest of the elected officers of the Tierra Amarilla land grant. The NMSP moved twenty-five police cruisers into the area on Thursday, June 1, in a huge manhunt for the twelve Aliancistas. Sanchez and New Mexico State Police Chief Joe Black ordered roadblocks on all highways leading to Coyote beginning on Friday. Police searched vehicles, recorded license plate numbers, and told occupants to skip the meeting or face arrest for unlawful assembly or extortion. Sanchez went on local radio stations to warn Alianza members to stay away from Coyote. In an appeal tone-deaf to New Mexico's colonial history, he told listeners, "Attempting to take over by force is a Communist philosophy, and I'm not kidding."[86]

On Friday evening officers arrested Felix Martínez and found pistols, rifles, walkie-talkies, and gas masks in his trunk. He was booked into the Santa Fe County jail on a charge of conspiracy. Meanwhile, police agents were serving arrest warrants all over Rio Arriba County. José María Martínez arrived at his daughter's house for Friday-night dinner just before a police cruiser pulled into the driveway. He was handcuffed and arrested. Juan Martínez was arrested later that night. On Saturday morning Cristobal Tijerina was arrested north of Hernandez. In his trunk police found a rifle, maps that Sanchez would later call "battle plans," and filing boxes that contained hundreds of Alianza membership cards. By noon five others had been arrested, including Anselmo, and Sanchez was back on the radio reiterating his promise to arrest anyone who went to Coyote.[87] Cargo was furious at what he considered harassment on the part of the police. Despite the threats a steady stream of people drove to Coyote to attend the meeting, while police and FBI agents waited. While the FBI searched cars, the NMSP distributed slips of paper to each car on which Sanchez had handwritten that "anybody who wanted the land was a Communist."[88]

Sanchez was convinced that he had dodged a bullet. He congratulated himself and wrote in his memoirs, "Everyone has cooperated and appreciated the information."[89] Cargo, meanwhile, demanded that Sanchez vacate the arrest warrants and dismiss the charges. Sanchez ignored him.[90] "I should have added

A handcuffed José María Martínez being led into the Tierra Amarilla jail, June 2, 1967. (From negative in Peter Nabokov Photo Collection, Center for Southwest Research, University Libraries, University of New Mexico. Courtesy of Peter Nabokov.)

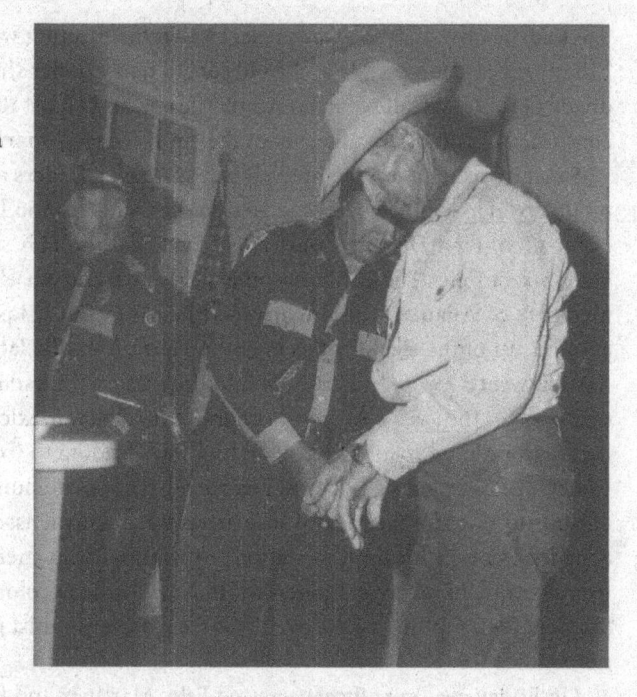

the name of Governor David F. Cargo to the list of Defendants," wrote Sanchez.[91] On Sunday, with eleven members of Alianza and Colonia in jail and Tijerina in hiding, Sanchez met with Judge Scarborough to discuss plans to petition the court for a contempt of court charge based on the 1964 permanent injunction.

On Monday morning Sanchez met with his staff in Santa Fe. Arraignments for the eleven arrested Aliancistas were scheduled for 2:00 p.m. at the courthouse in Tierra Amarilla. Plans were changed, however, when an informant called to say that Tijerina was hiding at a ranch in the village of Canjilon, east of Tierra Amarilla. Instead of going to the arraignment hearing in Tierra Amarilla, Sanchez sent an aide and moved the hearing up so that he could spend the morning trying to convince the state police to raid the ranch and arrest Tijerina. Had police moved into Canjilon, they would have found Tijerina with his daughter Rose and eighteen men armed with rifles and pistols racing along dirt roads leading from Canjilon toward the county courthouse in Tierra Amarilla in a caravan of four cars and one truck.

In Tierra Amarilla Sheriff Benny Naranjo looked out the window in his office just before 2:00 p.m. and saw four men pulling rifles out of their car trunks. Meanwhile, state police officer Nick Sais was loitering in the front lobby of the

Tijerina (*right, front*) after his arrest following the courthouse raid, June 1967. (Photo 000-093, Peter Nabokov Photo Collection, Center for Southwest Research, University Libraries, University of New Mexico. Courtesy of Peter Nabokov.)

courthouse, standing with his back to the front entry. Upstairs in his second-floor courtroom Scarborough was doing paperwork. The courthouse raiders, as the press came to call them, rushed into the courthouse en masse. When Scarborough heard the gunshots, he locked himself in an anteroom. Sais turned around too late and was shot in the arm. The county jailer, Eulogio Salazar, was shot in the face. As Sais fell to the ground, the panicked jailer turned and launched himself out a second-story window and onto the street, where he was shot again in the shoulder as he ran. While raiders established a perimeter around the courthouse, others inside ransacked the building looking for Sanchez. Sheriff Benny Naranjo was held at gunpoint on the floor outside his office. "Ya no están tan bravos [Now they're not so brave]," said one of the gunmen to Naranjo.[92]

When it was finally clear that Sanchez was not in the building and the arrested Aliancistas had already been arraigned and moved back to jail, they fled into the surrounding mountains, taking two hostages with them. Scarborough, from inside his chambers, got word to Santa Fe that the courthouse was under siege. Cargo was in Michigan at a governor's meeting when he received word. He quickly called in the National Guard, while he raced to the airport to catch a flight back to New Mexico. By 3:00 p.m. helicopters were buzzing Canjilon as NMSP officers were storming the ranch where Tijerina was thought to be hiding. Dozens were arrested, including young children. They were held in corrals for more than twenty-four hours without charges. Tijerina's daughter Rose was among those arrested. Meanwhile, tanks fitted with 40 mm canons and .50-caliber machine guns prowled the dirt roads around Tierra Amarilla, while National Guard troops moved into positions at roadblocks throughout the grant. FBI agents closed off Tierra Amarilla and refused access to all but the police and the military. Five hundred police officers and guardsmen hunted Tijerina and the other courthouse raiders.

By the day after the raid seventeen Aliancistas were in jail. On Wednesday Tijerina was still at large, but the National Guard demobilized and left Tierra Amarilla. "I think we've accomplished what we brought them in here for," Chief Black explained. "That was to show the people of Rio Arriba County that we mean business."[93] Three days later police pulled over a car just north of Albuquerque and discovered Tijerina hiding in the backseat. He was arrested and charged with a series of crimes including unlawful assembly, obstruction of justice, and kidnapping.

The Aftermath

The raid made Tijerina a national figure almost overnight. Only the Six-Day War between Egypt and Israel, which started the same day as the raid, diverted attention from the coverage of what the press called the New Mexico Land Grant War. Tijerina, unknown outside New Mexico on Sunday, suddenly became a key figure in the Chicano movement by Tuesday. The raid also elevated Tijerina's status for the FBI. All those arrested, including the officers of Colonia, were universally described by the press as Alianza members; there was no mention of the La Corporación or Colonia in any press coverage. In the wake of the raid the FBI ramped up intelligence operations against Alianza, and Hoover ordered agents to evaluate Tijerina's inclusion on the Rabble Rouser Index.[94] In February 1968 his listing was made official.[95]

Tijerina was now an official "rabble rouser," and thus became one of the FBI's most important targets. Agents doggedly tailed him everywhere. They followed him on a national speaking tour in the fall of 1967. In September, just months after the raid, Tijerina met with Elijah Muhammad in Chicago. The FBI filed a series of reports on the visit. He traveled to Austin, Texas, to

The official FBI "Rabble Rouser Index" form for Reies Lopez Tijerina. (From Box 3, folder 7, Reies Lopez Tijerina Papers, Center for Southwest Research, University Libraries, University of New Mexico.)

appear at a rally in support of farm workers. Agents milled about in the crowd. An undercover FBI agent attended a Tijerina speech in El Paso, Texas, and described it as of the "rabblerousing variety," telling Hoover that it reminded him of speeches "given by Mussolini and Hitler."[96] Tijerina made a series of appearances in Southern California, giving speeches and meeting with civil rights organizations. At his invitation, representatives of various civil rights and black power groups, the United Slaves and members of the Southern Non-Violent Coordinating Committee among them, attended the 1967 Alianza convention in Albuquerque. Tijerina met with Rodolfo "Corky" Gonzalez. Gonzalez, a former champion featherweight boxer, poet, and charismatic political leader, had founded a Denver-based Chicano movement organization called La Cruzada por Justicia (The Crusade for Justice), and he was also a target of FBI surveillance.[97] Tijerina gave a speech at a meeting celebrating the first anniversary of La Cruzada in which he declared that Alianza would look to the United Nations for justice in its struggle.[98]

His provocative speeches throughout this period frequently attacked the structures of power in New Mexico, attributed the social problems confronting land grant communities to racism, and always promised to meet violence with violence. In February 1968 Tijerina appeared with Stokely Carmichael at a Black Panther "Free Huey" rally in Oakland, California. An FBI agent in the crowd recorded the speech. "Oh, I don't hate the white man," he told the crowd. "No, of course not. I'm not going to be violent against him. All I'm going to do if I'm sleeping and he breaks down my door, I'm going to shoot him between the eyes and I'm going to keep on sleeping. Oh, he wants to make you believe that I'll go after them, no, no, no. I trap them like a spider."[99]

Shortly after Tijerina's appearance with Carmichael, the Baltimore FBI office reported that it had learned through reliable sources that Tijerina had received numerous death threats from the American Nazi Party and the John Birch Society.[100] Throughout 1967 the Birch Society magazine, *The American Opinion*, had published rabid anti-Alianza opinion pieces on Tijerina passed off as research reports. In one article titled "Reies Tijerina: The Communist Plot to Grab the Southwest," the author, Alan Stang, dismissed Tijerina's land claims as unfounded and the rantings of a "terrorist." The article included a picture of Tijerina above a caption that read, "Marxist Reies Tijerina is guerilla leader." Stang compared Alianza to the Vietcong and described Alianza tactics as "standard Communist operating procedure."[101] Hoover sent a copy of Stang's article to the SAC in Albuquerque and directed the office to prepare a brief on Alianza for the Office of Economic Opportunity based on the article. In the order Hoover directed the SAC to "conduct no active investigation." The brief was to be based entirely on the opinions of the John Birch Society.¹⁰²

In late 1968, with Alianza's prominence in local and statewide politics established and Tijerina's stature in the civil rights movement growing, Tijerina went to trial for his role in the courthouse raid. During the month-long trial Tijerina acted as his own lawyer. In his defense he claimed a constitutional right to make a citizen's arrest of any law enforcement officer who obstructed the right to free assembly. He was acquitted of all charges on December 13, 1968.

Days after his acquittal the home of Tijerina's ex-wife was bombed.¹⁰³ In January 1969 Alianza's headquarters were also bombed. The day following that bombing the local FBI field office wrote to Hoover arguing, "Because of [the] controversial nature of the organization and the pending prosecution in state court of several of its members, it is recommended that no investigation [of the bombing] should be conducted."¹⁰⁴ Alianza member Thomas Gallegos's house was bombed the same day. The following month a ranch north of Taos was firebombed and destroyed just hours after a sympathizer offered its use to Alianza.¹⁰⁵ In March 1969 an explosive device destroyed Alianza member Santiago Anaya's car. According to an FBI memo describing the explosion, parts of the automobile were found one hundred feet away. The blast drove a hole through the pavement to a depth of more than twelve inches.¹⁰⁶

Though they never offered any evidence, Tijerina and Alianza members held the NMSP and the Albuquerque Police Department responsible for the bombings. "The police harassed our people daily during 1967 and 1968. In those days, paid police spies trying to learn our every step plagued the Alianza. They wanted to find flaws. They did not let us rest. The police were waging a campaign of terror against the Alianza."¹⁰⁷ A memo from the FBI Albuquerque Field Office to the U.S. attorney in Albuquerque shared Tijerina's suspicions: "Following the confiscation of [a] membership list of [Alianza] in the summer of 1967 by state authorities numerous members of [Alianza] have been harassed and bombings have occurred."¹⁰⁸

In addition to official campaigns of state violence, groups linked to law enforcement also targeted Alianza. A March 1968 NMSP report indicates that authorities knew that Tiny Fellion, a former state trooper and federal marshal who was also a demolitions expert, was now a paid assassin operating out of Española, New Mexico.¹⁰⁹ Less than two months later Fellion blew off his left hand while placing an explosive device at Alianza headquarters in downtown Albuquerque. The report on the explosion noted that Fellion was a member of the John Birch Society and friendly with other Birch Society members in the

NMSP, various sheriffs' departments in the state, the office of District Attorney Sanchez, and the office of State Attorney General Boston Witt.[110]

By the early 1970s members of La Corporación/Colonia had been so thoroughly harassed by police and law enforcement officials that no official organization existed. Tijerina, meanwhile, eventually went to jail on charges of destroying federal property when he and his wife set fire to a Forest Service sign. By the time Tijerina was released from prison in the mid-1970s, Alianza was no longer operative.

Less than three years after Tijerina's acquittal and during the violent backlash against Tijerina and Alianza, COINTELPRO was finally exposed when an organization that called itself the Citizen's Committee to Investigate the FBI broke into a Media, Pennsylvania, FBI field office and stole thousands of classified documents. Under fire the FBI suspended all COINTELPRO activities. In 1975 the U.S. Senate initiated a detailed investigation of COINTELPRO. The subsequent Church Committee Report concluded that the FBI "violated the law and fundamental human decency. . . . The Bureau went beyond the collection of intelligence to secret action defined to 'disrupt' and 'neutralize' target groups and individuals. COINTELPRO tactics ranged from the trivial (mailing reprints of *Reader's Digest* articles to college administrators) to the degrading (sending anonymous poison-pen letters intended to break up marriages) and the dangerous (encouraging gang warfare and falsely labeling members of a violent group as police informers)."[111]

The Church Committee examined FBI harassment of numerous domestic organizations, but no part of this official investigation considered the history of police repression and violence against Alianza. As this chapter shows, however, La Corporación/Colonia members were prime targets of NMSP officers and law enforcement personnel, and Tijerina and Alianza were targets also of federal law enforcement agencies via COINTELPRO. Most importantly, the interest those agents and agencies expressed through surveillance, harassment, and arrests translated into violent campaigns against land grant activists. It is important to note that this turn from legal interpretation to violent suppression began at the very moment when land grant activists refused to accept the legitimacy of private property rights.

Confronted by Alianza's challenge to racial inequality and economic injustice, the state construed Alianza as a generalized, and racialized, threat to social order and responded with the use of intimidation and physical violence. Despite this history analyses of the struggle over property in New Mexico rarely include a consideration of the role that violence played in imposing private property rights. Dramatic changes in land law, property claims adjudication, and the patterns of bureaucratic administration that came with U.S. control over the territory are generally offered as a sufficient explanation for land loss.[112] In this explanation the law mediated social conflict over property claims, and acts of legal interpretation produced land grant dispossession. But this explanation obscures more than it reveals. The story of the violent enforcement of private property rights offered in this chapter suggests a much different explanation for land loss. The courts constructed private property rights on the grant and then gave way to the police, who ensured that Alianza and La Corporación/Colonia understood that "the violence of the law is utterly real."[113]

The patterns of state violence against Alianza would not end with Tijerina's incarceration. As the next chapter illustrates, the years after the courthouse raid were marked by continued patterns of violence against land grant activists. The logic of repression shifted, however, from the 1960s, when land grant activism was construed as a form of racialized anti-Americanism, to the 1970s, when land grant activism became a marker for what the FBI considered "domestic terrorism."

CHAPTER SIX

Terrorists and Tourists in Tierra Amarilla

THE EXPLOSIONS THAT DETONATED SIMULTANEOUSLY in Manhattan on October 26, 1974, destroyed four banks and announced the start of a bombing campaign by a group called Fuerzas Armadas de Liberación Nacional (Armed Forces of National Liberation, or FALN), a clandestine paramilitary group that advocated Puerto Rican independence from the United States. Born the same year as the beginning of the bombing campaign, the FALN was formed when the Comandos Armados de Liberación (Armed Commandos of Liberation) joined forces with the Movimiento de Independencia Revolucionario (Revolutionary Independence Movement). As the names suggest, the merger created a group committed to an armed struggle to evict the United States from Puerto Rico and destroy "the imperialist power base on the island to hasten a crisis which would shake the foundation of the Puerto Rican colonial world."[1] Although bombings by Puerto Rican nationalists were not uncommon in the late 1960s, they were largely limited to attacks on U.S. businesses and military installations located on the Puerto Rican archipelago. The October 1974 explosions were the first attacks on the U.S. mainland since the March 1, 1954, attack on the U.S. Congress, when four armed assailants infiltrated the Capitol building and launched a barrage of gunfire from the visitor's gallery into a packed assembly on the floor of the House of Representatives, wounding five congressmen.[2]

Beginning in 1974 the terrain of conflict shifted back to the U.S. mainland. Between 1974 and 1983 the FALN claimed responsibility for more than 120 attacks on targets throughout the United States, 58 of which came during an intense three-year bombing campaign that began with the October 1974 explosions in Manhattan. Among the targets during the campaign were New York banks and department stores, the State Department in Washington, D.C., the headquarters of the Newark city police department, and the Standard Oil Building in Chicago.[3]

On the morning of April 3, 1977, two bombs exploded, one right after the other, in New York. One bomb destroyed the entire floor of a Madison Avenue building housing offices of the Department of Defense, while the other destroyed one floor of the Mobil Oil Building on Forty-Second Street, killing one man and injuring seven others. Hundreds of additional bomb threats flooded emergency channels. Authorities evacuated hundreds of thousands of office workers from buildings throughout Manhattan, including the World Trade Center, where tens of thousands of office workers streamed out onto the street and blocked traffic in Lower Manhattan for most of the day. Authorities later found a communiqué from FALN at the Central Park statue of Cuban revolutionary Jose Martí that threatened more bombings against U.S. corporations.

Despite nearly sixty bombings by early 1977, New York and Chicago police and the FBI had no leads, nor did they know the identity of any members of the FALN. But just months prior to the April attack, in November 1976, a Chicago drug addict and small-time thief unwittingly interrupted FALN plans and gave FBI investigators a break in the case when he kicked in his neighbor's door looking for drugs and found instead a FALN bomb-making lab.

According to the Chicago Police Department, the addict had been watching his neighbor, a schoolteacher named Carlos Torres, bring large packages into his apartment late at night. When he kicked in Torres's door one evening looking for money or drugs, he found instead 211 sticks of dynamite. He was quickly arrested when police found him trying to sell or trade the dynamite for drugs on the street. When police raided Torres's apartment, they found FALN communiqués among the bomb-making materials. The FBI took over the investigation.

Sporadically throughout 1976 dynamite left by FALN at targets in New York or Chicago had failed to detonate. Authorities claimed that the dynamite in Torres's apartment matched the FALN duds. Agents pursued the lead aggressively and eventually claimed that they had traced the dynamite to a cache of explosives allegedly stolen in the late 1960s from the Bureau of Reclamation's Heron Dam construction site west of Tierra Amarilla. The FBI and the attorneys general in New York and Illinois believed that two New Mexico activists, Moises Morales, one of the twenty courthouse raiders from 1967, and a thirty-year-old resident of Tierra Amarilla named Pedro Arechuleta, were somehow linked to the FALN.[4]

According to the FBI Morales and Arechuleta were domestic terrorists, part of a huge underground network of militant Chicano activists who funneled money and smuggled fugitives along an underground network linking Chicano movement groups with radical, nationalist organizations like the FALN. The government viewed Tierra Amarilla as "a center of Chicano political activity," and the FBI spent years trying to prove the connection between Tierra Amarilla and the FALN.[5]

Morales, a former Tijerina protégé, was well known to authorities, including the FBI. And it was not the first time Arechuleta had drawn FBI interest. As a young activist in Tierra Amarilla in the mid-1960s, he had come to the attention of the FBI after forming a group called Los Comancheros del Norte. The FBI described it, quoting Arechuleta, as a group committed to protesting the "'rotten politicians and rich people'" who allegedly had denied Spanish Americans their civil rights.[6] Arechuleta described it as the "militant vanguard of the New Breed," a reference to the Indo-Hispano legacy that Tijerina used as a way to claim an indigenous identity for grant heirs in the land struggle. The FBI believed that Arechuleta's work with community organizations in Tierra Amarilla in the early 1970s brought him into contact with Chicano activists from Denver and Chicago and eventually into the FALN's inner circle.

The case against Arechuleta was based on his work with a group called the Hispanic Affairs Commission. In the mid-1970s the Episcopal Church, the sponsor of the commission, asked Arechuleta to join the board. He agreed and was introduced to a wide network of Chicano activists. Arechuleta recalled, "Going to Chicago and meeting the Puerto Ricans there we started to learn about the struggle in Puerto Rico and we started to see the United States was using the Mexicano people against the Puerto Rican movement struggle for liberation, for independence."[7] Arechuleta also joined a group called the Movimiento de Liberación Nacional (Movement for National Liberation, or MLN). The MLN was a group that first formed in June 1977 and was an umbrella organization that brought together Chicano activists from the U.S. Southwest and Puerto Rican activists. According to the FBI and various government reports, the MLN served as the key link between the FALN and land grant activists in Tierra Amarilla. The FBI suspected that Arechuleta, via the Hispanic Affairs Commission, was the link that connected the Heron Dam dynamite to Carlos Torres and the FALN. FBI agents monitored activities in Tierra Amarilla throughout the 1970s and 1980s and made frequent reports on Tierra Amarilla to the FBI's Domestic Terrorism Unit.[8]

Arechuleta became the prime target of the FBI's Domestic Terrorism Unit. After his appointment to the Hispanic Affairs Commission, he was considered for inclusion on its notorious ADEX list, a catalog that Hoover created in 1967 of more than one hundred thousand people identified as subversive.[9] Agents had earlier tried to recruit Arechuleta in September 1975 to work as an informant for the agency, but he angrily threw the FBI out of his Tierra Amarilla house, yelling, "I'm a Communist and I have no intentions of talking to the FBI or any representative of the United States Government."[10]

According to the FBI Arechuleta worked briefly in 1968 on the Heron Dam construction site before being fired. He became a focal point of the investigation when the attorneys general in New York and Illinois convened grand juries in 1977 to investigate the FALN, MLN, and the Hispanic Affairs Commission. During the investigation Episcopal Church officials initially gave the FBI access to its files. The decision caused a deep schism among bishops and lay leaders of the church, many of whom refused to cooperate with the federal inquiry. The FBI quickly subpoenaed all the members of the commission, but none agreed to cooperate. Maria Cueto, an Arizona activist and chair of the commission, was jailed in March 1977 when she refused to testify before the grand jury and a federal district court judge rejected her claims of First Amendment privilege.[11] Her secretary was jailed when she also refused to cooperate.

In April 1977 the *New York Times* called Arechuleta, who by that time had been subpoenaed to appear before grand juries in Chicago and New York, the FBI's "prime suspect in the theft of the Heron Dam dynamite."[12] By June he was in a Manhattan jail for refusing to cooperate with the grand jury. In August he refused to cooperate with the Chicago grand jury. "You can put me in jail for a year or ten years and I will never talk," said Arechuleta to a federal judge in Chicago. "In me you see the spirit of Emiliano Zapata, Francisco Villa and Pedro Albizu Campos ... fighting for justice."[13] Between Chicago and New York, Arechuleta spent eleven months behind bars, from June 1977 until his release in May 1978, when the terms of the two grand juries expired.

The inclusion of Morales on the list of grand jury witnesses, however, was more curious and suggests that the FBI thought the land grant movement in general was somehow connected to the FALN. Morales had no connection whatsoever to the Hispanic Affairs Commission, nor had he ever worked at the Heron Dam construction site. In the spring of 1977 the FBI acknowledged that its agents had tried repeatedly to recruit Morales as a paid informant during the investigation of Arechuleta.[14] The FBI tried to "bribe and intimidate" Morales, and when he refused to cooperate he was subpoenaed by the Chicago grand jury.[15]

Land Grant Activism as Terrorism

The FBI investigation of Chicano activists in the 1970s and 1980s, in which race and dissent became a marker for terrorism, was a continuation of the agency's racialized practices from COINTELPRO in the 1960s. Scholars who study political violence, particularly the violence of the state, argue that dissent often serves as the compelling factor in the application of covert repressive action by law enforcement authorities.[16] The history of COINTELPRO, however, shows that dissent is often sorted and repression focused along racial lines. Tierra Amarilla mapped nicely into the FBI's imaginary racialized geography of subversion, in which race was the key marker for anti-American militancy. In the 1960s this was reflected in the many FBI departments, categories, and acronyms that either linked race to subversiveness or used race as a key marker for militancy.

The hidden racial assumptions of programs like COMINFIL, however, which based its investigation of leaders like Martin Luther King Jr., Malcolm X, and Reies Lopez Tijerina on the notion that race and subversion were one and the same, were buried more deeply in the years after J. Edgar Hoover when "domestic terrorism" rather than a racialized anti-Americanism became the rubric through which subversion was sorted. The scores of bombings by FALN in New York and Chicago in the early 1970s, violent conflicts between police and various black power groups, and a spike in airplane hijackings from the United States to Cuba — an average of nearly 20 per year between 1969 and 1973 — created a state of emergency among law enforcement agencies such as the FBI, which deployed the threat of terror by Chicano groups as a way to relegitimize the use of racialized covert and coercive violence.

In this chapter I continue the examination of state violence begun in the last chapter by focusing on the way land grant and land grant–allied groups organized against the patterns of police violence. As discussed in previous chapters La Corporación offered stiff legal and rhetorical resistance to land loss from the 1930s until the early 1970s. The intense opposition to the rhetoric of Alianza and the claims of La Corporación included significant patterns of covert, as well as open, violence or harassment. The 1970s marked a shift in the conflict. I focus in this chapter on two organizations, La Raza Unida (RUP), a Chicano political party that mobilized an organized political response to police brutality and to a lesser degree development issues in Rio Arriba County in the 1970s, and El Consejo de la Tierra Amarilla, a land grant organization that adopted a paramilitary approach to the land grant struggle in the late 1980s. The emergence of RUP and El Consejo marked a shift in the mode of resistance among land grant activists in Tierra Amarilla; local activists now turned their attention to the patterns of police and state violence as the new terrain of property struggle.

La Raza Unida and the Patterns of Police Violence in Rio Arriba County

El Partido Nacional de La Raza Unida was first formed as a political third party in 1970 in Texas, where a group of Chicano activists ran for, and were elected to, city council seats in three towns. Chapters in Colorado, California, and New

Mexico quickly sprang up.[17] Unlike elsewhere, Chicano activists in New Mexico had recent experience organizing third parties. Drawing on his notoriety after the courthouse raid, Tijerina and Alianza supporters overcame legal challenges in 1968 to establish the People's Constitutional Party (PCP) of New Mexico.[18] Pedro Arechuleta and Moises Morales, among others, participated in conventions around the state that eventually produced a PCP platform calling for bilingual education, civilian police review boards, and an increase in welfare payments. Tijerina, however, was disqualified as a candidate for governor based on a felony conviction, and the party received less than 2 percent of the vote. After his incarceration in 1969, the PCP dissolved.

In 1971 the Chicano Associated Student Organization at New Mexico Highlands University in Las Vegas, New Mexico, formed an RUP chapter in San Miguel County.[19] Two Highlands students, Juan José Peña and Manuel Archuleta, organized the San Miguel chapter and, in the following year, joined with others to establish a statewide organization. While both were influenced by the writings of Daniel de Leon, a leader of the Socialist Labor Party at the turn of the century, they "didn't present them as ideas to the Hispano Community where there was a history of anti-Communism."[20] Instead they organized clothing drives, offered legal aid services to local residents, and focused on welfare rights and job discrimination.[21]

They also confronted long-standing patterns of police brutality against Chicano youth in San Miguel County. In addition to an elections committee, a voter registration committee, a publicity committee, a finance committee, a fundraising committee, and a student outreach committee, the San Miguel County chapter maintained what members half-jokingly called a violence committee.[22] The violence committee maintained covert surveillance of the county sheriff's posse, an auxiliary force composed largely of Anglo ranchers from San Miguel County that operated in the early 1970s as an anti-Chicano paramilitary strike force. Posse members, who used photos of RUP members in target practice at local gun ranges, frequently harassed RUP leaders. One RUP officer recalled being frequently attacked by sheriff's posse members. "I was shot at in my car several times. I had bullet holes in my car. I had my house shot at. I had bullet holes in my back window that faces the alley. People shot at that. I had people throw rocks through the windshield of one of my cars."[23]

The violence committee operated as an early-warning system for local activists and a vehicle for retaliation and intimidation (members once raked with gunfire the unoccupied house of a particularly violent posse member). The violence committee also monitored FBI activity. As Peña recalled, "[We] had people stationed all over town, at all the different entrances into Las Vegas so we knew who was coming and going. The FBI was always trying to infiltrate us with people, but the thing was they couldn't recruit local people so they'd send people from Texas, California, and they stood out like a sore thumb."[24]

In 1972 Manuel Archuleta recruited a childhood friend named Antonio "Ike" DeVargas to start an RUP chapter in Rio Arriba County. DeVargas was an imposing figure. Made strong from years working in the woods as a logger, he had a huge head of curly black hair and was skilled at skewering opponents with his quick wit. He had served in Vietnam as a Force Recon Marine and worked briefly upon returning to New Mexico in union organizing. Archuleta introduced DeVargas to the writings of Daniel de Leon and to Rudolfo Acuña's landmark study of Chicano history, *Occupied America: A History of Chicanos*. Inspired, DeVargas spent the next ten years working as the RUP chairman in Rio Arriba County.

DeVargas and RUP led a political assault against county sheriff Emilio Naranjo, a man whom the *Santa Fe New Mexican* called "the last *patron*" when he died in November 2008.[25] The term is a reference to the more than forty years that Naranjo spent in a variety of official capacities in Rio Arriba County as state senator, county sheriff, chairman of the Democratic Party, and U.S. marshal. From these posts Naranjo, a small, stocky man with an unusual squeaky voice, built a Chicago-style patronage machine through which he dominated local politics. For Barbara Manzanares, an RUP leader, Emilio Naranjo represented a kind of Chicano "of the type who prefers to call themselves Spanish-American." She asserted, "This force is on the brink of completely selling out our people and the little land left un-developed and intact to the big business interests who want to develop the area."[26]

In addition to protecting the interests of commercial developers, Naranjo controlled all public-sector hiring in the county. In the second poorest county in the third poorest state in the United States, public-sector jobs were, for most residents, the only jobs available, and Naranjo controlled hiring at all levels. He filled the assessor's office and the Office of the County Clerk with supporters. His loyalists held jobs as school janitors, principals, bus drivers, and teachers. The pattern sacrificed the public interest for Naranjo's political ambitions. A 1964 National Education Association report on Rio Arriba County schools called its districts among the worst in the United States and blamed the problem on "the Chairman of the major political party in the County."[27]

When patronage failed to produce political results, Naranjo deployed an army of sheriff's deputies as enforcers. "Emilio has become the sort of man," one Rio Arriba County resident remarked in the late 1970s, "no one will say anything about except that he's a very kind and generous man we're afraid of."[28]

DeVargas's experience in Vietnam galvanized his opposition to Naranjo. "When I got back from the military and I could see his machine and his thugs and all that stuff, I thought to myself, well, shit, they ship me off ten thousand miles away to fight the dictators and I come home and we have a freaking dictator right here."[29]

Moises Morales joined DeVargas in 1973 to bring concerns from the northern part of the county in Tierra Amarilla into La Raza Unida. With the collapse of Alianza and title to the grant quieted in the hands of private owners, land speculators had rediscovered northern New Mexico. Developers, with support from elected officials, spent the early 1970s buying up extensive swaths of land within the grant. They proposed airports, ski resorts, and huge commercial developments in a series of plans that promised to transform the small land grant village of Tierra Amarilla into a tourist mecca to rival Taos or Santa Fe, which, according to Pedro Arechuleta, would condemn land grant residents to a life of "cleaning up the shit of tourists and hunters who have no respect for our culture and get mad when we speak Spanish."[30]

The possibility of a future Tierra Amarilla that "would benefit only rich Anglos" galvanized Morales, who, along with Pedro Arechuleta, joined a small cadre of community activists. Together with a core group of activists, they organized a series of community-based organizations that offered an alternative to tourist-oriented development.[31] A legal aide office called La Oficina de Ley provided free and low-cost legal services out of offices in Tierra Amarilla. La Cooperativa Agricola (The Agricultural Cooperative) launched cooperative farming projects throughout the land grant area. La Cooperación del Pueblo (The Unified People) developed sustainable economic projects in the county, La Clínica del Pueblo de Río Arriba (The People's Clinic of Rio Arriba) provided the only free or low-cost medical clinic to residents within a hundred miles, and La Gente Unida Para El Progreso Controlado (The People United to Control Progress) coordinated efforts among other organizations to oppose the development of tourist-based industries and infrastructure in Rio Arriba County. The groups worked alone and in concert in various campaigns to oppose the Naranjo regime and plans for the tourist development of Tierra Amarilla. "The idea," according to one RUP ally, "was that if you could get a really progressive county government then you could do something with the land grant issue and the subdivision sales and stuff like that. That was certainly the idea at the time in the midseventies. The idea was to be able to tackle the land grant after you were able to succeed politically."[32]

Activists maintained that it was because of their political opposition to Naranjo and tourist-based development that law enforcement officials began to target La Raza Unida, Morales, Arechuleta, and DeVargas. The years in which RUP actively opposed Naranjo and tourist development were among the most violent and contentious in the long and bitter fight over Tierra Amarilla. Between April 1974 and May 1976 eighteen reported beatings or shootings by sheriff's deputies produced official complaints in the county. Dozens more, according to RUP activists, went unreported.[33] The Rio Arriba County Sheriff's Department had become, according to one RUP activist, "an instrument of Emilio's rule."[34] "What do you expect," explained a lawyer who represented RUP activists, "when you have a law agency where the positions are based on political allegiance and rewards."[35]

Naranjo responded to criticism by cracking down on political opposition and harassing RUP members with frequent arrests; he once arrested both candidates running against him for sheriff in the days before the election. The most violent deputies and key Naranjo loyalists eventually became targets themselves.[36] Throughout the 1970s Naranjo operated a large network of informants. The patterns of police violence against activists produced a retaliatory pattern against police collaborators. A Rio Arriba man known as informant number 69 was killed in August 1973, less than a month after information he provided to deputies resulted in a series of raids and arrests of residents in the southern Rio Arriba County village of Truchas.[37]

While RUP called attention to police violence in southern Rio Arriba County, allied activists ramped up opposition efforts against development projects in Tierra Amarilla. Andres Valdez and Henrietta Esquibel of La Gente Unida Para Progreso Controlado, along with Pedro Arechuleta, then working with La Cooperación del Pueblo, frequently disrupted meetings of local business leaders and elected officials who were trying to build a commercial airport in Tierra Amarilla. The location of the airport, within the boundaries of the grant, also drew the ire of former Alianza and La Corporación members. Fernanda Martínez, a longtime land grant activist and the wife of Juan Martínez, threatened the county commission: "[If] they make this airport inside the land grant, we might confiscate this land with the airport."[38] Naranjo's deputies provided security for controversial meetings surrounding the development of the Chama–Tierra Amarilla airport and Naranjo, who was known to "take someone right outside a conference room during a county meeting and slap him around," patrolled the meetings, shouted at protestors, and at times ejected people who he thought opposed the airport too vehemently.[39]

While activists in Tierra Amarilla were fighting airport plans, DeVargas was circulating a petition to dismiss five of Naranjo's deputies after three members of RUP were arrested in June 1975 on drug charges.[40] Ernesto Valdez and his two brothers, all active members of RUP, were arrested for possession of eight ounces of marijuana after police searched their Petaca homes.[41] In July RUP gave the sheriff's department a petition signed by more than five hundred residents asking for the dismissal of deputies for "'frame-ups' and criminal acts of brutality." Naranjo staffed the sheriff's office with deputies who, according to DeVargas, were "natural headbeaters."[42] The same week that DeVargas filed the petition to fire deputies the Valdez brothers were released from jail. Shortly after their release deputies arrested, beat up, released, and then rearrested their brother-in-law in an effort, according to RUP, to intimidate the brothers.[43]

In Tierra Amarilla Gregorita Aguilar, a former La Corporación member from Rutheron, just west of Tierra Amarilla, joined members of El Gente in a lawsuit against the county and the airport commission.[44] With the help of Oficina de Ley lawyer Richard Rosenstock, they secured a temporary restraining order against the county commission preventing it from holding more closed-door meetings regarding the airport. Chama mayor Benny Medina, the chair of the county's airport commission, admitted that he had convened closed meetings in order to evade protestors ("I wanted to bar the public," he admitted to the local newspaper).[45] In response to the lawsuit the county commission disbanded the airport commission and instead hired a private consultant to conduct a "scientific study" of the airport question.[46] The airport was planned for Ensenada, a small village north of the town of Tierra Amarilla that was at one time the heart of La Corporación membership and organizing. Airport boosters imagined a future of ski resorts, golf courses, bed and breakfasts, and vacation homes dotting a valley where land grant sheepherders would no longer live.

Meanwhile, the New Mexico chapter of the American Civil Liberties Union (ACLU) agreed to review RUP's claims of police brutality. It began its investigation by examining the case of a southern Rio Arriba County man left paralyzed when a sheriff's deputy shot him in the back.[47] In October another man filed a lawsuit claiming that the same five sheriff's deputies named in RUP's petition had beat him with clubs and chains in December 1974 and then took him into custody for resisting arrest. Deputies beat another man in September 1975 until his eardrums ruptured.[48] Naranjo dismissed the allegations of institutionalized police violence, saying only that crime in the county was down now that "there [was] law enforcement in Rio Arriba County."[49]

Tensions reached a head in November 1975, when a bar owned by the former undersheriff of Rio Arriba County blew up in an explosion authorities called suspicious.[50] Naranjo blamed RUP and claimed that the bombing was designed "to discourage tourism in the area."[51] In the wake of the bombing Naranjo's deputies embarked on a weeklong campaign of "searches, seizures and arrests" of RUP members.[52] The few vocal members not arrested protested the arrests by parading through Española streets chanting "La Raza, sí! Emilio, no!"[53]

Deputies arrested Andres Valdez, Pedro Arechuleta, Morales, and others and held them for days without charges. Deputies also raided the offices of the medical clinic in Tierra Amarilla. The search warrant claimed that a confidential informant had told police that the basement of La Clínica was full of weapons. When deputies came up empty handed, they broke into the adjacent offices of La Oficina de Ley and ransacked legal files.[54] Following the raids Naranjo claimed that his deputies had seized "an air force bomb shell and 1,000 rounds of ammunition" from the houses of RUP members. According to inventories filed by deputies, however, they confiscated only "a whip, bags of herbs, Tylenol aspirin, a sewing machine and rifles" during the raids.[55]

Naranjo said that deputies raided RUP members because the description of a car seen at the site of the explosion matched the vehicle of an RUP member.[56] But informants of an investigator who had been working in New Mexico since 1967 with HELP (Home Education Livelihood Program), a federal War on Poverty program, suggested that the explosion may have been a setup. The bar's owner had been removing valuables from the building in the days before the explosion.[57] "Naranjo wants to destroy us," said Arechuleta. "We are a threat to him and he is using the bombing as an excuse to get us."[58]

In early 1976 RUP gained access to county documents in a lawsuit it filed to force the county to release information regarding the distribution of federal funds. According to the documents the county had diverted more than five hundred thousand dollars that should have been spent on health, recreation, and services for low-income residents.[59] Naranjo responded by arresting RUP members and then arresting their lawyers when they came to meet their clients.[60] In response to the police crackdown DeVargas hung Naranjo in effigy at an RUP rally held in the parking lot outside an Española building that Naranjo owned and leased to the county.[61] In February La Cooperación presented reporters with a list of twenty-six criminal violations by Naranjo and his deputies including police brutality, illegal searches and seizures, "frame-ups," extortion, and tampering with evidence.[62] The *Rio Grande Sun* newspaper editorialized against Naranjo that the "unprovoked beatings, illegal property seizures, improper searches of private homes and downright terrorism are too numerous and well-documented to be ignored any longer."[63]

As Morales and DeVargas increasingly became the face of RUP, they experienced increased harassment. In lawsuits over the county's raids on RUP members the previous November, a district court judge ordered Naranjo to reveal the name of the anonymous informants he used to secure search warrants. At a July hearing a sheriff's lieutenant claimed Morales was in fact the informant on the raids of La Clínica and various RUP members the previous November. A laughing Morales denied the charge, recognizing an old FBI COINTELPRO tactic; he told the court and the local press, "People know me, they don't believe it."[64] That same month a federal grand jury began investigating the sheriff's department for civil rights violations. The grand jury heard testimony from a former deputy who claimed that Naranjo planned to frame Morales and DeVargas on drug charges and even discussed the possibility of ordering deputies to kill both men.[65] Later in the year another former deputy testified in Morales's drug trial that deputies in Naranjo's sheriff's department routinely framed perceived political enemies with phony drug busts.[66]

Claims that RUP was a terrorist organization were fueled by the violent spring of 1976, when Naranjo and his deputies experienced a pattern of retaliation against police brutality.[67] In April police officials found a huge bomb under Naranjo's home in Gallina made from twenty-six sticks of dynamite.[68] Alcohol, Tobacco and Firearms agents found that the fuse had been lit, but the dynamite had failed to detonate.[69] In May two shots were fired into the home of one deputy, while another's house burned to the ground the same night. Two weeks later a patrol car came under fire while in a remote area of the county. Bullets careened through the back of the squad car as the deputy fled the scene.[70]

In September sheriff's deputies responded to a late-night 911 call to find one of their own unconscious and bleeding from the head outside the Chamisa Inn in Española, a popular bar in town. DeVargas was arrested two days later. In October a grand jury indicted DeVargas for assault. The officer first claimed that six men jumped him but later changed his story and said that DeVargas alone was responsible for his beating. DeVargas stole his gun, he told investigators, and beat him until he was unconscious. DeVargas told authorities that he was going from bar to bar that night recruiting people to attend an RUP rally on Sunday when an off-duty sheriff's deputy began harassing him and challenged him to a fight. According to DeVargas when the two walked out of the bar, the deputy made a move for his gun. DeVargas lunged at the weapon and disarmed the deputy in a brief struggle that ended with DeVargas pistol-whipping the deputy to the ground.[71] DeVargas was held without bail for two days at the state penitentiary; all sides thought he would be safe from reprisal in Santa Fe, far from Rio Arriba County. Despite the precaution eight correctional officers beat DeVargas for hours when he refused to shave his moustache and sideburns.[72] The charges were eventually dropped after DeVargas passed a lie detector test. The sheriff's deputy, who needed emergency cranial surgery after the fight, declined to take a lie detector test and later signed an affidavit refusing to testify against DeVargas.[73]

After DeVargas was released, cracks in the Naranjo political machine began to appear. In the 1976 elections, with only 2 percent of the County registered with La Raza Unida, RUP won 11 percent of the vote. Though the percentage was small, the impact was significant. Naranjo resigned as sheriff and was named "law enforcement coordinator." The position came with a salary greater than that for sheriff but without a clear job description or, it seems, any duties. Complaints by RUP and editorials by the local newspaper led to investigations by the New Mexico attorney general and eventually a lawsuit against the county. By 1977 the sheriff who had replaced Naranjo and the local district attorney, an office that had long supported Naranjo at any cost, abandoned him. The lawsuits and defections eroded the sense of invulnerability that had for forty years sustained Naranjo's political authority.

Through its provocative tactics and frequent lawsuits, RUP revealed the political nature of police violence in Rio Arriba County. Disguised as law enforcement, policing under the Naranjo regime had become a political act in which violence became a means to political ends. Much research on police violence suggests that the police often ignore the law, stretch it, or only provisionally apply it, and that understanding the origins and politics of police violence requires understanding the unique subculture of police.[74] The history of police violence in New Mexico in the 1970s, however, suggests that police violence can be explained not only as an effect of police culture but also through an examination of the relation between law and violence.

According to German social critic Walter Benjamin, law's monopoly on violence vis-à-vis the individual is not a cultural artifact but rather an effort to preserve law itself.[75] And police violence, according to Jacques Derrida, is not merely a form of legal enforcement but a form of lawmaking itself. Derrida argues that "today the police are no longer content to enforce the law, and thus to conserve it; they invent it."[76] In the mid-1970s the police in Rio Arriba County were not the instruments of law's violence but rather, in the wake of COINTELPRO and the covert war by the state against Alianza, were themselves both enforcers *and* makers of law. According to a lawyer with Oficina de Ley, the police in Rio Arriba "were free to wreak whatever havoc they wanted on their community against people they didn't like."[77] As a result the violence of law remained hidden in its enforcement, legitimized by law's monopoly of violence. For La Raza Unida and allied organizations such as La Cooperación, however, it was clear that law and violence were linked to the land grant struggle. The construction of a private property regime on the grant served development interests over land grant residents, and Naranjo's sheriff's department enforced that arrangement.

For Pedro Arechuleta and a group he would organize in the 1980s called El Consejo de la Tierra Amarilla, the law vested authority in the hands of capital and against the interests of land grant heirs. As I examine in the next section, they would match the law's violence with their own to make the point.

El Consejo de la Tierra Amarilla

In 1966 a Tierra Amarilla man named Amador Flores built an eighteen-acre enclosure on a five-hundred-acre property adjacent to his family's land in Tierra Amarilla and waited to see what would happen. "I said to my dad," he recalled, "nobody is saying nothing about the fence posts."[78] Following his father Rafael's advice, he wrote a deed for the entire five hundred acres and began paying property taxes.[79] He planted a small garden and used the property to graze cattle, sheep, and goats. Three years later he offered a portion of the land to La Cooperativa to plant gardens. In 1982 Flores, short and stocky with jet-black hair, began building a house on the property.[80]

Flores was the grandson of Roque Flores. When Roque Flores lost access to the land that Abeyta and La Corporación had deeded him in the 1940s after the *Flores v. Brusselbach* case, he acquired another small parcel of land from La Corporación located just southwest of the village of Tierra Amarilla. Flores and his family lived on and worked the land unmolested. After his death Roque's son, Rafael, inherited the property. Amador expanded the small ranch in 1969 and used it without interruption until the morning of September 25, 1985, when he found a surveyor from a Chama title insurance company walking the land. Flores threw the surveyor off the land and, with his sons, removed the stakes and destroyed the monuments marking the surveyor's property boundaries.

Two months earlier Vista del Brazos, a development corporation, had filed a quiet title lawsuit in district court for a 1,900-acre parcel that included Flores's 500 acres. Flores and his wife were named among a long list of defendants. Vista, an Arizona company, intended to subdivide the land and develop the lots as vacation homes to serve the adjacent ski area proposed by a company called Peñasco Amarilla Ski Corporation. In August La Corporación de Abiquiú filed a motion to intervene.[81] Vista opposed the motion by La Corporación to intervene, pointing out that not only was its interest based on a common property claim to the grant that five courts had rejected, but also a permanent injunction meant that "allowing an intervention of the Corporación de Abiquiú . . . [was] a violation of the Court decree."[82] District court judge Bruce Kauffman agreed, citing the 1964 permanent injunction, or "Tackett Decree," and refused to allow the group to intervene.[83]

In March 1986 lawyers for Flores made arrangements to have him give an oral deposition in May in the Chama offices of Vista's attorney, Peter Holzem. On the same day the oral deposition was to occur, however, the court allowed Flores's attorney, Wilbert Maez, to withdraw. Without an attorney Flores skipped the May deposition. The court ordered Flores to appear for another oral deposition within twenty days. In August, after Flores had missed the second deposition, Judge Kaufmann issued a partial final decree for Vista. In January 1987, with the lawyerless Flores supposedly refusing to comply with court orders and requests, Kaufmann issued a summary judgment in favor of Vista.[84]

But Flores refused to leave the property. In February Holzem sent an agent of the title insurance company to Flores's home to investigate the situation. Flores told the agent he was not aware of any judgment and had never received notice of any hearings after Maez had withdrawn from the case. Vista persisted and sent a local land manager from Chama to threaten Flores with eviction. By this time the case had become local news and a group of supporters, led by Pedro Arechuleta, formed a group called El Consejo de la Tierra Amarilla to coordinate efforts in support of Flores. El Consejo advised Flores to ignore the courts altogether. "We didn't see that we were going to get justice on our behalf," explained Arechuleta. "The deeds given to the people here were never recognized by the government or the courts."[85]

Flores, however, decided to fight the case in court. "This property is mine and does not belong to any Arizona Corporation," he wrote in an angry response to the threat of eviction. Vista asked the court for a temporary restraining order to remove Flores from the land. A hearing was scheduled in Santa Fe in late March.[86] Instead of attending the hearing himself, Flores sent Pedro Arechuleta's brother, Belarmino, to the court to represent him. The court issued a temporary restraining order. In April Flores hired Santa Fe attorney Steve Herrera, who, like Maez before him, agreed to work pro bono. In August Herrera filed a motion to vacate the judgment against Flores. A hearing was scheduled for April 1987. Herrera, however, failed to file supporting documentation for the hearing, and Flores never appeared.

The case dragged on through late 1987; in March 1988 Judge Kauffman determined that Flores's intransigence merited Vista a judgment in the case. He issued the judgment on March 25 and then allowed Herrera to withdraw on March 28. Days after the judgment Holzem asked Kauffman for a permanent injunction against Flores. Kaufmann agreed to prepare the order to show cause for Flores. Holzem later claimed he sent the order to Flores, but Flores said he

Amador Flores (*middle*) during a court hearing, May 1, 1990. (Photo by Leslie Tallant; © 2008 The New Mexican, Inc. Reprinted with permission. All rights reserved.)

never received it, and no record with the post office or sheriff's department was ever found.[87] Despite the lack of notice the permanent injunction was granted in early April.

On the afternoon of April 11 a sheriff's deputy drove to the property to serve Flores with the permanent injunction. When he arrived the deputy found nearly two dozen supporters holding semiautomatic machine guns and standing behind Flores as he held a press conference with Albuquerque TV stations and print journalists from throughout the state. With cameras running Flores took the order from the deputy and threw it into the campfire.[88]

A furious Judge Kaufmann ordered Flores to court. On May 1 Richard Rosenstock, the Oficina de Ley attorney who had represented La Raza Unida in the 1970s, agreed to represent Flores. He filed an affidavit for Flores four days later that claimed Holzem never sent notices after Herrera withdrew. Two days before the contempt hearing, the New Mexico chapter of the ACLU filed an amicus brief with the court arguing that Holzem had violated Flores's constitutional right to procedural due process. After a delay Flores came before the court in late June. Kaufmann found him in contempt of court and remanded him to the Santa Fe County detention facility, where he was jailed for nearly a month.[89]

While Flores was in jail, two dozen supporters made permanent the occupation of the land that they had begun on April 11. Over what would become a fourteen-month armed occupation, El Consejo barricaded the entrance, built five fortified bunkers on the land, organized armed patrols of the property, and enforced a trespassing order.[90] They built and installed "Vietnam-type booby traps." Arechuleta described the traps: "You know we soaked willows in about twenty-four or sixteen inches of human waste and then we put them facing a trail with a trip wire; if you trip and you hit one of those things, it's going to poison you. We also put shotguns with moss traps on trees. We had aluminum cans; if someone would hit them, we would know."[91] Despite the show of force El Consejo rarely had more than a handful of members at the site at one time. Often only Pedro Arechuleta and a young activist from an adjacent village named Daniel Aguilar stood guard.

A state police tactical team considered storming the encampment. "The use of force," said a police spokesman, "is absolutely the last possible thing that anyone wants considered. But in the final analysis we are responsible for the

An armed Amador Flores (*right*) and his son, Vincent Flores, stand in front of one of the five bunkers built during a fourteen-month standoff, May 7, 1988. (Photo by Larry Beckner; © 2008 The New Mexican, Inc. Reprinted with permission. All rights reserved.)

Rafael Flores, the son of Roque Flores (*Flores v. Brusselbach*) and the father of Amador Flores, reacts to news about his son's legal issues, August 12, 1988. (Photo by Sydney Brink; © 2008 The New Mexican, Inc. Reprinted with permission. All rights reserved.)

public safety."[92] Police considered El Consejo a general threat to public safety and the governor's Organized Crime Task Force agreed. In January 1989 the task force leaked a report in which it linked El Consejo to MLN and the FALN and claimed it was a terrorist organization. The report described Daniel Aguilar and Pedro Arechuleta as having ties to terrorist organizations. "I feel they're trying to get the basis for getting us [off the land] by trying to get us connected to these terrorist organizations," said Arechuleta, adding, "The people here know me, they know I'm not a terrorist."[93] Holzem too played on fears of Chicano subversiveness, telling a Denver television station, "These people are nothing but terrorists."[94]

While land grant activists were digging in for a long fight, Flores and his attorneys were negotiating a settlement with Vista. In August 1989, a little more than a year after Flores had been released from jail, El Consejo announced that a settlement with Vista had been reached. Flores would receive two hundred acres and $117,250. Rosenstock and another attorney would split $164,000. The settlement came after Rosenstock had filed a series of civil lawsuits against Holzem, Vista, and Judge Kaufmann claiming that they conspired to obstruct Flores's right to a fair hearing. Flores said that the land would be turned over to

El Consejo. "This is the first piece of the Tierra Amarilla Land Grant that has been free," said Arechuleta.[95]

When you drive north from Abiquiú to Tierra Amarilla on U.S. 84, the road crests a bluff just north of a little ranching village called Cebolla. From there it descends into the Tierra Amarilla valley. The massive granite face of the Brazos Cliffs looms to the east, and the huge southern San Juan peaks are visible to the north in southern Colorado. The road drops quickly into the valley, and just before the town of Tierra Amarilla begins, a huge billboard welcomes visitors with an image of the Mexican revolutionary Emiliano Zapata beneath the painted slogan he made famous, "Tierra O Muerte" (Land or Death). The sign marks the site of the fourteen-month standoff between El Consejo and Vista del Brazos. It was erected during the conflict and remains standing today, a sign of the ongoing struggle over property in the Tierra Amarilla land grant. There are other signs as well. A series of structures stand behind bunkers arrayed along the eastern edge of the property, a reminder of the years of armed struggle waged for land on the grant. Other, more recent signs, offer a different way to view the legacy of the fight. "There are six people buried there," explained Cruz Aguilar, a member of La Corporación and El Consejo. "Two of my sons and the parents of Amador Flores and Pedro Arechuleta."

At the press conference announcing the settlement victory, members of El Consejo talked about plans for a cultural center and a museum, but neither today stands on the site. "The activists didn't pass it on to their kids," explained Pedro Arechuleta. "They went to school and they forgot Spanish and they learned English."[96] The lack of economic opportunities, particularly in agriculture, has led to fewer young people staying in Tierra Amarilla. "They want to get involved in the whirlwind of the city and things like that," explained Gregorita Aguilar, a longtime member of La Corporación.[97]

The Rio Arriba County La Raza Unida chapter folded in 1984, when the majority of members decided to register as Democrats and support Jesse Jackson in the Democratic primary. Despite the failure of the party to put members in elected positions, many former members have since found electoral success within the Democratic Party. "Over the years we've had a number of those people who have been in office. Moises Morales is one of them. Valdez he's county manager. Alfredo Montoya, county commissioner."[98] Morales served two terms as a county commissioner in the 1990s and the first decade of the twenty-first century. His work in public office, however, often frustrated longtime land grant activists. "He is county commissioner," said one former member active in La Corporación from its inception, "and has forgotten that when he was young he

The sign with the image of Mexican revolutionary Emiliano Zapata alongside the phrase "Tierra O Muerte" (Land or Death) and "Zapata Vive" (Long Live Zapata) was erected during the standoff. It remains standing today, greeting visitors along the road into Tierra Amarilla. (Photo by Eric Shultz used with permission.)

worked with us in the struggle for the land against the state. And now he has [allowed the grant to be] divided into parts, and sold."[99]

The years prior to and following *Vista del Brazos v. Flores* were years in which La Corporación splintered into competing groups. While La Corporación de Abiquiú remained active well into the 1970s, other heirs split off and formed different groups. El Consejo focused its work on supporting Flores. Another group called the Heirs of Manuel Martínez formed in the mid-1970s and organized protests of land sales within the boundary of the grant, often interrupting public meetings with signs that read, "Whoever buys land in Tierra Amarilla buys trouble."[100] A fourth group called the Tierra Amarilla Community Land Grant was formed during the legal fight with Vista. Many of the same people served at various times and in various capacities in these different groups.

Although the claims by the FBI and the State of New Mexico that Arechuleta was a terrorist failed to dislodge El Consejo from the land, it exacerbated existing tension between various land grant groups. Danny Martínez, a leader of the Tierra Amarilla Community Land Grant, distanced himself from Arechuleta after the Organized Crime Task Force report in 1989. He explained, "They have never worked with the land grant, only their own claim-jumping, you know? All the time we've been supporting Pedro and Amador, but it's just this thing with the terrorists. We don't want the people to think we're involved in that."[101]

Claims by federal officials of terrorist activity among land grant activists in Tierra Amarilla are surprisingly persistent. They began in the early 1960s, and as recently as 2004 the Counterterrorism Unit of the FBI's Domestic Terrorism Operations Unit considered conducting aerial surveillance of the Flores ranch. An FBI memo recommended focusing any possible investigation on Arechuleta:

> [Pedro Arechuleta and others] reside in Tierra Amarilla, New Mexico, a locale centered within a Spanish land grant. Captioned subjects are among the heirs of the original land grant, and, have subscribed to a militant viewpoint concerning the legality of the area being considered a part of the United States. Further, they are believed to have identified with the Ejercito Zapatista de Liberation National (EZLN) and the Mexican National Liberation Movement (MLMN). These are known rebel movements within Mexico that believe in reclaiming the lands originally ceded to the United States from Mexico in 1848.[102]

Given the long history of efforts to remove land grant heirs from Tierra Amarilla, it is important to take seriously the ways in which legal authorities have reworked tactics of removal. The police violence of the Naranjo regime and the frequent use of the claim that land grant activists are domestic terrorists call into question the claim of law enforcement officials that they do nothing more than merely uphold the law. Any distinction between lawmaking and law preserving or claims of law's objectivity and neutrality collapse under the weight of a history of violence against land grant members. Against the police and the official story of land grant heirs being militant radicals, domestic terrorists, and obstacles to progress, RUP and El Consejo offered acts of resistance that disrupted development and police brutality in ways that brought the violence of the law into view.

EPILOGUE

Rare Earth

IT'S AUGUST 2011, and I'm in the backseat of a four-wheel-drive Ranger, a gas-powered, off-road "golf" cart with huge tires and plenty of cup holders. We're tearing along a rutted gravel road that leads to the land at the heart of the *Martínez v. Mundy* dispute. Mike Plant is driving, drinking a Tecate and smoking a Cuban cigar. Nagging knee injuries have turned the former Olympic speed skater into a pudgy fifty-two-year-old land developer. Actually, land development in Tierra Amarilla is just his hobby. He spends most of his time in Atlanta, where he serves as the executive vice president of Major League Baseball's Atlanta Braves. His route into sports management dates to just after the 1980 Olympics, when he was a teammate of six-time gold-medal speed skater Eric Heiden. After the Olympics Plant took up competitive cycling, as did Heiden. Unlike Heiden, however, Plant found his greatest success in organizing athletic events rather than competing in them. With a partner he started a sports promotion company in the late 1980s and convinced Donald Trump to pitch in millions of dollars. The Tour de Trump was the result, an East Coast U.S. version of the Tour de France. The tour folded after a few years, but not before the Atlanta Braves' billionaire owner Ted Turner bought Plant's company.

Plant holds out a Cuban cigar to me. "Have you ever smoked a Cuban?" he asks. When I say no, he pulls it back. "It'll make you sick then. Better not." He takes another sip from his can of Tecate and returns to the conversation he's having with his front-seat passenger, former Atlanta Braves slugger Ryan Klesko. Klesko hit nearly three hundred home runs in a sixteen-year career spent mostly with the Braves and now, in retirement, hosts his own hunting show on cable. He's in Tierra Amarilla to film an episode about elk hunting on the former land grant.

I can barely hear the two of them over the roar of the engine, but I make out that they're discussing elk habitat and the best place to locate a hunting blind. I turn to watch the scenery fly by. "For sale" signs in front of small ranchettes populate the roadside alongside "no trespassing" signs and, occasionally, massive western-style ranch entrances with huge metal gates and names like The Landings at Chama and Mundy Ranch. Fences are everywhere we look, and

One of the many entry gates to Canyon Ridge: A Rare Earth Community, August 2011. (Photo by author.)

they define new boundaries of property that today divide the former land grant into thousands of smaller private holdings. Wealthy out-of-state vacationers own many of the ranchettes, a real estate euphemism for upscale second homes. We drive past Jim Mundy's ranch, and Plant hollers back that Jim, the son of Bill Mundy, is building an exclusive residential development complete with an artificial-turf golf course and a firing range that can accommodate .50-caliber machine guns, a gun so large that the rounds are as big as small bananas.

We're on our way to Plant's 5,800-acre ranch/development, which he named Canyon Ridge, a Rare Earth Community. The glossy real estate brochures that promote Canyon Ridge describe an idyllic setting for million-dollar homes set in a mountaintop, conservation-friendly, master-planned community. Promotional materials narrate a history of untrammeled wilderness and peaceful seclusion that elide the long history of conflict and property struggle in Tierra Amarilla. Plant's website doesn't even include the villages that made up the Tierra Amarilla land grant. Like the sheepherders that the story of Canyon Ridge ignores, they're off the map.

Canyon Ridge comprises part of the land that Bill Mundy first bought in 1951. Since acquiring the property in 2007, Plant has reduced whole ridgelines to rubble in order to build roads through thick forests. Soon, if all goes as planned, the roads will be choked with construction equipment building scores of multimillion-dollar homes with breathtaking views of the Tierra Amarilla valley — a valley that Plant's maps have renamed the Chama Valley.

We finally reach the ranch entrance, and Plant idles the four-wheeler in front of a huge gate. Klesko hops out to open the fence, and Plant turns around to tell me the story of how he came to buy the ranch. He came west more than five years earlier, he says, to find a hunting ranch somewhere in southern Colorado. He ended up buying a seventy-acre ranch near Pagosa Springs, Colorado, but quickly grew bored with it. It was exactly what he wanted, he says, except not big enough. He decided that what he really wanted was a "legacy property," as he put it, and he found his ideal site in the mountains above Tierra Amarilla. In June 2007 he paid a doctor (who had bought the ranch from Mundy years earlier as a private hunting preserve) $8.6 million. He was determined, he said, to reserve most of the fifty-eight hundred acres for wildlife habitat and, in an ironic reiteration of the commons, reserve most of the land as an amenity for the scores of homeowners who would eventually live on the grant in multimillion-dollar mansions. "I donated the conservation easement to the Rocky Mountain Elk Foundation," Plant says. "When the place is all built out, you'll only be able to enter the conservation easement by horseback or on an electric cart." When they do visit their "commons," the residents will find nicely appointed hunting cabins nestled along the Chavez and Brazos Rivers.

Klesko gets back in the Ranger, and we drive into Canyon Ridge. The gravel road curves to the north as we head toward the massive Cañon Creek gorge at the northern edge of the development. We stop briefly at the future site of the clubhouse, where Plant shows us a view of the Tierra Amarilla valley from more than ten thousand feet. It begins to rain as we climb back into the Ranger for the short drive to the gorge. When Plant bought the ranch, he found it crisscrossed with a network of sheep trails and decided to turn them into a system of hiking trails. We're driving around in the rain so Plant can install signs marking trailheads. After a brief stop at the gorge to place a sign, we turn south. The land slopes slowly down the length of the ranch until it reaches Chavez Creek. We're passing lots where future houses will be built. Each residential lot clings to a cliff-top ridge that offers impressive views of the entire property. We stop at one of the most expensive lots. The views are breathtaking. To the north a ridgeline sweeps across to the west enclosing a deep, forested valley at its center. The master plan includes eighty-one lots with prices between $445,000 and $745,000. Each comes with a bird's-eye view of the Tierra Amarilla valley to the west, the interior valley to the east, and the Brazos cliffs looming above from the southeast. For many of the lots even the massive southern Colorado San Juan Mountains are visible to the north.

The view looking north from Canyon Ridge over the Cañon Creek Gorge. The southern San Juan Mountains in Colorado are visible in the distance, August 2011. (Photo by author.)

    We climb back into the Ranger for a short drive to another trailhead. Plant describes in words full of anticipation how the woods we're about to enter look and feel like a rainforest. We drive through open pastures and climb back above ten thousand feet before stopping at a trailhead at the edge of a forest thick with mature Douglas fir dripping with moss. Rotting nurse logs litter the forest floor, and grass shoots up in spots nearly to our waist. Klesko's just back from South America, where he filmed an episode of his hunting show. He's filmed episodes all over the world he tells me, but he's awestruck by the grant. He asks me to email him all the photos I'm taking.
    We're hiking toward a rocky ridge where Plant says we'll find what he calls Sheepherder's Monument. He's still smoking his Cuban cigar as we walk and talking about the monument when we get lost in a huge rock field. It takes nearly an hour of backtracking and climbing over boulders to find our way back to the trail. Plant mentions that he got permission from Rio Arriba County to start his own sand and gravel operation on the grant in order to make the roads. "There are enough rocks here to pave the whole property and then some," he says. When we finally get to the monument, we find an eight-foot obelisk made of rocks the size of bowling balls. With a start I realize that it's an old property boundary marker. I can't tell if it's a rock cairn placed by sheepherders in the

The view looking east from one of the eighty-one lots in the Canyon Ridge development. The Brazos cliffs are in the middle. To the right in the distance is the abandoned ski area, August 2011. (Photo by author.)

nineteenth century or by Mundy in the twentieth. Either way I mention to Plant the irony of the very thing that came to define the commons in ways that would eventually exclude sheepherding — private property — is now the very thing memorializing sheepherders.

While Plant and Klesko screw trail markers into adjacent trees, I take pictures of the monument and the huge valley that drops away from the ridge and slopes back up on the other side toward the Brazos cliffs, the uplift that marks the eastern edge of the San Juan Basin. Earlier in the day, before Klesko arrived, Plant and I sat on the deck of his modular home perched above the road between Tierra Amarilla and Chama, which serves as Canyon Ridge's temporary headquarters. We talk about sports mostly, his time in the Olympics and the Braves' chances in the 2011 pennant race. I ask him about the trouble he's had getting development approvals from the county. Getting the green light from the county took nearly two years, he tells me. In December 2007 the county commission rejected his master plan application after dozens of land grant heirs packed the hearing room. One grant heir testified that Plant was nothing more than "a thief and a crook." Plant is laughing when he tells me this. "And then he comes up to me afterwards and asks me for a job, can you believe that?" he remarks.

A trail sign marks the site of Sheepherder's Monument, August 2011. (Photo by author.)

I mention the history of conflict over the land grant, and Plant seems interested. "Yeah, when I bought the property, Jim Mundy told me all about it. He said the only way to get things done around here is to bribe people. These guys I'm telling you are programmed to do everything they can to stop progress in the county." The progress that Plant has in mind is the progress that developers since the mid-1970s have promised for Tierra Amarilla: tourist-related jobs in retail, construction, and hospitality. Plant hires locals to serve as hunting guides, mostly sheriff's deputies.

"I've read a few things about the land grant," Plant tells me, "but the land grant issue had zero to do with our submission." It's a planning issue, he contends, and one he intends to win. "I've negotiated with the Russians. I've done projects in China. I'm not going to get my ass whipped by a bunch of local sheepherders."

This book has traced the long history of struggle over property in Tierra Amarilla. My focus has been on the struggles waged by a variety of groups, such as the night riders of the 1920s, La Corporación from the 1930s through the 1960s, Alianza in the 1960s, and El Consejo and La Raza Unida in the 1970s. By examining these struggles I have tried to interrupt the idea of law as objective and independent of society and the notion of property as a "natural" part of the landscape. As the claims of various groups demonstrate, law is both an object of ownership and an arena of social struggle, and conflict over property claims is always marked by violence.

The inherent violence of property in Tierra Amarilla has been one permeated by a persistent and racialized colonial geography reinforced through state violence. The legal construction of private property in Tierra Amarilla obscured histories of colonial violence and Indian removal and required violence to sustain it. Nicholas Blomley has made a similar argument about law when he examined what he referred to as property's geographies of violence: "Law tends to deflect questions of its own innate violence to the violence that makes law necessary."[1]

The struggles that dominate current conflicts over property in Tierra Amarilla, however, are not strictly legal ones. The rhetoric and practice of community development have largely replaced the law as the site of conflict. It is an arena in which planning and development operate as a kind of "anti-politics machine," where planning, like the law, presents itself as rational, scientific, and thus beyond challenge.[2] A development like Canyon Ridge follows the logic of the market in which property is merely a technical problem of land use and an object wholly legible to the state.[3]

Even though places like Mundy Ranch and Canyon Ridge have the feeling of finality to them — the feeling that they represent a kind of inexorable climax condition of private property — it would be a mistake to imagine the current struggles over planning and property in Tierra Amarilla as a final resolution to the conflict. To argue that property is more than an object but also a set of social relations constituted through political struggle means that property is never finished. What we call property, therefore, is something that never finds completion.

Perhaps one reason Canyon Ridge feels like the end of the conflict has something to do with it being a product of the logic of planning that has considered Tierra Amarilla an underdeveloped place in need of private investment and upscale residential development projects such as Canyon Ridge. The idea that New Mexico's land grant villages such as Tierra Amarilla are underdeveloped is not new. It was first elaborated by federal agencies such as the United States Forest Service (USFS). The USFS manages millions of acres in northern New Mexico, most of it the former common lands of Mexican land grants that were either rejected by U.S. adjudicators in the nineteenth century or sold to the government by speculators in the twentieth.

From its very beginning the USFS defined the poverty it found in land grant communities as a cultural deficiency of land grant society. *A Dependency Study of Northern New Mexico*, authored in 1935 by a Forest Service grazing assistant named Roger Morris, concludes that "[Hispanos] are sedentary in character living in the present and with no thought for the future. They accept conditions as they are and make the best of them with no idea of conserving the natural resources much less enhancement of them. They would remain in place to the point of extinction by starvation and disease before they would migrate."[4] The study, which relied on surveys of local economic conditions by the Soil and Water Conservation Service, suggested that the Forest Service should regulate and limit local resource use for local land grant families. Morris observes, "It is noted . . . that the diet . . . is exceedingly plain, and the clothing supply very meager, and also that there has been no provision for medical attention. It is thus felt that the indicated income figure of $426.25 can very well be raised to an even $500.00."[5] Ultimately, the Forest Service elected to transform the subsistence economy of the region in ways more conducive to industrial resource use.[6] According to the report, "in the matter of determining the proper relationships between inhabitants and existing natural resources there is a certain ratio of the population such as merchants and laborers deriving their living indirectly from the said resources to those deriving a direct living from them and this ratio should be determined in all cases."[7]

The Morris report describes New Mexico's land grant communities as welfare cases, whole communities completely dependent on the state for subsistence. And in this Morris was right. The conversion of land grants to either private lands or publicly managed forests placed most former common lands off limits to land grant communities or at best beyond the financial reach of most small cattle ranchers or sheepherders. In place of land grant property relations, the logic of rational planning prescribed economic development based on private interests: industrial forestry, tourism, and, most recently, oil and gas exploration. The irony is that the very thing that created the economic crisis for land grant communities — the power of private interests over collective rights and the enclosure of the commons — became the centerpiece of antipoverty planning by agencies such as the USFS. When the plan failed to reduce poverty, the Forest Service blamed land grant communities and intensified its stock reduction program and industrial forestry focus.[8]

The courthouse raid of 1967 interrupted the logic of planning that blamed poverty on local communities. Alianza attributed poverty to land grant dispossession and directly challenged the legitimacy and authority of the federal government in New Mexico. In response, the Forest Service adopted even more punitive and paternalistic management policies and practices. The version of economic development that the agency embraced was the liberal economic theory premised on the idea that poverty creates "underdevelopment" and is a consequence of weakly developed market relations or a result of communities not fully enrolled in capitalist social relations.[9] This notion of development has been powerful in its ability to make the subjects of development—the poor, depicted as beneficiaries of the gift of development—subordinate to a capitalist rationality depicted as the only alternative to poverty.[10]

For scholars of development, planning is similar to the law in its ability to disguise power relations as "natural." Canyon Ridge appears as a kind of permanence because it reflects a logic of development that agencies like the Forest Service assume is common knowledge. "Perhaps no other concept," according to anthropologist Arturo Escobar, "has been so insidious, no other idea gone so unchallenged" than planning.[11] For Escobar, it is through the practice of planning that the conditions of "domination and social control" are created and maintained. And though the question of land use is at the heart of planning theory and practice, concern about tenure and ownership is largely absent. Private property is not a legal or historical issue for planning but is instead a depoliticized, logistical one. To its critics, therefore, land use planning is a "quiet redistributive mechanism" that reinforces patterns of economic domination.[12]

A few months after my visit with Mike Plant, I visited Jim Mundy, one of Bill Mundy's two sons, to try to better understand how upscale residential development was transforming the land grant. We spent the day driving around what's left of the Mundy ranch in his huge black Hummer SUV. At its height the Mundy ranch exceeded thirty-five thousand acres. Today only fifty-five hundred acres remain; the rest has been sold off to developers or has been developed by Jim Mundy. Like his father, Bill, Jim Mundy is a thin, opinionated man with a penchant for political incorrectness. He lacks all sentimentality about the ranch and still nurses grudges from more than a half century ago. In 2009 Mundy received approval from the Rio Arriba County Commission for a Master Plan application for the Mundy Ranch, a development that, once completed, would mark the end of Mundy ownership of land in Tierra Amarilla. Like Canyon Ridge, to which it is adjacent, it is a development with plenty of exclusive land set aside for the common use of the owners of huge homes on large lots behind gated entrances.

At the hearing to consider Mundy's application, his engineer gave a short presentation before the planning director offered the staff's opinion. "This is exactly the kind of development we want for Tierra Amarilla," the planner said. A land grant heir interrupted him by angrily condemning the proceedings, calling it "a criminal conspiracy." Flustered, the planning director backtracked, stammered through an explanation of procedure and standards, and reminded those in the packed hearing room, just across the street from the courthouse made famous by the raid, that everything was preliminary, that nothing was set in stone. "Recommending the approval of the master plan," he said, "in no way means the development is going to happen." During discussion each county commissioner took the same care to celebrate the history of the land grant before reminding the audience in the hearing room that they were procedurally and administratively compelled to approve the development.

The moment seemed similar to the many legal hearings and court battles waged by land grant heirs in which legal procedures produced an accumulation of case law that conspired against land grant claims. Only now it was elected officials instead of judges who used planning documents instead of case law to reinforce the rights of private owners over the history of common use. Sitting in the room and listening to the hearing, I was struck by the realization that the difference between planning and law is planning's ability to resolve the contentious struggles over property into a boring and abstract exercise. Planning's conflicts remain cloistered in hearing rooms and zoning offices.

But cracks have recently appeared in the solid edifice of planning and development looming over Tierra Amarilla. While planning has been able to clear the way for development and has transformed the grant into a commodity available for developers like Plant to buy and sell, it has been unable to resolve the contradictions of upscale residential development in remote northern New Mexico. By the end of 2007, when Plant and his partners finished the design work, they began a series of launch marketing events in Phoenix, Albuquerque, Denver, and Boston. Plant's partners flew wealthy prospects into New Mexico on private planes and spent huge sums of money on advertising and parties. But in 2008, after sinking more than one million dollars into their marketing campaign, the luxury real estate market collapsed. After the crash Plant bought out his partners and found local financing for the project: no more private planes, launch marketing, or fancy parties. The ranch, however, still required enormous investments in infrastructure, so Plant spent millions of dollars, he told me, bringing electricity to the remote ranch, constructing miles of gravel roads, building elaborate entrance fences, and digging all the wells necessary for the eighty-one lots. By the summer of 2011 the only lot he'd sold was the one he bought himself.

Mundy has also suffered from the housing market crash. His planning approvals came just before the collapse and just as his marriage ended. The divorce settlement left him with land but without the money to develop it. He began shopping the development to potential buyers or partners, hoping to either finish or cut his losses. His situation illustrates a final irony regarding the long property struggle for Tierra Amarilla. Over the past few years Mundy has been negotiating with the Jicarilla Apache Nation to buy the Mundy Ranch.

If the story of the Tierra Amarilla land grant begins with a story of Indian removal and sheepherders from the Genízaro land grant of Abiquiú, it seems appropriate that it ends with the Jicarilla Apaches buying it back. Over the last thirty years the Jicarillas have been quietly buying up land adjacent to the reservation and within the boundary of the Tierra Amarilla land grant. In my interview with Mundy he told me that he'd been waiting for the Jicarilla Apache Nation to buy his ranch. "Why would they buy your ranch?" I asked him. "The rumor is that they have over a billion dollars in a land acquisition fund, and they're ready to start buying back the land grant. I'm negotiating with them to sell my 5,500-acre ranch for $30 million."

In the late nineteenth century Jicarilla Apaches settled on lands near Tierra Amarilla in order to receive annuity goods from the Indian agency there. In the early 1870s Jicarilla chief Ignacio negotiated a treaty with the U.S. government for a reservation west of Tierra Amarilla and east of the massive Navajo reservation. The nine-hundred-square-mile reservation was made official in March 1874, but many of the Jicarillas who were camped near Tierra Amarilla refused to settle on the new lands. It was easy to understand why. The new reservation encompassed the badlands of northern New Mexico, a region the Spanish called *tierra baldía*, or waste lands. At the time the rugged lands west of Tierra Amarilla were all but impossible to travel through, much less settle, hunt, or farm. Despite the resistance, however, the Jicarilla Apaches were forcibly moved from Tierra Amarilla in 1881.

Though the Jicarillas didn't know it at the time, the Jicarilla Apache Reservation, at the center of the San Juan Basin, sat on top of an energy bonanza that, one hundred years later, would make them major players in regional resource extraction and land acquisition. Oil and gas extraction began in earnest in the 1930s, after an extensive network of pipelines and hubs linked the region to outside markets. For natural gas the network meant that operators could finally capture, rather than flare, methane. The Jicarilla Apaches took full advantage of this expanding oil and gas infrastructure and dotted the reservation with oil and gas wells. Today nearly one-third of the reservation, 377,000 acres, is devoted to resource extraction. Nearly 2,200 wells have produced more than 300,000 barrels of oil and almost 35 billion cubic feet of natural gas.[13]

Historically, natural resource administration on tribal lands has been developed in accordance with procedures strictly dictated by the federal government. The Bureau of Indian Affairs administers the leasing of tribal land to non-Indian developers on behalf of Indian nations. This arrangement has largely rejected Native authority over resource management, particularly in the administration of mineral resources. In the late 1970s, however, the Jicarilla Apache tribe threatened BIA authority and energy profitability when it imposed a severance tax on all oil and gas leases on reservation land. It was the first such tax ever imposed by a tribe in the history of BIA authority. Nearly a dozen oil and gas companies with leases on the reservation filed suit against the tribe. The case eventually reached the Supreme Court in 1982 as *Merrion v. Jicarilla Apache Tribe*, 455 U.S. 130 (1982). In a decision authored by Thurgood Marshall, the court held that tribes have the sovereign power to tax nonmember oil and gas lessees on reservations. A "nonmember's presence," concluded the court, "and conduct on Indian lands are conditioned by the limitations the tribe may choose to impose." The *Merrion* decision sanctioned a new and expansive view of tribal sovereignty over natural resources on reservation lands and for the Jicarillas produced a lucrative new income stream.[14]

Royalties and severance tax revenues from the more than five hundred oil and gas producers on the reservation have transformed the Jicarilla Apaches into land speculators and developers. In January 1982, the same month that the Supreme Court ruled in *Merrion*, the Jicarilla Apache tribe purchased a tract of land known as El Poso Ranch and conveyed it to the United States to be held in trust for the tribe. Under federal law Indian nations can purchase land and, if it lies adjacent to the existing reservation, can convey the land to the BIA to be held in trust for the tribe. Such an arrangement transforms private property into public as the federal government holds legal title for the beneficial interest of the tribe.

Though it garnered little notice at the time, the purchase was significant for the land grant as well. El Poso had been the property at the center of the *HND Land Company v. Suazo* lawsuit. The trustee-beneficiary arrangement is particularly ironic in the case of El Poso because this was precisely what La Corporación attorney Robert La Follette tried to argue existed between the United States and the land grant in the late 1930s. Three years after the El Poso purchase, the tribe bought the 54,843-acre Horse Lake Ranch for $24 million. As with El Poso, Horse Lake was also once part of the former common lands of the grant. Like El Poso, Horse Lake was adjacent to the reservation; therefore the Jicarillas could convey the land to the United States. It too was converted from private property into trust land.[15] By the time the tribe purchased its third land grant property, Willow Creek Ranch in the early 1990s, it had spent $40 million and added 94,000 acres to the 800,000-acre reservation. The acquisitions comprised more than 15 percent of the original acreage of the Tierra Amarilla

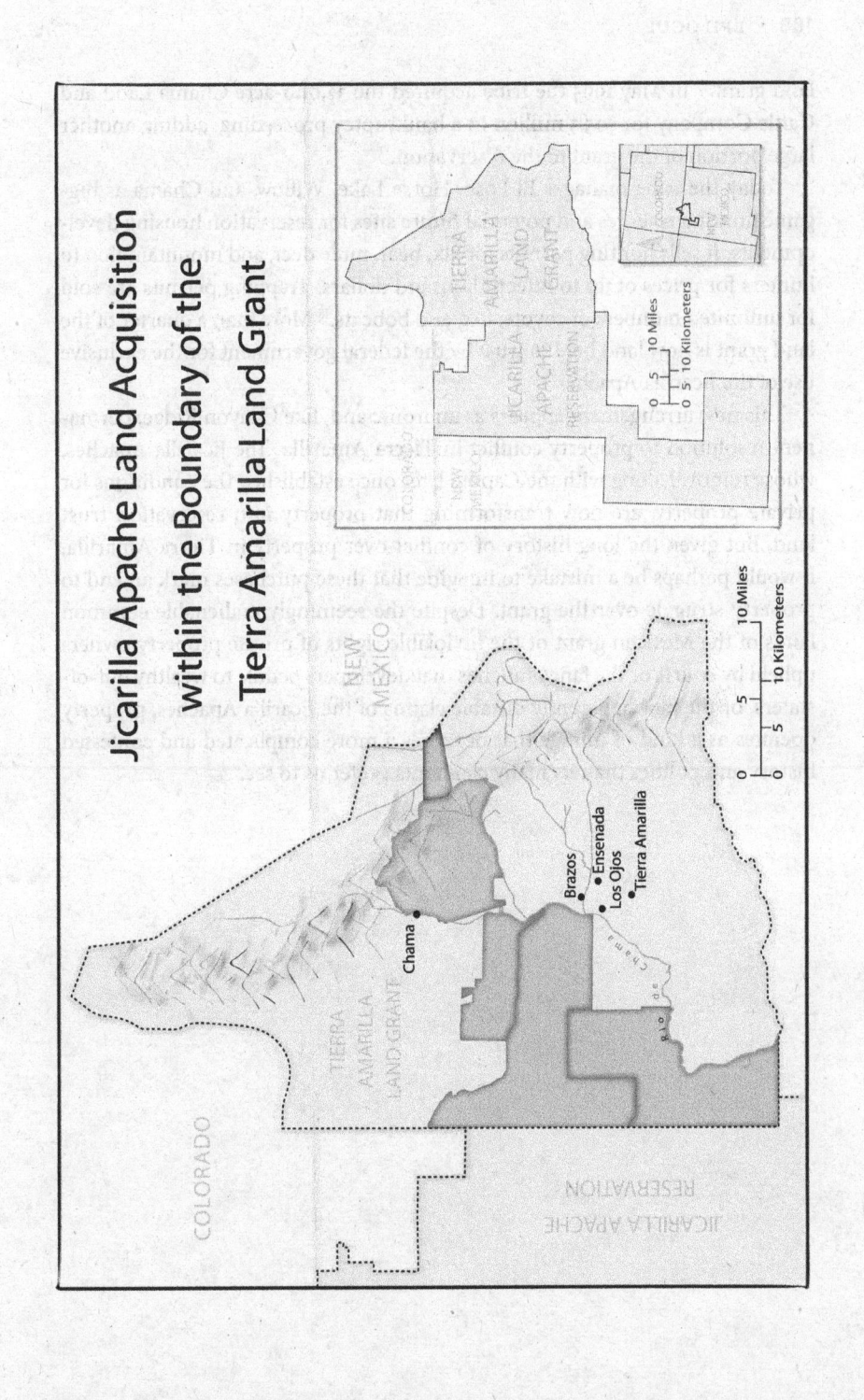

Jicarilla Apache Land Acquisition within the Boundary of the Tierra Amarilla Land Grant

land grant.[16] In May 1995 the tribe acquired the 32,000-acre Chama Land and Cattle Company for $25.5 million in a bankruptcy proceeding, adding another large portion of the grant to the reservation.[17]

Today the tribe manages El Poso, Horse Lake, Willow, and Chama as big-game hunting reserves and potential future sites for reservation housing developments. It sells hunting permits for elk, bear, mule deer, and mountain lion to hunters for prices of up to fifteen thousand dollars. Trapping permits are sold for unlimited numbers of coyote, fox, and bobcats.[18] More than a quarter of the land grant is now land held in trust by the federal government for the exclusive use of the Jicarilla Apaches.

This new arrangement appears as an ironic and, like Canyon Ridge, permanent resolution to property conflict in Tierra Amarilla. The Jicarilla Apaches, whose removal along with the Capote Utes once established the conditions for private property, are now transforming that property into reservation trust land. But given the long history of conflict over property in Tierra Amarilla, it would perhaps be a mistake to imagine that these purchases mark an end to property struggle over the grant. Despite the seemingly inalienable common lands of the Mexican grant or the inviolable rights of private property owners upheld by courts or the fancy ranches that developers peddle to wealthy out-of-staters, or the new apparently durable claims of the Jicarilla Apaches, property operates as a kind of mirage that obscures a more complicated and contested history and politics than its many claimants prefer us to see.

NOTES

INTRODUCTION. *Property and the Legal Geographies of Violence in Northern New Mexico*

1. White, Koch, Kelly, and McCarthy, *Land Title Study* (Santa Fe: New Mexico State Planning Office, 1972).
2. Westphall, *Public Domain in New Mexico*.
3. Ebright, *Land Grants and Lawsuits*.
4. In addition to Alianza the land grant resistance of Las Gorras Blancas on the Las Vegas land grant in San Miguel County, New Mexico, in the 1890s is a story of resistance well known among land grant heirs and scholars.
5. Ebright, *Land Grants and Lawsuits*, 4.
6. Montoya, *Translating Property*, 9.
7. Ibid., 75.
8. Lamar, *Far Southwest*; Ebright, *Tierra Amarilla Grant*; Ebright, *Spanish and Mexican Land Grants*; Westphall, *Mercedes Reales*; Van Ness and Van Ness, *Spanish and Mexican Land Grants*.
9. Briggs, Briggs and Van Ness, *Land, Water, and Culture*; Hall, *Four Leagues of Pecos*; Sunseri, *Seeds of Discord*.
10. Blomley, "Law, Property," 135.
11. Delaney, *Spatial*; Blomley, *Law, Space*.
12. Blomley, "Simplification Is Complicated," 1840.
13. Blomley, *Unsettling the City*, 37.
14. Blackhawk, *Violence over the Land*.
15. Ibid.
16. Cover, "Violence and the Word," 1602n16.
17. Ibid., 1608.
18. Tilly, *Politics of Collective Violence*, 4; Cover, "Violence and the Word," 1607.
19. Delaney, *Law and Nature*, 94.
20. Mitchell, *Rule of Experts*, 56.
21. Benjamin. "Critique of Violence," 295.
22. Derrida, "Force of Law," 989.
23. Blackhawk, *Violence over the Land*, 7.

PROLOGUE. *Yellow Earth*

1. Blackhawk, *Violence over the Land*, 90.
2. Simmons, *Last Conquistador*, 145.

3. Wilcox, *Pueblo Revolt*.
4. Blackhawk, *Violence over the Land*, 27–35.
5. Frank, *From Settler to Citizen*, 50.
6. Ibid., 42.
7. John, *Storms Brewed*, 475.
8. Ibid., 474.
9. Ibid., 102.
10. Jefferson, Delaney, and Thompson, *Southern Utes*, 6–7.
11. Brooks, *Captives and Cousins*, 157.
12. Blackhawk, *Violence over the Land*, 46.
13. Ibid., 92.
14. Petitions for Land Grants, Surveyor General Case Files, Tierra Amarilla Grant, Spanish Archives of New Mexico (hereafter SANM) I, 12:564–72, New Mexico State Records Center and Archive (hereafter NMSRCA), Santa Fe.
15. Hurt, *Indian Frontier*, 34.
16. Blackhawk, *Violence over the Land*, 93.
17. Hämäläinen, *Comanche Empire*, 46; John, *Storms Brewed*, 322.
18. Swadesh, *Los Primeros Pobladores*, 35.
19. Blackhawk, *Violence over the Land*, 79.
20. Ebright and Hendricks, *Witches of Abiquiu*.
21. T. Warner, *Dominguez-Escalante Journal*, 7.
22. Blackhawk, *Violence over the Land*, 125.
23. Wilson and Kammer, *La Tierra Amarilla*; Tórrez, "Jacal in the Tierra Amarilla."
24. Ebright, *Tierra Amarilla Grant*.
25. Petition for Abiquiu by Manuel Martin and Pablo Romero, SANM I, roll 3, frames 1583–85, NMSRCA, Santa Fe.
26. Ebright, *Tierra Amarilla Land Grant*, 10.
27. Swadesh, *Los Primeros Pobladores*, 46.
28. Ebright and Hendricks, *Witches of Abiquiu*, 97.
29. In addition to being a military leader and a local elected official in Abiquiú, Chavez was also involved in frontier trade, which included slave raids in Ute territory. See Bailey, *Indian Slave Trade*, 171.
30. Petitions for Land Grants, Surveyor General Case Files, Tierra Amarilla Grant, SANM I, 12:564–72, NMSRCA, Santa Fe.
31. Request of Manuel Martínez, April 25, 1832, Surveyor General Case Files, Tierra Amarilla Grant, SANM I, 12:566, NMSRCA, Santa Fe.
32. Ibid.
33. Abreu not only served as Mexico's territorial governor for New Mexico but he was also the president of the territorial legislature *and* the president of the Santa Fe *ayuntamiento*, or city council.
34. Report of La Corporación de Abiquiú, May 15, 1832, Surveyor General Case Files, Tierra Amarilla Grant, SANM I, 12:567, NMSRCA, Santa Fe.

35. Appeal of Manuel Martínez, Surveyor General Case Files, Tierra Amarilla Grant, SANM I 12:568–69, NMSRCA, Santa Fe.
36. Report of the Committee Appointed by the Territorial Deputation, SANM I, 6:37, Center for Southwest Research, University of New Mexico, Albuquerque.
37. Decree, Surveyor General Case Files, Tierra Amarilla Grant, SANM I 12:569, NMSRCA, Santa Fe.
38. Bowden, "Private Land Claims," 1054.
39. Tórrez, "El Campo."
40. Alcalde report, March 25, 1836, Surveyor General Case Files, Petaca Grant, SANM I, 23:228, NMSRCA, Santa Fe.
41. Ibid.
42. Weber, *Mexican Frontier*, 92.
43. Testimony of Juan Antonio Pena, Court of Private Land Claims, 18:821–78, Thomas B. Catron Collection, Center for Southwest Research, University of New Mexico, Albuquerque.
44. Hernandez, "Indian Slave Trade," 162.

CHAPTER ONE. *Colonizing the Lands of War*

1. Julian, "Land Stealing in New Mexico," 25.
2. Lamar, *Far Southwest*.
3. Montoya, *Translating Property*, 11.
4. During negotiations to end the war, Mexico insisted on language that would have required the United States to recognize, prima facie, the property claims of Mexican citizens. Prior to ratification, however, the article in which this language appeared was eliminated from the treaty.
5. Lamar, *Far Southwest*, 232.
6. Ibid.; Ebright, *Land Grants and Lawsuits*.
7. DeLay, *War of a Thousand Deserts*; Blackhawk, *Violence over the Land*; Brooks, *Captives and Cousins*; Hämäläinen, *Comanche Empire*.
8. See Ebright, *Tierra Amarilla Grant*; Ebright, *Land Grants and Lawsuits*; Westphall, *Mercedes Reales*.
9. Ebright, *Land Grants and Lawsuits*, 43.
10. Ibid., 3.
11. Montoya, *Translating Property*, 4.
12. Letter to the New Mexico Surveyor General from Ramon Salazar, Geronimo Gallegos, and Pedro Salazar, July 7, 1861, Surveyor General Letters Received, August 5, 1854–March 8, 1876, SANM I, 60, Center for Southwest Research, University of New Mexico, Albuquerque.
13. For a discussion of the role of Locke's theories of property in the development of liberal notions of property in the U.S. context, see Arneil, *John Locke and America*; and Huyler, *Locke in America*.

14. Locke, *Second Treatise of Government*.
15. Joseph McKnight, "Law Books."
16. Locke, *Second Treatise of Government*, 17.
17. Ibid., 20.
18. Thompson, *Customs in Common*, 164.
19. Speech by L. Bradford Prince at the Territorial Exposition in Albuquerque, September 15, 1891, box 13999, folder 10, L. Bradford Prince Papers, NMSRCA, Santa Fe.
20. Julian, "Land Stealing in New Mexico," 31.
21. MacPherson, *Property*, 5.
22. Van Ness, "Hispanic Land Grants."
23. Hale, *Mexican Liberalism*, 179.
24. Ibid., 180.
25. Petition of Francisco Martínez, Surveyor General Report, Tierra Amarilla Grant, SANM 12:570, NMSRCA, Santa Fe.
26. Chap. 167, 12 Stat. 71 (1860).
27. Plaintiff's Exhibit 14, transcript of trial, Martínez v. Mundy, 61 N.M. 87, 295 P. 2d 209 (1956), p. 643, National Archives and Records Administration (hereafter NARA), Denver.
28. Ebright, *Tierra Amarilla Grant*, 22n62.
29. On the use of *hijuelas*, see Will de Chaparro, *Death and Dying*; Louis Warner, "Conveyance of Property"; L. Warner, "Wills and Hijuelas."
30. New Mexico, Laws (1875–1876), chap. 3.
31. Defendant's findings of facts, transcript of trial, p. 123, H.N.D. Land Co. v. Suazo, 44 N.M. 547, 105 P.2d 744 (1940), NARA, Denver.
32. See Arny, *Interesting Items Regarding New Mexico*, for a collection of Arny's writings on economic development in New Mexico and Indian removal.
33. Murphy, *Frontier Crusader*.
34. *Santa Fe Weekly Gazette*, February 19, 1853.
35. *Santa Fe Weekly Gazette*, August 12, 1865.
36. *Santa Fe Weekly Gazette*, May 28, 1864.
37. Report of the Superintendent of Indian Affairs, New Mexico, A. B. Norton to D. N. Cooley, Commissioner of Indian Affairs, July 29, 1866, in "Report of the Commissioner of Indian Affairs (Washington, D.C.: U.S. Government Printing Office, 1866).
38. Report of D. N. Cooley, Commissioner of Indian Affairs, to O. H. Browning, Secretary of the Interior, in *Annual Report of the Commissioner of Indian Affairs*, October 11, 1866 (Washington, D.C.: U.S. Government Printing Office, 1866).
39. *Santa Fe New Mexican*, February 7, 1870; February 8, 1870.
40. Murphy, *Frontier Crusader*, 150.
41. Murphy, *Indian Agent in New Mexico*.
42. Ibid., 14.
43. Report of J. B. Hanson, in Annual Report of the Commissioner of Indian Affairs to the Secretary of the Interior, September 3, 1870.

44. Robert Tórrez, "Southern Ute Agency," 16.
45. Murphy, *Indian Agent in New Mexico*, 10.
46. Bender, "Battle of Tierra Amarilla."
47. Blackhawk, *Violence over the Land*, 218.
48. Ibid., 219.
49. Bender, "Battle of Tierra Amarilla," 248.
50. Jefferson, Delaney, and Thompson, *Southern Utes*, 32.

CHAPTER TWO. *"Under the Malign Influence of Land-Stealing Experts"*

1. Tórrez, "El Bornes," 164.
2. Ibid., 167.
3. Westphall, *Thomas Benton Catron*.
4. Lamar, *Far Southwest*, 131.
5. Westphall, *Thomas Benton Catron*, 71.
6. See Lamar, *Far Southwest*, 121–50.
7. Correia, "Making Destiny Manifest"; Robbins, *Colony and Empire*.
8. "New Mexican Land Thieves: Further Flagrant Examples of Unblushing Plunder, Tools of the Cattle Kings, How Cowboys Perjure Themselves in Pre-empting Public Lands," *New York Herald*, April 10, 1886, 3.
9. "Editorial: We Are Being Robbed," *New York Herald*, April 10, 1886, 4.
10. Julian, "Land Stealing in New Mexico," 29.
11. Ebright, *Land Grants and Lawsuits*.
12. Gonzalez, "Struggle for Survival."
13. Weber, *Mexican Frontier*.
14. Correia, "'Retribution Will Be Their Reward.'"
15. Duran, "Francisco Chavez."
16. Julian, "Land Stealing in New Mexico," 28.
17. Ebright, *Land Grants and Lawsuits*; Westphall, *Mercedes Reales*.
18. Lamar, *Far Southwest*.
19. Westphall, *Mercedes Reales*, 282, appendix 3.
20. Ellison petition, May 20, 1875, Surveyor General Reports, Petaca Grant, SANM I, 23:536–40, NMSRCA, Santa Fe.
21. Transcript of 1875 Ellison petition, Surveyor General Reports, Vallecito Grant, SANM 51:654–63, NMSRCA, Santa Fe.
22. Proudfit report, October 13, 1875, Surveyor General Reports, Vallecito Grant, SANM 51:663, NMSRCA, Santa Fe; Proudfit report, October 13, 1875, Surveyor General Reports, Petaca Grant, SANM 23:577–78, NMSRCA, Santa Fe.
23. Letter from William Blackmore to L. H. Lloyd, Esq., February 14, 1872, William Blackmore Collection, NMSRCA, Santa Fe.
24. Letter from Amado Chavez, box 1, Amado Chavez Papers, NMSRCA, Santa Fe.
25. Letter from Amado Chavez to L. Bradford Prince, n.d., L. Bradford Prince Collection, 13980:10, NMSRCA, Santa Fe.

26. Legal contract for George Hill Howard and Petaca claimants, January 14, 1893, L. Bradford Prince Collection, NMSRCA, Santa Fe.

27. Petition, box 2, folder 17, Amado Chavez Collection, NMSRCA, Santa Fe.

28. Letter from Amado Chaves to George Hill Howard, July 21, 1903, Amado Chavez Collection, NMSRCA, Santa Fe.

29. Robbins, *Colony and Empire*, 77.

30. Ibid., 62–63.

31. Myrick, *New Mexico's Railroads*.

32. Athearn, *Rebel of the Rockies*.

33. Quoted in Fisher, *Builder of the West*, 127.

34. Correia, "Taking Timber, Earth, and Water," 954.

35. Ralph Edgel, "Brief History of Banking."

36. Schweikart, "Early Banking."

37. Winther, "Promoting the American West."

38. Spence, "British Investment."

39. Spence, "When the Pound Sterling Went West." The conversion into dollars is derived from the average exchange rate from 1860 to 1900 of U.S.$5.42 = £1; see L. H. Officer, "Dollar-Pound Exchange Rate from 1791," Measuring Worth, accessed May 2010, http://www.measuringworth.org/exchangepound.

40. Spence, "British Investment," 137. The conversion is derived from the average exchange rate from 1886 to 1900 of U.S.$4.87 = £1.

41. Frost, *New Mexico*.

42. Seligman, "El Paso."

43. Letter from the Secretary of the Interior Transmitting Copies of reports upon the subject of fraudulent acquisition of titles to lands in New Mexico, March 3, 1885, Senate Report, 48th Cong., 2nd sess., Ex. Doc. no. 106.

44. Report of the Governor of New Mexico to the Secretary of the Interior 1885, Territorial Archives of New Mexico New Mexico (hereafter TANM), 102:279–84, NMSRCA, Santa Fe.

45. Ibid., 102:281.

46. Ibid.

47. Ibid., 102:283.

48. Ibid.

49. Julian, *Land Stealing*, 28.

50. Ibid., 17.

51. Ibid., 29.

52. Ibid., 18.

53. Ibid., 38.

54. Ibid., 31.

55. T. D. Burns store ledgers, Thomas D. Burns Collection, NMSRCA, Santa Fe.

56. Baxter, *Las Carneradas*.

57. Parish, *Charles Ilfeld Company*.

58. Knowlton, "Patron-Peon Pattern," 13.
59. Baxter, *Las Carneradas*.
60. Weigle, "Sharecropping with Sheep."
61. Charles, "Development."
62. Weigle, "Sharecropping with Sheep."
63. Tórrez, "El Bornes," 171.
64. William Parish, in particular, argues in *The Charles Ilfeld Company* that *partido* production benefited both *partidarios* and *patrons* alike.
65. Tórrez, "El Bornes," 171.
66. Weigle, "Sharecropping with Sheep," 217.
67. I arrived at this figure by comparing the names of *hijuela* holders with the records of the U.S. Territory, New Mexico District Courts for Rio Arriba in the Agreement of T. B. Catron with T. D. Burns, Rio Arriba County Civil Case 246, box 8, NMSRCA, Santa Fe.
68. Letter from Robert Goshorn to Ben Thomas Moore, April 16, 1893, box 14, folder 5, Ben Thomas Moore Papers, Fray Angelico Chavez Library, Santa Fe.
69. Burns, Biggs Co. royalty statements, 1890–1906, MSS 29BC, box 6, folders 4–5, Thomas B. Catron Papers, Center for Southwest Research, University of New Mexico, Albuquerque. Board feet is a measure of lumber; 1 board foot is a volume equivalent to a board that is 1 inch thick, 1 foot wide, and 1 foot long, or 144 cubic inches. An average wood home requires around 12,000 board feet of lumber.
70. Correia, "Taking Timber, Earth, and Water," 957.
71. Goshorn to Moore, April 16, 1893.
72. Tórrez, "El Bornes," 170.
73. Letter from Thomas D. Burns to Eugene Fiske, n.d., box 3, folder 28, Eugene A. Fiske Papers, NMSRCA, Santa Fe.
74. Westphall, *Thomas Benton Catron*, 281. He later partnered with Catron in a land and cattle company in New Mexico that served as a vehicle for land investments.
75. Tórrez, "Park View."
76. Westphall, *Thomas Benton Catron*, 281.
77. The commissioner of the General Land Office had long hesitated to allow a survey of Tierra Amarilla. By 1874 the GLO had extensive experience translating Spanish and Mexican grant boundaries into the abstract metes and bounds of U.S. survey language, but the surveys often produced spectacular inconsistencies. Questions also remained about the legitimate size of a community land grant. The GLO's interim commission on this issue limited current owners to a property claim not in excess of eleven leagues, a limit found in the Mexican colonization laws of 1824. Brevoort sent a pointed letter to New Mexico surveyor general Henry Atkinson on May 13, 1876: "I will assist in any official effort to properly establish those boundaries, but I cannot consent to any departure therefrom for the mere purpose of selection some specified quantity of land which the GLO may invite me to take in full satisfaction of my legitimate claim. . . . Nothing more, nothing less" (SANM, 1:589–91, NMSRCA, Santa Fe). With

Henry Atkinson in the office of surveyor general, less was not a problem. Anticipating difficulties, the commissioner sought a compromise. If the survey proved larger than eleven leagues, the owners could carve out any eleven-league portion of the grant they chose. Following previous legal cases, however, the GLO had no sound legal basis for such a requirement. The *Tameling* case confirmed the rights of land grant owners to claim property in their full extent, even in excess of the eleven-league standard. Atkinson's assistants completed their survey of Tierra Amarilla in 1876. The grant, according to the notoriously bad surveyors, was massive, nearly six hundred thousand acres.

78. Westphall, *Thomas Benton Catron*.

79. Records of U.S. Territorial/New Mexico District Courts for Rio Arriba, Rio Arriba County Civil Case 46, box 8, NMSRCA, Santa Fe.

80. Catron's close relationship with Burns and Fiske, however, suggests he knew the names of local settlers. Every single *hijuela* had passed through the hands of Burns's translator, Alexander Read, who later served as an attorney for Catron while also serving as the Rio Arriba County sheriff (Alexander Read to Catron, reel 11, 367; itemized list of U.S. Land and Colonization Company Alexander Read (Dr.), reel 11, 496. It is more likely that Catron feigned ignorance of the names of settlers with adverse claims in order to quickly and quietly secure a quiet title.

81. Westphall, *Thomas Benton Catron*.

82. Letter from G. Smiley to Thomas Catron, April 8, 1883, Thomas Catron Collection, 11:226; letter to Catron, January 5, 1883, Thomas B. Catron Collection, 11:217–18, Center for Southwest Research, University of New Mexico, Albuquerque.

83. Theodore Seth et al. vs. Thomas B. Catron, series 202, Miscellaneous Case Records [ca. 1884–1925], box 2, folder 5, Thomas B. Catron Collection, Center for Southwest Research, University of New Mexico, Albuquerque.

84. Westphall, *Thomas Benton Catron*, 56.

85. Letter from Thomas Catron to Wilson Waddingham, August 9, 1897, Thomas B. Catron Collection, 11:516, Center for Southwest Research, University of New Mexico, Albuquerque.

86. Seth et al. vs. Catron.

87. Report on TA grant by W. G. Manson, October 19, 1901, Thomas B. Catron Collection, 11:278–81, Center for Southwest Research, University of New Mexico, Albuquerque.

88. Summons and complaint, signed by County Clerk Bergere, January 1901, Thomas B. Catron Collection, 11:448, Center for Southwest Research, University of New Mexico, Albuquerque.

89. Letter from Jarmuth to Catron, October 17, 1902, Thomas B. Catron Collection, 11:487, Center for Southwest Research, University of New Mexico, Albuquerque.

90. Thomas B. Catron Collection, 11:489, Center for Southwest Research, University of New Mexico, Albuquerque.

91. He nearly convinced John D. Rockefeller and Jay Gould to purchase the grant, but their interest was short lived.

92. "Thomas D. Burns Old Resident and Pioneer Merchant Passes Away," *New State*, March 13, 1916.

93. "Chama Is Bustling Town for Sheepmen, Thousands of Lambs to Be Shipped," *New State*, October 8, 1917.

94. Deutsch, *No Separate Refuge*, 109.

95. Deutsch, "Labor, Land," 274.

CHAPTER THREE. *The Night Riders of Tierra Amarilla*

1. Letter from Captain Serna to Governor Octaviano Larrazolo, June 28, 1920, box 4, 64, Correspondence, Governor Octaviano Larrazolo Papers, NMSRCA, Santa Fe.

2. Report of Alcario Montoya to Governor Larrazolo, May 28, 1920, Correspondence, Governor Octaviano Larrazolo Papers, NMSRCA, Santa Fe.

3. Ibid.

4. Ibid.

5. Tórrez, *La Mano Negra*, 9.

6. Ibid., 10.

7. *El Nuevo Estado*, May 9, 1921.

8. Letter from Kenneth Heron to Governor James Hinkle, April 24, 1924, Governor James Hinkle Papers, 6:220, NMSRCA, Santa Fe.

9. Letter from Mary Emma Burns Becker to Governor Hinkle, May 2, 1924, Governor James Hinkle Papers, 6:220, NMSRCA, Santa Fe.

10. "Rio Arriba Night Riders Out: Homes Fired, Death Threats," *Santa Fe New Mexican*, May 2, 1924.

11. "Handfull [sic] of Men Causing Trouble in Rio Arriba Country, Believe," *Santa Fe New Mexican*, May 5, 1924.

12. "Houses Burned, Threats Posted by Terrorists," *Albuquerque Morning Journal*, May 3, 1924.

13. Letter from Heron to Hinkle, April 24, 1924.

14. Letter from Becker to Hinkle, May 2, 1924.

15. Letter from Kenneth Heron to Governor James Hinkle, April 29, 1924, Governor James Hinkle Papers, 6:220, NMSRCA, Santa Fe.

16. Letter from Heron to Hinkle, April 24, 1924.

17. Ibid.

18. "Rio Arriba Night Riders Out: Homes Fired, Death Threats," *Santa Fe New Mexican*, May 2, 1924.

19. Letter from Kenneth Heron to Governor James Hinkle, May 15, 1924, Governor James Hinkle Papers, 6:220, NMSRCA, Santa Fe.

20. Despite these obvious differences, histories of Las Gorras Blancas have described the movement in terms similar to histories of the Klan. Both groups developed a similar repertoire of images, symbols, and tactics. As conservative social movements, they enforced rural traditions and defended local practices against the onslaught of Progressive Era social change. The White Caps, for example, whose name land grant activists translated into Las Gorras Blancas, was a conservative rural anti-enclosure movement in Indiana that eventually spread westward. The white robes and hoods worn by New Mexico's Las Gorras Blancas bore an uncanny resemblance to the dramatic disguises of the once and future Klan. Despite these similarities, the possibility of any cooperation between the Klan and land grant settlers or even Klan influence in Tierra Amarilla seems as yet uninvestigated.

21. Schlesinger, "Las Gorras Blancas," 90.

22. See Esenwein, *Anarchist Ideology*.

23. Swadesh, *Los Primeros Pobladores*, 231n42.

24. Rio Arriba County Census records from 1910 through 1940 record only one immigrant from Spain living in Rio Arriba County, and none in Tierra Amarilla.

25. Uria, "Myth of the Peaceable Peasant"; Esenwein, *Anarchist Ideology*; Lida, "Agrarian Anarchism in Andalusia."

26. Deutsch, *No Separate Refuge*, 26.

27. Ibid., 222n52.

28. Arellano, "Through Thick and Thin"; Correia, "'Retribution Will Be Their Reward.'"

29. Gardner, *Grito!*

30. Tórrez, "La Mano Negra," 9.

31. "Klan to Be in Saddle," *Santa Fe New Mexican*, May 8, 1924; *Santa Fe New Mexican*, June 28, 1924. Similarly, at the same time night riders were posting threatening handbills with ominous black hands, the *Santa Fe New Mexican* was reporting on threats by an Italian criminal syndicate known as La Mano Negra in Louisiana; see "Black Hand by Threats Seeks to Put Stop to Execution," *Santa Fe New Mexican*, April 30, 1924; "More Threats by Friends of Doomed Sextet," *Santa Fe New Mexico*, May 2, 1924.

32. Robert Rosenbaum, *Mexicano Resistance in the Southwest: "The Sacred Right of Self-Preservation"* (Austin: University of Texas Press, 1981). Rosenbaum uses the term "Mexicano" to refer to native, Spanish-speaking New Mexicans.

33. Gomez, *Manifest Destinies*, 55.

34. Nieto-Philips, *Language of Blood*.

35. Montgomery, *Spanish Redemption*, 13.

36. Nieto-Phillips, "Spanish American Ethnic Identity," 99.

37. Montgomery, *Spanish Redemption*, 8.

38. Menchaga, "Anti-Miscegenation History," 279.

39. Ibid., 289.

40. Ibid.

NOTES TO CHAPTER THREE · 191

41. Barrett and Roediger, "Inbetween Peoples," 14.
42. Harris, "Whiteness as Property," 1713.
43. Deutsch, *No Separate Refuge*, 109–10.
44. Nieto-Phillips, "Spanish-American Ethnic Identity," 134.
45. Wade, *Fiery Cross*.
46. MacLean, *Behind the Mask of Chivalry*.
47. McVeigh, "Structural Incentives for Conservative Mobilization," 1466; Jackson, *Ku Klux Klan in the City*.
48. McVeigh, "Power Devaluation," 2.
49. Lay, "Imperial Outpost on the Border," 67; Lay, *War, Revolution, and the Ku Klux Klan*, 53.
50. Alexander, *Ku Klux Klan in the Southwest*, 76.
51. Goldberg, *Hooded Empire*, 86.
52. Goldberg, "Denver," 39–40.
53. Goldberg, *Hooded Empire*, 30.
54. Ibid., 33.
55. Vargas, *Labor Rights Are Civil Rights*, 33.
56. Goldberg, *Hooded Empire*, 79.
57. Jackson, *Ku Klux Klan in the City*, 237.
58. Lay, *War, Revolution, and the Ku Klux Klan*, 153.
59. Letter from Governor Merritt Mechem to F. C. H. Livingston, Esquire, August 28, 1922, Governor Merritt Mechem Papers, 6:217, NMSRCA, Santa Fe.
60. Correspondence, Governor Dillon Archive, Fray Angelico Chavez Library, Santa Fe.
61. Chalmers, *Hooded Americanism*, 224.
62. Deutsch, *No Separate Refuge*, 164.
63. Vargas, *Labor Rights Are Civil Rights*, 27.
64. Ibid., 29.
65. Ibid., 31.
66. Barrett and Roediger, "Inbetween Peoples," 16.
67. Melzer, "Exiled in the Desert."
68. Forrest, *Preservation of the Village*, 99–100.
69. "Houses Burned, Threats Posted by Terrorists," *Albuquerque Journal*, May 3, 1924.
70. "Klan to Be in Saddle," *Santa Fe New Mexican*, May 8, 1924.
71. McVeigh, "Power Devaluation," 10.
72. *Santa Fe New Mexican*, June 28, 1924.
73. Moore, "Historical Interpretations," 19.
74. The word "watchers," for example, reflected the intense surveillance of Tierra Amarilla in language commonly used to describe anti-Klan monitoring. This became a key tactic against the El Paso Klan chapter. While they were recruiting in New Mexico, the local anti-Klan paper, the *El Paso Times*, surveilled suspected Klan meetings

though the use of surreptitious "watchers," who collected license plates and names of participants. Thus anti-Klan efforts of surveillance and infiltration were commonly referred to as done by "watchers." See Lay, "Imperial Outpost on the Border," 86.

CHAPTER FOUR. *An Unquiet Title*

1. Certificate of Incorporation, September 15, 1937, Archives of the State Corporation Commission, Santa Fe.
2. "Los Mercendado en Operación," *La Opinión de Río Arriba*, January 13, 1938.
3. These included Phil Gallegos and Ralph Gallegos of Chama; Roman Salazar, Fidel Martínez, and Manuel Trujillo of Parkview; Alfredo Esquibel of Nutrias; Pedro Lopez and Sabino Salazar of Tierra Amarilla; Jesus Atencio of La Puente; Frank Gallegos of Brazos; and Celesino Lobato of Ensenada.
4. Article II: "Object," Certificate of Incorporation, September 15, 1937, Archives of the State Corporation Commission, Santa Fe.
5. "Aviso Legal," *La Opinión de Río Arriba*, December 23, 1937.
6. "Los Mercendado en Operación."
7. Minutes of the February 16, 1940, meeting of La Corporación de Abiquiú, in author's possession.
8. "La Corporación de la Merced de Tierra Amarilla Dia por Dia mas Fuerte," *La Opinión de Río Arriba*, May 12, 1938.
9. Gardner, *Grito!*
10. Ibid., 71–76.
11. Ibid., 76.
12. HND Land Co. v. Suazo, 44 N.M. 547, 105 P.2d 744 (1940); Flores v. Brusselbach, 149 F.2d 616 (3d Cir., 1945); Martínez v. Rivera, 196 F.2d 192 (10th Cir., 1952); and Martínez v. Mundy, 61 N.M. 87, 295 P.2d 209 (1956).
13. Rose, "Possession," 82.
14. "Junta Entucista de Los mercenados el 16 de este mes," *La Opinión de Río Arriba*, January 27, 1938.
15. The complaint named the Arlington Land Company, the Mosoto Land Company, and the El Vado Oil and Royalty Company as defendants. A quiet title lawsuit of the kind HND filed is one in which one party seeks to establish a claim as the rightful owner of a piece of real property against other possible parties, or claimants. Quiet title lawsuits frequently go unanswered, a kind of fishing expedition in which a claimant names unknown heirs or claimants. If a complaint goes unanswered, the court finds for the plaintiff and quiets title.
16. "Los Mercendado de la Merced de Tierra Amarilla principiaran su contienda," *La Opinión de Río Arriba*, March 17, 1938.
17. In a reference to the crucifixion, Abeyta implored the members to intervene in the HND case using the phrase "adelante con la cruz," which literally translates as "forward with the cross" (ibid.).

18. "Una Gran Junta en Park View el Domingo por los Mercenados," *La Opinión de Río Arriba*, June 2, 1938.

19. "Historia Breve de la Merced de Tierra Amarilla," *La Opinión de Río Arriba*, May 26, 1938.

20. HND Land Company v. Suazo et al., and Medardo Abeyta et al., Appeal from District Court of Rio Arriba, Transcript of Record, Supreme Court of New Mexico, p. 16, NARA, Denver.

21. Ibid., p. 12.

22. "Answer to Cross Complaint of Juan Suazo et al., Transcript of Record, Supreme Court of New Mexico, p. 27, NARA, Denver.

23. "Admission of Facts upon Issues of Adverse Possession," Transcript of Record, Supreme Court of New Mexico, pp. 89–90, NARA, Denver.

24. Ibid., p. 90.

25. Appellant's Brief to the Supreme Court, Transcript of Record, Supreme Court of New Mexico, p. 18, NARA, Denver.

26. Final Decree, Transcript of Record, New Mexico Supreme Court, pp. 166–88, NARA, Denver.

27. Opinion, J. Mabry, September 18, 1940, Transcript of Record, New Mexico Supreme Court, NARA, Denver.

28. Tameling v. United States Freehold and Emigration Company, 93 U.S. 644 (1876).

29. Opinion, J. Mabry, September 18, 1940.

30. Ibid.

31. Plaintiff's Exhibit 6, Flores v. Brusselbach, Transcript of Record, p. 102, NARA, Denver.

32. *La Opinión de Río Arriba*, first publication, March 8, 1943; last March 29, 1943.

33. Letter to Ed Sargent from Medardo Abeyta, March 20, 1944, Presidente Comision Ejecutiva, Manuel Trujillo, and Nicolas Abeyta, Exhibit 5, Flores v. Brusselbach, Transcript of Record, p. 101, Tenth Circuit Court, no. 3075, NARA, Denver.

34. See Correia, "From Agropastoralism."

35. The local newspaper in Tierra Amarilla, the *New State*, with a Spanish-language version (*El Nuevo Estado*), followed the comings and goings of prominent and wealthy stock growers in Tierra Amarilla. April 24, 1916; and August 14, 1916, updates of Kinderman's comings and goings placed at residences in Colorado and Tierra Amarilla; see also *El Republicano*, December 20, 1901; *El Nuevo Estado*, April 25, 1921; Transcript of District Court Hearing, Flores v. Brusselbach, NARA, Denver.

36. Testimony of Herquilano Herrera, Flores v. Brusselbach, Transcript of Record, p. 30, NARA, Denver.

37. Flores v. Brusselbach Complaint, Transcript of Record, p. 4, NARA, Denver.

38. "Answer," Transcript of Record, p. 8, NARA, Denver.

39. Testimony of Karl Brusselbach, Transcript of Record, p. 29, NARA, Denver.

40. Testimony of Roque Flores, Transcript of Record, p. 45, NARA, Denver. Note:

194 • NOTES TO CHAPTER FOUR

The NARA-Denver transcript of the case includes a page number that corresponds to the entire trial archive. The page numbers of testimony from the trial refer to this number and not the page numbers of the trial transcript.

41. Testimony of Roque Flores, Transcript of Record, p. 45, NARA, Denver.
42. Testimony of Medardo Abeyta, Transcript of Record, pp. 48–51, NARA, Denver.
43. Answer and Cross-Complaint of the Corporacion de Abiquiu, Merced de Tierra Amarilla, Transcript of Record, pp. 13–14, NARA, Denver.
44. Transcript of Record, p. 52, NARA, Denver.
45. Charles Allen, Transcript of Record, p. 53, NARA, Denver.
46. In other words, although Abeyta rejected any private claim to land within the grant, the legal strategy implied otherwise and suggests that La Corporación chose a much more pragmatic approach to dealing with the courts.
47. Testimony of José M. Trujillo, Transcript of Record, p. 55, NARA, Denver.
48. Testimony of Juan Martínez y Lopez, Transcript of Record, p. 57, NARA, Denver.
49. Testimony of Medardo Abeyta, Transcript of Record, p. 63, NARA, Denver.
50. Ibid., p. 64.
51. Charles Allen, Transcript of Hearing, Transcript of Record, p. 54 (30), NARA, Denver.
52. Testimony of Medardo Abeyta, Transcript of Record, pp. 51–52, NARA, Denver.
53. *La Opinión de Río Arriba*, July 13, 1944.
54. *La Opinión de Río Arriba*, August 24, 1944.
55. "Proceedings of the Board of County Commissioners," Rio Arriba County, March 1, 1951, on file in the Office of the County Clerk, Rio Arriba County Courthouse, Tierra Amarilla.
56. Complaint, Transcript of Record, Martínez v. Rivera, p. 2, NARA, Denver.
57. Ibid.
58. Temporary Injunction, Transcript of Record, p. 12, NARA, Denver.
59. Martínez v. Rivera pretrial conference, Transcript of Proceedings, p. 21, NARA, Denver.
60. Ibid., 26.
61. Martínez v. Rivera hearing, Transcript of Proceedings, p. 27, NARA, Denver.
62. Ibid., 30.
63. Martínez v. Rivera, Transcript of Trial, p. 64, NARA, Denver.
64. Ibid., p. 15.
65. Opinion of the Court, Transcript of Proceedings, p. 267, NARA, Denver.
66. Ibid.
67. Ibid., p. 265.
68. Ibid.
69. Gardner, *Grito!*, 48.
70. Testimony of Bill Mundy, Martínez v. Mundy, Transcript of Record, pp. 315–34, NARA, Denver.
71. Ibid., p. 324.

72. Ibid., p. 340.
73. Ibid., p. 362.
74. Ibid., p. 348.
75. Ibid., 352.
76. Ibid., p. 345.
77. Olivia Cordova, interview with author, May 7, 2009, Ensenada, N.M.
78. Testimony of Bill Mundy, Transcript of Record, p. 356.
79. Ibid., p. 348.
80. Complaint, Transcript of Record, pp. 1–3, NARA, Denver.
81. Order of Judge David Carmody on Motion for Change of Venue, August 5, 1952, Transcript of Record, NARA, Denver.
82. Memorandum of Opinion of Judge David Carmody, July 30, 1953, Transcript of Record, NARA, Denver.
83. Carmody all but apologized in his opinion. "The Court, very definitely, does not want the plaintiffs or their attorneys," he explained "to feel that their case is being prejudged." See Memorandum of Opinion of Judge David Carmody, July 30, 1953.
84. "Judge Rules against Jury of Advisors," *Santa Fe New Mexican*, August 24, 1953.
85. "State Police Avert Bloody Chama Battle," *Santa Fe New Mexican*, June 29, 1953.
86. Ibid.
87. Ibid.
88. HND was an acronym for Hall, Nossman, and Dudrow, three ranchers who sold land in 1930 that eventually became the property that Mundy claimed.
89. José María Martínez Brief, Transcript of Record, p. 15, NARA, Denver.
90. Defendant's Exhibit 3, Transcript of Record, NARA, Denver.
91. José María Martínez Brief, Transcript of Record, p. 46. Bigbee also playfully claimed that it would be absurd for the court to interpret the Martínez-to-Manzanares deed as a conveyance of the entire grant. It would be like believing that "the story of Jack and the Beanstalk and Alice in Wonderland were Gospel truth" (p. 45).
92. Bill Mundy Brief, Transcript of Record, p. 32.
93. Ibid., p. 33.
94. August 18, 1871, duly filed for record and recorded in book 2 at pages 390, 392 of the Record of Rio Arriba County, New Mexico.
95. Bigbee Brief, Transcript of Record, p. 453, NARA, Denver.
96. Transcript of Record, p. 12.
97. Olivia Cordova, interview with author, May 7, 2009, Ensenada, N.M.
98. Testimony of José María Martínez, Transcript of Record, p. 462, NARA, Denver.
99. Ibid., p. 436.
100. Testimony of José Remigio Martínez, Transcript of Record, p. 391, NARA, Denver.
101. Testimony of Manuel Gallegos, Transcript of Record, p. 506, NARA, Denver.
102. Testimony of José María Martínez, Transcript of Record, p. 459.
103. Ibid.

104. Testimony of Bill Mundy, Transcript of Record, pp. 325–53, NARA, Denver.
105. Testimony of Joe Turner, Transcript of Record, p. 233, NARA, Denver.
106. Testimony of Brother Rowland, Transcript of Record, p. 614, NARA, Denver.
107. Ibid., p. 617.
108. Ibid.
109. Plaintiff's Requested Findings of Fact and Conclusions of Law, December 17, 1953, Transcript of Record, NARA, Denver.
110. Findings of Fact and Conclusions of Law, Transcript of Record, p. 61, NARA, Denver.
111. Court's Findings of Fact and Conclusions of Law, December 17, 1953, Transcript of Record, pp. 56–63, NARA, Denver.
112. McManus Opinion, Transcript of Record, p. 5, NARA, Denver.
113. "High Court Rules for Mundays (*sic*) in Old Tierra Amarilla Land Grant Struggle," *Santa Fe New Mexican*, March 20, 1956.
114. Blomley, *Law, Space*, 76.
115. Blomley, "Law, Property," 135.
116. McManus Opinion, Transcript of Record, p. 9, NARA, Denver.
117. Ibid.

CHAPTER FIVE. *The New Mexico Land Grant War*

1. Payne was registered as a corporation in Delaware, thus making a federal filing possible.
2. Ebright, *Tierra Amarilla Grant*; Golten, "Lobato v. Taylor." The first four cases were discussed in the previous chapter.
3. Golten, "Lobato v. Taylor," 472.
4. Affidavit of Bernardo Rivera, January 31, 1958 (filed on February 9, 1959), Transcript of Record, NARA, Denver.
5. Opinion of the Court, Judge Waldo Rogers, filed February 1, 1960, Transcript of Record, NARA, Denver.
6. This is not to say that claims based on the Mexican grant have not appeared since *Payne*. In the summer of 1989 a Tierra Amarilla man sued to quiet title in district court for the grant under a claim that he owned much of the grant based on deeds original to the Mexican claim. The court's reaction, however, demonstrates that it considered the question of property in Tierra Amarilla resolved. "This case" the judge wrote, "is another episode in the seemingly endless saga of the Tierra Amarilla Land Grant. Questions regarding the Land Grant were largely laid to rest in previous litigation" (Rivera v. Brazos Lodge Corp. 808 P.2d 955 [1991]).
7. Scott, *Seeing Like a State*.
8. Ibid., 49.
9. Mitchell, *Rule of Experts*, 57.

10. King, "Keeping People in Their Place," 2.
11. Cover, "Violence and the Word," 1607.
12. Alfonso Sanchez, interview with author, September 9, 2009, Santa Fe.
13. Ibid.
14. Ibid.
15. An abstract is a compendium of the various legal documents, deeds, mortgages, wills, etc., that chronicle the particular history of a given piece of land.
16. Unpublished memoir, box 1, folder 4, Alfonso Sanchez Papers, Center for Southwest Research, University of New Mexico, Albuquerque.
17. Ibid.
18. Nabokov, *Tijerina and the Courthouse Raid*.
19. Tijerina, *They Called Me King Tiger*, 7.
20. Reies Lopez Tijerina, interview with author, May 5, 2009, El Paso.
21. Tijerina, *They Called Me King Tiger*, 8.
22. Gardner, *Grito!*, 94.
23. Ibid., 97.
24. "Naranjo Denies Chama Vandalism," *Rio Grande Sun*, July 30, 1964.
25. Gardner, *Grito!*, 100.
26. Eviction letter, 1888–2003, box 46, folder 22, Inventory of the Reies Tijerina Papers, Center for Southwest Research, University of New Mexico, Albuquerque.
27. "'We're Forgotten People' Grant Chief Says," *Rio Grande Sun*, August 13, 1964.
28. "Land Grant Officials 'Evict' Bureau," *Rio Grande Sun*, August 6, 1964.
29. "Partial Report on Tierra Amarilla Dispute," box 2, folder 24, Peter Nabokov Papers, Center for Southwest Research, University of New Mexico, Albuquerque.
30. Pearl Holmquist, "Congress May Get Grant Question," *Rio Grande Sun*, August 20, 1964.
31. "Grant Corp. Decides against Taking Its Case to Congress," *Rio Grande Sun*, August 27, 1964.
32. Sanchez, interview with author.
33. "Notes" of October 8, 1963, meeting between Sanchez and Tijerina, box 1, folder 4, Alfonso Sanchez Papers, Center for Southwest Research, University of New Mexico, Albuquerque.
34. Letter from Alfonso Sanchez to J. Edgar Hoover, July 22, 1964, box 2, folder 24, Peter Nabokov Papers, Center for Southwest Research, University of New Mexico, Albuquerque.
35. "Partial Report on Tierra Amarilla Dispute," Peter Nabokov Papers.
36. Pearl Holmquist, "DA to Seek Injunction in T.A. Land Grant Dispute," *Rio Grande Sun*, October 1, 1964.
37. Ibid.
38. Gardner, *Grito!*, 102.
39. Petition of Alfonso Sanchez, October 9, 1964, First Judicial District Court of New Mexico Case 9258.

40. Doyle Akers, "Judge Strips Abiquiu Power," *Santa Fe New Mexican*, October 18, 1964.

41. Doyle Akers, "In T.A. Land Grant Case: Judge Enjoins 'Corporation,'" *Santa Fe New Mexican*, October 16, 1964.

42. Akers, "Judge Strips Abiquiu Power."

43. Ibid.

44. Hoover memo, box 2, folder 13, Reies Lopez Tijerina Papers, Center for Southwest Research, University of New Mexico, Albuquerque.

45. Report of the United States Senate Select Committee to Study Governmental Operations with Respect to Intelligence Activities, April 26, 1976, book 2, Final Report, section 3 (a)(i) "Covert Action and the Use of Illegal or Improper Means," Church Committee Archive, Assassination Archives and Research Center (hereafter AARC), Washington, D.C.

46. Memo from Charles Brennan, FBI, to William Sullivan, Assistant Director of Domestic Intelligence Division, FBI, May 9, 1968, Church Committee Archive, AARC.

47. Memo from San Diego Field Office to J. Edgar Hoover, September 15, 1969, Senate Report, "Using Covert Action to Disrupt and Discredit Domestic Groups," Subheading (d)(b), Church Committee Archive, AARC.

48. Cunningham and Browning, "Emergence of Worthy Targets," 359.

49. Memo from Hoover to all SACs, August 4, 1967, "The Development of FBI Intelligence Investigations", 511, Church Committee Archive, AARC.

50. Final Report, Church Committee, "The Development of FBI Intelligence Investigations," 513, Church Committee Archive, AARC.

51. Final Report, Church Committee, "COINTELPRO: The FBI's Covert Action Programs Against American Citizens," (II)(b)(8), Church Committee Archive, AARC.

52. Final Report, Church Committee, "The Development of FBI Intelligence Investigations," 518, Church Committee Archive, AARC.

53. Memo from Hoover to Albuquerque SAC, February 12, 1964, box 2, folder 13, Reies Tijerina Papers, Center for Southwest Research, University of New Mexico, Albuquerque.

54. Albuquerque SAC memo, box 2, folder 13, Reies Tijerina Papers, Center for Southwest Research, University of New Mexico, Albuquerque.

55. Memo from Albuquerque SAC to Hoover, June 16, 1964, box 2, folder 13, Reies Tijerina Papers, Center for Southwest Research, University of New Mexico, Albuquerque. FBI documents reveal that undercover agents attended every annual Alianza convention.

56. Memo from Hoover to Albuquerque SAC, April 10, 1964, box 2, folder 13, Reies Tijerina Papers, Center for Southwest Research, University of New Mexico, Albuquerque.

57. Memo from Hoover to Albuquerque SAC, May 20, 1964, box 2, folder 13, Reies Tijerina Papers, Center for Southwest Research, University of New Mexico, Albuquerque.

58. Memo from J. Edgar Hoover to all SACs, August 28, 1964, Senate Report, "The Development of FBI Intelligence Investigations," 479, Church Committee Archive, AARC.

59. Memo from SAC Albuquerque to Hoover, November 16, 1964, box 2, folder 15, Reies Tijerina Papers, Center for Southwest Research, University of New Mexico, Albuquerque.

60. "Domestic Intelligence Division: informative note," October 20, 1966, box 2, folder 15, Reies Tijerina Papers, Center for Southwest Research, University of New Mexico, Albuquerque.

61. Records of the New Mexico Corporation Commission. The name change is apparently a function of the belief that it would void the permanent injunction.

62. Letter from Colonia Mejicana to Assistant District Attorney E. E. Chavez, October 25, 1966, box 1, folder 5, Alfonso Sanchez Papers, Center for Southwest Research, University of New Mexico, Albuquerque.

63. Exhibit A of December 31, 1965, Petition for Contempt by Alfonso Sanchez, Transcript of Record, Court of Appeals, p. 42, State of New Mexico et al. v. Corporación de Abiquiú, no. 10939.

64. Oropeza, "Heart of Chicano History," 57.

65. Letter from Reies Lopez Tijerina to Corky Gonzalez, March 25, 1967, quoted in Vigil, *Crusade for Justice*, 30.

66. Kosek, "Deep Roots and Long Shadows."

67. Letter from Andrew Brenman, State Department Office of the Legal Advisor, to Ramona Brusseau, New Mexico Governor's Office, May 23, 1968, box 1, folder 6, Alfonso Sanchez Papers, Center for Southwest Research, University of New Mexico, Albuquerque.

68. Letter from Victorino Chavez to Lyndon Johnson, January 3, 1967, box 1, folder 6, Alfonso Sanchez Papers, Center for Southwest Research, University of New Mexico, Albuquerque.

69. United Press International, "Cargo to Confer with Rio Arriba Police Officials," *Albuquerque Journal*, May 23, 1967; Nabokov, *Tijerina and the Courthouse Raid*, 27–28; "Notes," box 1, folder 6, Alfonso Sanchez Papers, Center for Southwest Research, University of New Mexico, Albuquerque.

70. Nabokov, *Tijerina and the Courthouse Raid*, 28.

71. Governor David Cargo, interview with author, October 8, 2009, Santa Fe.

72. Confidential report by Freddie Martínez and Robert Romero, NMSP, box 34, folder 706, Governor David Cargo Papers, NMSRCA, Santa Fe.

73. Nabokov, *Tijerina and the Courthouse Raid*, 31.

74. Confidential report by Freddie Martínez and Robert Romero, NMSRCA.

75. Gardner, *Grito!*, 146.

76. Unpublished memoirs, box 1, folder 6, Alfonso Sanchez Papers, Center for Southwest Research, University of New Mexico, Albuquerque.

77. Ibid., p. 77.

78. Ibid., p. 79.
79. Cargo, interview with author.
80. Gardner, *Grito!*, 139.
81. Memo from Hoover to Albuquerque SAC, June 6, 1967, box 2, folder 15, Reies Tijerina Papers, Center for Southwest Research, University of New Mexico, Albuquerque.
82. Nabokov, *Tijerina and the Courthouse Raid*, 36.
83. Associated Press, "Former Alliance Grant May Try to Take Over Vast Southwest Areas," *Albuquerque Journal*, May 28, 1967.
84. FBI report, May 29, 1967, box 1, folder 6, Alfonso Sanchez Papers, Center for Southwest Research, University of New Mexico, Albuquerque.
85. Report by Fred Martínez, NMSP, June 1, 1967, box 1, folder 8, Alfonso Sanchez Papers, Center for Southwest Research, University of New Mexico, Albuquerque.
86. Transcript of radio address, box 1, folder 8, Alfonso Sanchez Papers, Center for Southwest Research, University of New Mexico, Albuquerque; Gardner, *Grito!*, 150.
87. Gardner, *Grito!*, 151.
88. Ibid., 154.
89. Unpublished memoir, box 1, folder 8, p. 86, Alfonso Sanchez Papers, Center for Southwest Research, University of New Mexico, Albuquerque.
90. Ibid., p. 88.
91. Ibid., p. 91.
92. Gardner, *Grito!*, 5.
93. Ibid., 165.
94. Memo from Hoover to SAC Albuquerque, November 3, 1967, box 2, folder 22, Reies Tijerina Papers, Center for Southwest Research, University of New Mexico, Albuquerque.
95. "Rabble Rouser," box 3, folder 1, Reies Tijerina Papers, Center for Southwest Research, University of New Mexico, Albuquerque.
96. Memo from SAC El Paso to Hoover, October 27, 1967, box 2, folder 23, Reies Tijerina Papers, Center for Southwest Research, University of New Mexico, Albuquerque.
97. Vigil, *Crusade for Justice*.
98. Ibid., 41.
99. Memo from SAC Albuquerque to Hoover, April 26, 1968, box 3, folder 1, Reies Tijerina Papers, Center for Southwest Research, University of New Mexico, Albuquerque.
100. Baltimore SAC memo, box 3, folder 2, Reies Tijerina Papers, Center for Southwest Research, University of New Mexico, Albuquerque.
101. Box 2, folder 22, Reies Tijerina Papers, Center for Southwest Research, University of New Mexico, Albuquerque.
102. Memo from Hoover to SAC Albuquerque, November 15, 1967, box 2, folder

22, Reies Tijerina Papers, Center for Southwest Research, University of New Mexico, Albuquerque.

103. Tijerina, *They Call Me King Tiger*, 127.

104. Memo from SAC Albuquerque to Hoover, January 24, 1969, box 3, folder 17, Reies Tijerina Papers, Center for Southwest Research, University of New Mexico, Albuquerque.

105. U.S. Forest Service intelligence, box 6, folder 3, History of the Forest Service Archive, Center for Southwest Research, University of New Mexico, Albuquerque.

106. Memo from SAC Albuquerque to Hoover, March 17, 1969, box 3, folder 17, Reies Tijerina Papers, Center for Southwest Research, University of New Mexico, Albuquerque.

107. Tijerina, *They Call Me King Tiger*, 105.

108. Memo from SAC Albuquerque to Hoover, May 16, 1969, box 3, folder 17, Reies Tijerina Papers, Center for Southwest Research, University of New Mexico, Albuquerque.

109. Intelligence report from Robert Gilliland to Chief Black, March 11, 1968, box 35, folder 11, Reies Tijerina Papers, Center for Southwest Research, University of New Mexico, Albuquerque.

110. Ibid.

111. Final Report, Church Committee, "The FBIs Covert Action Programs against American Citizens," book 3, Church Committee Archive, AARC.

112. Ebright, *Land Grants and Lawsuits*; Montoya, *Translating Property*.

113. Cover, "Bonds of Constitutional Interpretation."

CHAPTER SIX. *Terrorists and Tourists in Tierra Amarilla*

1. Silén, *We, the Puerto Rican People*, 127.

2. All five shooters were arrested and jailed. FALN communiqués, which came after nearly every bombing, routinely demanded their release. Three received a presidential pardon in 1979. See Torrez and Velázquez, *Puerto Rican Movement*.

3. Mary Breasted, "3-Year Inquiry Threads Together Evidence on FALN Terrorism," *New York Times*, April 17, 1977.

4. Originally spelled "Archuleta," he later changed his last name to "Arechuleta."

5. Sater, *Puerto Rican Terrorists*, 15.

6. Memo enclosure, from SAC, Albuquerque, to Director, FBI, December 31, 1969, FBI file (FOIA 1118360-000, released April 9, 2009), copy in author's possession.

7. Pedro Arechuleta, interview with author, June 10, 2008, Tierra Amarilla.

8. Memo from SAC, Albuquerque, to Director, FBI and Domestic Terrorism Unit, July 17, 1990, FBI File of Pedro Arechuleta (FOIA 118360-000), copy in author's possession.

9. Donner, *Age of Surveillance*, 166.

10. Memo from SAC, Albuquerque, to Director, FBI, October 20, 1975, FBI file of Pedro Arechuleta, (FOIA 1118360–000), copy in author's possession.

11. The FBI claimed that a bomb-sniffing dog reacted positively for dynamite in Cueto's New York apartment but could not confirm the claim through laboratory tests.

12. Breasted, "3-Year Inquiry."

13. Quoted in Nabokov, "'Remember Tierra Amarilla.'" Zapata and Villa were leaders of the Mexican revolution, while Campos was a leading figure in the Puerto Rican independence movement.

14. "FBI Money Offer 'No Bribe,'" *Santa Fe New Mexican*, July 27, 1977.

15. "Raza Official Says FBI Out of Line," *Santa Fe New Mexican*, July 21, 1977. Though subpoenaed Morales was never called to testify by the grand jury.

16. Davenport, "Understanding Covert Repressive Action."

17. Navarro, *La Raza Unida Party*.

18. People's Constitutional Party v. Evans, 491 P.2d 520 (1971).

19. Juan José Peña, interview with author, December 10, 2008, Albuquerque.

20. Ibid.

21. Navarro, *La Raza Unida Party*, 182.

22. Ibid.

23. Peña, interview with author.

24. Ibid.

25. Steve Terrel, "Emilio Naranjo, Rio Arriba County's Longtime Political Boss, Dead at 92," *Santa Fe New Mexican*, November 13, 2008.

26. Quoted in Rosenstock, "Death of a System."

27. Rosenstock, "Death of a System," 4.

28. Quoted in Nabokov, "Remember Tierra Amarilla," 339.

29. Antonio "Ike" DeVargas, interview with author, July 10, 2008, Sevilleta Plaza, New Mexico.

30. Quoted in Nabokov, "Remembering Tierra Amarilla," 338.

31. "Group Opposes Proposed Airport in Chama Area," *Rio Grande Sun*, March 6, 1975.

32. Richard Rosenstock, interview with author, December 20, 2008, Santa Fe.

33. Rosenstock, "Death of a System," n. 16.

34. Wilfredo Vigil, interview with author, January 28, 2009, El Duende, New Mexico.

35. Rosenstock, interview with author.

36. "RA Official Charged by Defendant," *Rio Grande Sun*, August 1, 1974.

37. "Warrants Issued on Informant's Information, Naranjo Testifies" *Rio Grande Sun*, August 22, 1974.

38. "Chama-Tierra Amarilla Airport Hassle Continues," *Rio Grande Sun*, April 10, 1975.

39. Quoted in Nabokov, "Remember Tierra Amarilla," 339; "Chama-Tierra Amarilla Airport Hassle Continues."

40. Rosemary Harvath, "Petition Asks for Deputies Dismissal," *Rio Grande Sun*, June 26, 1975.

41. The search warrant was issued for a search of property of a person named Edward Valdez and listed the possibility of thirty to forty marijuana plants.

42. "Petitions Asking Firing of 5 Deputies," *Rio Grande Sun*, July 7, 1975.

43. Ibid.

44. Bill Mundy served on the airport commission along with a number of realtors, elected officials, and developers. See Susan Scott-Mayer, "Airport Planned near Chama," *Rio Grande Sun*, February 6, 1975.

45. "Chama Meeting Cancelled in Face of Court Order," *Rio Grande Sun*, July 17, 1975.

46. "Airport Board Dropped," *Rio Grande Sun*, August 7, 1975.

47. "FBI Check Underway Of Brutality Claims," *Rio Grande Sun*, September 18, 1975.

48. "RA Sheriff, Deputies Face Brutality Suit," *Rio Grande Sun*, October 9, 1975.

49. "Naranjo Defends Officers," *Rio Grande Sun*, September 18, 1975.

50. "Bar Bombed, Sheriff Mum," *Rio Grande Sun*, November 6, 1975.

51. "Judge Frees Two after Sheriff Raids," *Rio Grande Sun*, November 13, 1975.

52. Ibid.

53. Photo caption, "Viva La Raza!," *Rio Grande Sun*, November 13, 1975.

54. "Judge Frees Two after Sheriff Raids."

55. Ibid.

56. "Rio Arriba Wary, Divided," *Albuquerque Journal*, December 7, 1975.

57. Memo from Dan Devereux to W. H. Ferry, November 12, 1975, Peter Nabokov Papers, Center for Southwest Research, University of New Mexico, Albuquerque.

58. "Rio Arriba Wary, Divided."

59. "La Raza Suit Gets Results," *Rio Grande Sun*, January 15, 1976.

60. "Federal Grand Jury Probe Asked," *Rio Grande Sun*, February 12, 1975.

61. "Naranjo Target of March by La Raza," *Rio Grande Sun*, February 26, 1976.

62. "TA Group Pushing for Grand Jury Study of Naranjo," *Rio Grande Sun*, February 12, 1976.

63. Editorial, *Rio Grande Sun*, March 11, 1976.

64. "Morales Planning $1 Million Suit," *Rio Grande Sun*, July 1, 1976. Despite the levity with which Morales handled the informant charge, other RUP members took the threat more seriously. DeVargas suggested that naming Morales as an informant was not just a "frame-up" but a prelude to more violent action. At a press conference DeVargas promised that if Naranjo's deputies made late-night visits to the houses of RUP members, "they would be treated as thieves and outlaws." See Rosenstock, "Death of a System."

65. "Grand Jury to Hear of Alleged Murder Plans," *Rio Grande Sun*, July 29, 1976. RUP members had been requesting an investigation of Naranjo for more than a year. The U.S. attorney and the New Mexico attorney general had refused. District Attorney Castellano, a Naranjo loyalist whom an Oficina de Ley attorney described as

"a mediocre attorney at best, unburdened by even the most minimal sense of justice and fairplay," routinely responded to calls for Naranjo investigations by launching investigations of RUP (see Rosenstock, "Death of a System", 19). In May 1976 two deputies shot a Rio Arriba man in the back. Castellano tried to indict the victim for resisting arrest. When New Mexico attorney general Toney Anaya launched an investigation of the shooting, Castellano threatened to file "obstruction of justice" charges against the attorney general. See Rosenstock, "Death of a System," 21.

66. "Ex-Deputy Testifies to Previous Marijuana 'Frames,'" *Rio Grande Sun*, December 2, 1976.

67. In addition to retaliation against police brutality, a bomb exploded on the ninth anniversary of the courthouse raid at the home of Marie Louise Quarles, the granddaughter of Thomas Burns. See "House near Chama Bombed," *Santa Fe New Mexican*, June 8, 1976.

68. "Facts Vague about Disturbance in RA," *Santa Fe New Mexican*, April 13, 1976.

69. "Bomb Found under House of RA Sheriff," *Santa Fe New Mexican*, April 6, 1976.

70. "RA Officer's Vehicle Shot at during Patrol," *Santa Fe New Mexican*, June 10, 1976.

71. DeVargas, interview with author; "DeVargas Bond Lowered; Injured Deputy Recovers," *Rio Grande Sun*, September 23, 1976.

72. "DeVargas Posts Bond on Assault Charges," *Rio Grande Sun*, September 30, 1976.

73. Rosenstock, "Death of a System," 38.

74. Steve Herbert, "Police Subculture Reconsidered," *Criminology* 36 (1998): 343–69.

75. Benjamin, "Critique of Violence," 281.

76. Derrida, "Force of Law," 1007.

77. Rosenstock, interview with author.

78. Karen Peterson, "Flores Tells of Claiming Land," *Rio Grande Sun*, May 19, 1988.

79. Exhibit 9, May 1988, Rio Arriba County Tax Notice, Case Record, Vista del Brazos v. Briggs, p. 494.

80. Exhibit 1, May 5, 1988, Affidavit of Amador Flores, Case Record, Vista del Brazos v. Briggs.

81. Motion to Intervene, August 14, 1985, Case Record, Vista del Brazos v. Briggs, p. 72.

82. "Memorandum of Points and Authorities in Support of Motion in Opposition to Corporacion de Abiquiu's Motion for Intervention," Case Record, p. 99.

83. Letter from Bruce Kaufmann to Peter Holzem, October 22, 1985, Transcript of Record, p. 194.

84. Flores claimed later that he never received the order for a rescheduled hearing. In November Holzem claimed that he had sent Flores documents regarding the case but had never received a reply. Summary Judgment, January 12, 1987, Transcript of Record, pp. 249–50.

85. Vista del Brazo v. Briggs, Transcript of Record, p. 310.
86. Order to Show Cause, March 18, 1987, Transcript of Record, p. 276.
87. Requested Findings of Fact, Transcript of Record, p. 632.
88. "Motion to Show Cause Why Defendant Should Not Be Held in Contempt of Court," Transcript of Record, p. 400.
89. Findings of Fact and Conclusions of Law, Transcript of Record, p. 644.
90. *Rio Grande Sun*, March 30, 1987.
91. Pedro Arechuleta, interview with author.
92. Peter Eichstaedt, "Lawyer Carrying Offer to Jailed Land Claimant," *Santa Fe New Mexican*, June 25, 1988.
93. Judy Xanders and Maureen Schein, "Tierra Amarilla Trespass Claim Depends on Legal Ownership," *Rio Grande Sun*, March 30, 1989.
94. Carolyn Hayes, *Tierra o Muerte: Land or Death*, a KBDI-TV production, 1991.
95. Maureen Schein, "Flores Claims Land Victory, Plans Home, Car Purchase," 31 August 1989, *Rio Grande Sun*.
96. Pedro Arechuleta, interview with author.
97. Gregorita Aguilar, interview with author, June 5, 2009, Rutheron, New Mexico.
98. Cruz Aguilar, interview with author, June 5, 2009, Rutheron, New Mexico.
99. Ibid.
100. Photo caption, *Santa Fe New Mexican*, April 27, 1976.
101. Judy Xanders and Maureen Schein, "Tierra Amarilla Trespass Claim Depends on Legal Ownership," *Rio Grande Sun*, March 30, 1989.
102. Memo from Albuquerque Squad 3 (Joint Terrorism Task Force) to Domestic Terrorism Operations Unit, January 28, 2004, Pedro Arechuleta FBI File (FOIA 1118360-001). The report is riddled with inaccuracies and based on an earlier report in which agents tried, almost comically, to come up with a tactical definition of Aztlan, a term generally understood as referring to the mythical Aztec homeland that Chicano activists in the 1960s valorized as a way to map a pre-Columbian heritage onto more recent political boundaries. Evocations of Aztlan became a powerful way for Chicano activists to claim the U.S. Southwest as the homeland of a Chicano nation. For Tijerina, for example, Aztlan was the geographical homeland to Indo-Hispanos, a new race "born when the East and the West were joined." See Tijerina, *They Called me King Tiger*, 35. The FBI misconstrued the language of Aztlan as Mexican nationalist rhetoric that they thought linked Chicano activists to Mexican separatist groups. And it didn't help that FBI agents were woefully ignorant about Mexican history or contemporary Mexican politics. In an earlier memo a Denver FBI agent explained the significance of a sign depicting Mexican revolutionary Emiliano Zapata in Tierra Amarilla as actual, material proof of a link to the Zapatista movement in Mexico, which the agent erroneously claimed "took over the Mexican government and reclaimed the lands of Mexico for the indigenous people," an assertion that, presumably, should have been easy for the agent to fact check. Memo from FBI Denver to (SAC) Albuquerque, January 13, 2004, Pedro Arechuleta FBI file (FOIA 1118360-001).

EPILOGUE. *Rare Earth*

1. Blomley, "Law, Property," 123.
2. Ferguson, *Anti-Politics Machine*.
3. Scott, *Seeing like a State*.
4. Morris, *Dependency Study of Northern New Mexico*, 1–2.
5. Ibid., 32–33.
6. See Correia, "From Agropastoralism."
7. Morris, *Dependency Study*, 36.
8. See Correia, "Sustained Yield Forest Management."
9. Goldstein, *Poverty in Common*.
10. Escobar, *Encountering Development*.
11. Escobar, "Planning," 132.
12. Harvey, *Social Justice and the City*, 100.
13. Statement of Levi Pesata, President of the Jicarilla Apache Nation, February 16, 2012, Senate Committee on Indian Affairs, Oversight Hearing on Indian Energy Issues.
14. Nordhaus, Hall, and Rudio, "Revisiting Merrion v. Jicarilla Apache Tribe."
15. On September 13, 1988, the secretary of the BIA issued a proclamation formally adding the El Poso Ranch and Horse Lake Ranch parcels to the reservation pursuant to federal law that allowed a federally recognized tribe to purchase land adjacent to the reservation and petition to have that land attached to the reservation. See *Proclamation of Certain Lands as Part of the Jicarilla Apache Reservation*, 53 Fed. Reg. 37355-02 (Sept. 26, 1988).
16. Phill Casaus, "Jicarilla Indians Expand Their Reservation," *High Country News*, May 16, 1994.
17. The following year the tribe established the Jicarilla Apache Energy Corporation (JAECO) and took over older well leases on the reservation. Also the oil and gas administration of the Jicarilla Apache Nation continued to receive royalties and severance taxes for the nearly 2,200 oil and gas wells on Jicarilla lands, 132 active leases, and 10 mineral development agreements on nearly 377,000 acres.
18. "Jicarilla Apache Nation 2012–13 Non-tribal member Hunting Proclamation," available at http://www.jicarillahunt.com, accessed March 15, 2012.

BIBLIOGRAPHY

Alexander, Charles. *The Ku Klux Klan in the Southwest*. Norman: University of Oklahoma Press, 1995.
Arellano, Anselmo. "Through Thick and Thin: Evolutionary Transitions of Las Vegas Grandes and Its Pobladores." PhD diss., University of New Mexico, 1990.
Arneil, Barbara. *John Locke and America: The Defence of English Colonialism*. Oxford: Clarendon Press; New York: Oxford University Press, 1996.
Arny, William F. M. *Interesting Items regarding New Mexico: Its Agricultural, Pastoral and Mineral Resources, People, Climate, Soil, Scenery, Etc*. Findlay, Ohio: Hubbard Press, 2008.
Athearn, Robert. *Rebel of the Rockies: A History of the Denver and Rio Grande Western Railroad*. New Haven, Conn.: Yale University Press, 1962.
Bailey, Lynn. *Indian Slave Trade in the Southwest*. Los Angeles: Westernlore Press 1973.
Barrett, James, and David Roediger. "Inbetween Peoples: Race, Nationality and the 'New Immigrant' Working Class." *Journal of American Ethnic History* 16 (1997): 3–44.
Baxter, John. *Las Carneradas: Sheep Trade in New Mexico, 1700–1860*. Albuquerque: University of New Mexico Press, 1987.
Bender, Norman. "The Battle of Tierra Amarilla." *New Mexico Historical Review* 63 (1988): 241–56.
Benjamin, Walter. "A Critique of Violence." In *Reflections: Essays, Aphorisms, Autobiographical Writings*, edited by Peter Demetz, 277–300. New York: Schocken Books, 2007.
Blackhawk, Ned. *Violence over the Land: Indians and Empires in the Early American West*. Cambridge, Mass.: Harvard University Press, 2008.
Blomley, Nicholas. "Law, Property, and the Spaces of Violence: The Frontier, the Survey, and the Grid." *Annals of the Association of American Geographers* 93 (2003): 121–41.
———. *Law, Space, and the Geographies of Power*. New York: Guildford Press, 1994.
———. "Simplification Is Complicated: Property, Nature, and the Rivers of Law." *Environment and Planning A* 40 (2008): 1825–42.
———. *Unsettling the City: Urban Land and the Politics of Property*. New York: Routledge, 2004.
Bowden, J. J. "Private Land Claims of the Southwest." MA thesis, Southern Methodist University, 1969.

Briggs, Susan, Charles Briggs, and John Van Ness, eds. *Land, Water, and Culture: New Perspectives on Hispanic Land Grants*. Albuquerque: University of New Mexico Press, 1987.

Brooks, James. *Captives and Cousins: Slavery, Kinship, and Community in the Southwest Borderlands*. Chapel Hill: University of North Carolina Press, 2001.

Chalmers, David. *Hooded Americanism: The History of the Ku Klux Klan*. Durham, N.C.: Duke University Press 1987.

Charles, Ralph. "Development of the New Mexico Sheep Industry." MA thesis, University of New Mexico, 1940.

Correia, David. "From Agropastoralism to Sustained Yield Forestry: Industrial Restructuring Rural Change and the Land Grant Commons in Northern New Mexico." *Capitalism Nature Socialism* 16 (2005): 25–44.

———. "Making Destiny Manifest: United States Territorial Expansion and the Dispossession of Two Mexican Property Claims in New Mexico, 1824–1899." *Journal of Historical Geography* 35 (2009): 87–103.

———. "'Retribution Will Be Their Reward': New Mexico's Las Gorras Blancas and the Fight for the Las Vegas Land Grant Commons." *Radical History Review* 108 (2010): 49–72.

———. "The Sustained Yield Forest Management Act and the Roots of Environmental Conflict in Northern New Mexico." *Geoforum* 38 (2007): 1040–51.

———. "Taking Timber, Earth, and Water: The Denver and Rio Grande Railroad and the Struggle for New Mexico's Land Grants." *Natural Resources Journal* 48 (2008): 949–62.

Cover, Robert. "The Bonds of Constitutional Interpretation: Of the Word, the Deed, and the Role." *Georgia Law Review* 20 (1986): 818–19.

———. "Violence and the Word." *Yale Law Journal* 95 (1986): 1601–29.

Cunningham, David, and Barb Browning. "The Emergence of Worthy Targets: Official Frames and Deviance Narratives within the FBI." *Sociological Forum* 19 (2004): 347–69.

Davenport, Christian. "Understanding Covert Repressive Action: The Case of the U.S. Government against the Republic of New Africa." *Journal of Conflict Resolution* 49 (2005): 120–40.

Delaney, David. *Law and Nature*. New York: Cambridge University Press, 2003.

———. *The Spatial, the Legal and the Pragmatics of World-Making: Nomospheric Investigations*. New York: Routledge, 2011.

DeLay, Brian. *War of a Thousand Deserts: Indian Raids and the U.S.-Mexican War*. New Haven: Yale University Press, 2009.

Derrida, Jacques. "Force of Law: The Mystical Foundation of Authority." *Cardozo Law Review*, 11 (1989–1990): 920–1045.

Deutsch, Sarah. "Labor, Land, and Protest since Statehood." In *Telling New Mexico: A New History*, edited by Marta Weigle, 269–84. Albuquerque: Museum of New Mexico Press, 2009.

———. *No Separate Refuge: Culture, Class, and Gender on an Anglo-Hispanic Frontier in the American Southwest, 1880–1940*. New York: Oxford University Press, 1989.

Donner, Frank. *The Age of Surveillance: The Aims and Methods of America's Political Intelligence System*. New York: Alfred Knopf, 1980.

Duran, Tobias. "Francisco Chavez, Thomas B. Catron, and Organized Political Violence in Santa Fe in the 1890s." *New Mexico Historical Review* 59 (1984): 291–310.

Ebright, Malcolm. *Land Grants and Lawsuits in Northern New Mexico*. Albuquerque: University of New Mexico Press, 1993.

———, ed. *Spanish and Mexican Land Grants and the Law*. Santa Fe: Sunflower Press, 1989.

———. *The Tierra Amarilla Grant: A History of Chicanery*. Guadalupita, N.M.: Center for Land Grant Studies, 1993.

Ebright, Malcolm, and Rick Hendricks. *The Witches of Abiquiu: The Governor, the Priest, the Genízaro Indians, and the Devil*. Albuquerque: University of New Mexico Press, 2006.

Edgel, Ralph. *A Brief History of Banking in New Mexico, 1870–1959*. Business Information Series 39. Albuquerque: University of New Mexico, Bureau of Business Research, 1962.

Escobar, Arturo. *Encountering Development: The Making and Unmaking of the Third World*. Princeton, N.J.: Princeton University Press, 1994.

———. "Planning." In *The Development Dictionary: A Guide to Knowledge as Power*, edited by Wolfgang Sachs, 132–45. New York: Zed Books, 1995.

Esenwein, George. *Anarchist Ideology and the Working-Class Movement in Spain, 1868–1898*. Berkeley: University of California Press, 1989.

Ferguson, James. *Anti-Politics Machine: Development, Depoliticization, and Bureaucratic Power in Lesotho*. Minneapolis: University of Minnesota Press, 1994.

Fisher, John. *A Builder of the West: The Life of General William Jackson Palmer*. Caldwell, Idaho: Claxton Printers, 1939.

Forrest, Suzanne. *The Preservation of the Village: New Mexico's Hispanics and the New Deal*. Albuquerque: University of New Mexico Press, 1998.

Frank, Ross. *From Settler to Citizen: New Mexican Economic Development and the Creation of Vecino Society, 1750–1820*. Berkeley: University of California Press, 2001.

Frost, Max, ed. *New Mexico: Its Resources, Climate, Geography and Geological Condition*. Report of the Bureau of Immigration. Santa Fe, 1888.

Gardner, Richard. *Grito! Reies Tijerina and the New Mexico Land Grant War of 1967*. New York: Harper Colophon, 1971.

Goldberg, Robert. "Denver: Queen City of the Colorado Realm." In Lay, *Invisible Empire in the West*, 39–49.

———. *Hooded Empire: The Ku Klux Klan in Colorado*. Champagne: University of Illinois Press, 1982.

Goldstein, Alyosha. *Poverty in Common: The Politics of Community Action during the American Century*. Durham, N.C.: Duke University Press, 2012.

Golten, Ryan. "Lobato v. Taylor: How the Villages of the Rio Culebra, the Colorado Supreme Court, and the Restatement of Servitudes Bailed Out the Treaty of Guadalupe Hidalgo." *Natural Resources Journal* 45 (2005): 457–94.

Gomez, Laura. *Manifest Destinies: The Making of the Mexican American Race.* New York: New York University Press, 2007.

Gonzalez, Phillip. "Struggle for Survival: The Hispanic Land Grants of New Mexico, 1848–2001." *Agricultural History* 77 (2003): 293–324.

Hale, Charles. *Mexican Liberalism in the Age of Mora, 1821–1853.* New Haven, Conn.: Yale University Press, 1968.

Hall, Emlen G. *Four Leagues of Pecos: A Legal History of the Pecos Grant, 1800–1933.* Albuquerque: University of New Mexico Press, 1984.

Hämäläinen, Pekka. *The Comanche Empire.* New Haven, Conn.: Yale University Press, 2008.

Harris, Cheryl. "Whiteness as Property." *Harvard Law Review* 106 (1993): 1707–91.

Harvey, David. *Social Justice and the City.* London: Edward Arnold, 1973.

Herbert, Steve. "Police Subculture Reconsidered." *Criminology* 36 (1998): 343–69.

Hernandez, Andrew. "The Indian Slave Trade in New Mexico: Escalating Conflicts and the Limits of State Power." PhD diss., University of New Mexico, 2003.

Hurt, Douglas, R. *The Indian Frontier, 1763–1846.* Albuquerque: University of New Mexico Press, 2002.

Huyler, Jerome. *Locke in America: The Moral Philosophy of the Founding Era.* Lawrence: University of Kansas Press, 1995.

Jackson, Kenneth. *The Ku Klux Klan in the City, 1915–1930.* New York: Oxford University Press, 1967.

Jefferson, James, Robert W. Delaney, and Gregory C. Thompson. *The Southern Utes: A Tribal History.* Salt Lake City: Southern Ute Tribe, 1972.

John, Elizabeth. *Storms Brewed in Other Men's Worlds: The Confrontation of Indians, Spanish, and French in the Southwest, 1540–1795.* Oklahoma City: University of Oklahoma Press 1996.

Julian, George. "Land Stealing in New Mexico." *North American Review* 145 (1887): 17–31.

King, Mary. "Keeping People in Their Place: An Exploratory Analysis of the Role of Violence in the Maintenance of 'Property Rights' in Race and Gender Privileges in the United States." *Review of Radical Political Economics* 31 (1999): 1–11.

Knowlton, Clark. "Patron-Peon Pattern among the Spanish Americans of New Mexico." *Social Forces* 41 (1962): 12–17.

Kosek, Jake. "Deep Roots and Long Shadows." *Environment and Planning D: Society and Space* 22 (2004): 329–54.

Lamar, Howard. *The Far Southwest, 1846–1912: A Territorial History.* Albuquerque: University of New Mexico Press, 2000.

Lay, Shawn. "Imperial Outpost on the Border: El Paso's Frontier Klan no. 100." In Lay, *Invisible Empire in the West,* 67–96.

———, ed. *The Invisible Empire in the West: Toward a New Historical Appraisal of the Ku Klux Klan of the 1920s*. Champagne: University of Illinois Press, 1992.

———. *War, Revolution, and the Ku Klux Klan: A Study of Intolerance in a Border City*. El Paso: Texas Western Press, 1985.

Lida, Clara. "Agrarian Anarchism in Andalusia." *International Review of Social History* 14 (1969): 315–52.

Locke, John. *The Second Treatise of Government*. 1690. Indianapolis: Bobbs-Merrill Company, 1976.

MacLean, Nancy. *Behind the Mask of Chivalry: The Making of the Second Ku Klux Klan*. New York: Oxford University Press, 1994.

MacPherson, C. B. *Property: Mainstream and Critical Positions*. Toronto: University of Toronto Press, 1999.

McKnight, Joseph. "Law Books on the Hispanic Frontier." *Journal of the West* 27 (1988): 74–84.

McVeigh, Rory. "Power Devaluation, the Ku Klux Klan, and the Democratic National Convention of 1924." *Sociological Forum* 16 (2001): 1–30.

———. "Structural Incentives for Conservative Mobilization: Power Devaluation and the Rise of the Ku Klux Klan, 1915–1925." *Structural Forces* 77 (1999): 1461–96.

Melzer, Richard. "Exiled in the Desert: The Bisbee Deportees' Reception in New Mexico, 1917." *New Mexico Historical Review* 67 (1992): 269–84.

Menchaga, Martha. "The Anti-Miscegenation History of the American Southwest, 1837 to 1970: Transforming Racial Ideology into Law." *Cultural Dynamics* 20 (2008): 279–318.

Mitchell, Timothy. *Rule of Experts: Egypt, Techno-politics, Modernity*. Berkeley: University of California Press, 2002.

Montgomery, Charles. *The Spanish Redemption: Heritage, Power, and Loss on New Mexico's Upper Rio Grande*. Berkeley: University of California Press, 2003.

Montoya, Maria. *Translating Property: The Maxwell Land Grant and the Conflict over Land in the American West, 1840–1900*. Berkeley: University of California Press, 2002.

Moore, Leonard. "Historical Interpretations of the 1920s Klan: The Traditional View and Recent Revision." In Lay, *Invisible Empire in the West*, 17–38.

Morris, Roger. *A Dependency Study of Northern New Mexico*. Taos, N.M.: United States Forest Service, 1935.

Murphy, Lawrence. *Frontier Crusader: William F. M. Arny*. Tucson: University of Arizona Press, 1972.

———, ed. *Indian Agent in New Mexico: The Journal of Special Agent WFM Arny, 1870*. Santa Fe: Stagecoach Press, 1967.

Myrick, David. *New Mexico's Railroads: An Historical Survey*. Albuquerque: University of New Mexico Press, 1990.

Nabokov, Peter. "'Remember Tierra Amarilla': Chicano Power in the Feudal West." *Nation*, October 8, 1977, 336–40.

———. *Tijerina and the Courthouse Raid.* Berkeley, Calif.: Ramparts Press, 1969.
Navarro, Armando. *La Raza Unida Party: A Chicano Challenge to the U.S. Two-Party Dictatorship.* Philadelphia: Temple University Press, 2000.
Nieto-Philips, John. *The Language of Blood: The Making of Spanish-American Identity in New Mexico, 1880s–1930s.* Albuquerque: University of New Mexico Press, 2004.
———. "Spanish-American Ethnic Identity and New Mexico's Statehood Struggle." In *The Contested Homeland: A Chicano History of New Mexico*, edited by Erlinda Gonzales-Berry and David Maciel, 97–142. Albuquerque: University of New Mexico Press, 2000.
Nordhaus, G., Em Hall, and Anne Alise Rudio. "Revisiting Merrion v. Jicarilla Apache Tribe: Robert Nordhaus and Sovereign Indian Control over Natural Resources on Reservations." *Natural Resources Journal* 43 (2003): 224–84.
Oropeza, Lorena. "The Heart of Chicano History: Reies Lopez Tijerina as a Memory Entrepreneur." *Sixties* 1 (2008): 49–67.
Parish, William. *The Charles Ilfeld Company: A Study of the Rise and Decline of Mercantile Capitalism in New Mexico.* Cambridge, Mass.: Harvard University Press, 1961.
Robbins, William G. *Colony and Empire: The Capitalist Transformation of the American West.* Lawrence: University Press of Kansas, 1994.
Rose, Carol. "Possession as the Origin of Property. *University of Chicago Law Review* 52 (1985): 73–88.
Rosenbaum, Robert. *Mexicano Resistance in the Southwest: "The Sacred Right of Self-Preservation."* Austin: University of Texas Press, 1981.
Rosenstock, Richard. "Death of a System." MS. 1978. Author's files.
Sater, William. *Puerto Rican Terrorists: A Possible Threat to U.S. Energy Installations?* Report prepared for Sandia Laboratories by the Rand Corporation, 1981.
Schlesinger, Andrew. "Las Gorras Blancas, 1889–1891." *Journal of Mexican American History* 1 (1971): 87–143.
Schweikart, Larry. "Early Banking in New Mexico from the Civil War to the Roaring Twenties." *New Mexico Historical Review* 63 (1988): 1–25.
Scott, James. *Seeing like a State: How Certain Schemes to Improve the Human Condition Have Failed.* New Haven, Conn.: Yale University Press, 1999.
Seligman, G. L. "The El Paso and Northeastern Railroad's Economic Impact on Central New Mexico." *New Mexico Historical Review* 61 (1986): 217–31.
Silén, Juan Angel. *We, the Puerto Rican People: A Story of Oppression and Resistance.* New York: Monthly Review Press, 1971.
Simmons, Marc. *The Last Conquistador: Juan de Oñate and the Settling of the Far Southwest.* Oklahoma City: University of Oklahoma Press, 1991.
Spence, Clark. "British Investment and the American Mining Frontier." *New Mexico Historical Review* 36 (1961): 121–37.
———. "When the Pound Sterling Went West: British Investments and the American Mineral Frontier." *Journal of Economic History* 16 (1956): 482–92.

Sunseri, Alvin. *Seeds of Discord; New Mexico in the Aftermath of the American Conquest, 1846–1861.* Chicago: Neslon-Hall, 1979.

Swadesh, Frances Leon. *Los Primeros Pobladores: Hispanic Americans of the Ute Frontier.* South Bend, Ind.: University of Notre Dame Press, 1974.

Thompson, E. P. *Customs in Common: Studies in Traditional Popular Culture.* New York: New Press, 1991.

Tijerina, Reies Lopez. *They Called Me King Tiger: My Struggle for the Land and Our Rights.* Houston: Arte Publico Press, 2000.

Tilly, Charles. *The Politics of Collective Violence.* New York: Cambridge University Press, 2003.

Tórrez, Andrés, and José Emiliano Velázquez. *The Puerto Rican Movement: Voices from the Diaspora.* Philadelphia: Temple University Press, 1998.

Tórrez, Robert. "El Bornes: La Tierra Amarilla and T. D. Burns." *New Mexico Historical Review* 56 (1981): 161–75.

———. "El Campo: Forgotten Sentinel of the Tierra Amarilla." MA, New Mexico Highlands University, 1973.

———. "The Jacal in the Tierra Amarilla." *El Palacio* 85 (1979): 14–18.

———. *La Mano Negra.* Center for Land Grant Studies Research Paper no. 46. Guadalupita, N.M.: Center for Land Grant Studies, 1994.

———. "Park View: A Chicago Agricultural Colony in Northern New Mexico." *New Mexico Historical Review* 76 (2001): 175–88.

———. "The Southern Ute Agency at Abiquiu and Tierra Amarilla, New Mexico." Working paper, Center for Land Grant Studies, 1994.

Uria, Jorge. "The Myth of the Peaceable Peasant in Northern Spain: Asturias, 1898–1914." *International Labor and Working-Class History* 67 (2005): 100–124.

Van Ness, John. "Hispanic Land Grants: Ecology and Subsistence in the Uplands of Northern New Mexico and Southern Colorado." In *Land, Water, and Culture: New Perspectives on Hispanic Land Grants*, edited by Susan Briggs, Charles Briggs, and John Van Ness, 141–214. Albuquerque: University of New Mexico Press, 1987.

Van Ness, John, and Christine Van Ness, eds. *Spanish and Mexican Land Grants in New Mexico and Colorado.* Santa Fe: Center for Land Grant Studies, 1980.

Vargas, Zaragosa. *Labor Rights Are Civil Rights: Mexican American Workers in Twentieth-Century America.* Princeton, N.J.: Princeton University Press, 2007.

Vigil, Ernesto. *The Crusade for Justice: Chicano Militancy and the Government's War on Dissent.* Madison: University of Wisconsin Press, 1999.

Wade, Wyn Craig. *The Fiery Cross: The Ku Klux Klan in America.* New York: Simon & Schuster, 1987.

Warner, Louis. "Conveyance of Property, the Spanish and Mexican Way." *New Mexico Historical Review* 6 (1931): 334–59.

———. "Wills and Hijuelas." *New Mexico Historical Review* 7 (1932): 75–89.

Weber, David. *The Mexican Frontier, 1821–1846: The American Southwest under Mexico.* Albuquerque: University of New Mexico Press, 1982.

Weigle, Marta. "Sharecropping with Sheep." In *Hispanic Villages of Northern New Mexico*, edited by Marta Weigle, vol. 2 of *Tewa Basin Study*. Santa Fe: Lightening Tree Press, 1975. Reprint of the 1935 *Tewa Basin Study*.

Westphall, Victor. *Mercedes Reales: Hispanic Land Grants of the Upper Rio Grande Region*. Albuquerque: University of New Mexico Press, 1984.

———. *The Public Domain in New Mexico, 1854–1891*. Albuquerque: University of New Mexico Press, 1965.

———. *Thomas Benton Catron and His Era*. Tucson: University of Arizona Press, 1973.

Wilcox, Michael. *The Pueblo Revolt and the Mythology of Conquest: An Indigenous Archaeology of Contact*. Berkeley: University of California Press, 2009.

Will de Chaparro, Martina. *Death and Dying in New Mexico*. Albuquerque: University of New Mexico Press, 2007.

Wilson, Chris, and David Kammer. *La Tierra Amarilla: Its History, Architecture, and Cultural Landscape*. Albuquerque: Museum of New Mexico Press, 1992.

Winther, Oscar. "Promoting the American West in England, 1856–1890." *Journal of Economic History* 16 (1956): 506–13.

INDEX

Abernathy, Ralph, 3
Abeyta, Medardo, 84–102, 108, 117, 192n17
Abiquiú: abandonment of, 19; Genízaro settlement of, 19; population of, 21; raid of, 18; settlers from, 24–27; as site of conflict, 16, 17, 42, 43
Abreu, Santiago, 22, 182n33
ACLU (American Civil Liberties Union), 155, 161
Acoma, siege of, 15
Acuña, Rudolfo, 152
Aguilar, Cruz, 164
Aguilar, Daniel, 162, 163
Aguilar, Gregorita, 155, 164
Alianza Federal de Mercedes: activism of, 1, 5, 174; Albuquerque to Santa Fe march of, 132; arming of, 135, 136; attacks against, 143–44; communist influence of, 131; constituency of, 2; Echo Amphitheater occupation by, 133, 134; implication of, 4; origins of, 124; surveillance of, 3, 14, 128–31
Allen, Charles, 97
American Civil Liberties Union (ACLU), 155, 161
American Nazi Party, 142
Apaches, Jicarilla, 1, 8, 12, 18, 32, 33, 40–46; land acquisition by, 177–80
Archuleta, Manuel, 151
Arechuleta, Pedro, 147–66
Arlington Land Company, 67, 68, 95
Armstrong, John, 45, 46
Arny, William F. M., 41–46
Arson, as resistance, 69–71, 113, 114, 124, 126, 134

Atkinson, Henry, 53, 64, 65, 187n77
Aztlan, 205n102

Banking, in New Mexico, 58, 59
Becker, George, 68–71
Benjamin, Walter, 10, 11, 158
Bigbee, Harry, 102–19, 126, 195n91
Biggs, Edgar, 63
Black, Joe, 137, 140
Black Hand, 13, 69–76, 190n31
Blackhawk, Ned, 11, 17
Blackmore, William, 54
Blomley, Nicholas, 6, 7, 173
Brazos, 19, 164, 171
Brevoort, Elias, 40, 64, 187n77
Brusselbach, Karl, 95–102, 105, 108
Bureau of Indian Affairs, 178
Burger, Warren, 2
Burns, Thomas, 47–50; speculation tactics of, 60–68

Cachupín, Tomás Vélez, policies of, 16–19
Campbell, Jack, 132, 135
Canyon Ridge, 168–72
Capital (finance): British, 58, 59; as racialized, 81
Cargo, David, 135–40
Carmichael, Stokely, 3, 142
Carmody, David, 108–17, 195n83
Catron, Charles, 67
Catron, Thomas Benton, 40, 70, 84, 90, 110, 120; speculation tactics of, 48–68, 188n80
Central Intelligence Agency (CIA), 3, 131

215

Chama Land and Cattle Company Ranch, 124, 180
Chavez, Amado, 55–57
Chavez, Dennis, 85
Chavez, José María, 21, 182n29
Chavez, Victorino, 133
Chicano/a movement, 3
Church Committee Report, 144
CIA (Central Intelligence Agency), 3, 131
Citizen's Committee to Investigate the FBI, 144
Class, 19, 73–78, 82
Cleveland, Grover, 59
Clínica del Pueblo de Río Arriba, 153
COINTELPRO (Counter Intelligence Program), 129, 150; exposed, 144–45; in New Mexico, 128–31; and violence, 129
Colonia Mejicana, 131
Color of title, 87–119
Comancheros del Norte, 148
Comanches, 1, 16, 18; raids of, 17
Comandos Armados de Liberación, 146
COMINFIL (Communist Infiltration of the Civil Rights Movement), 130, 131, 150
Comite Pro-Mercedes por la Corona Español, 129, 130
Confederación de Pueblos Libres, 135
Consejo de la Tierra Amarilla, 14, 150, 159–66
Cooperación del Pueblo, 153
Cooperativa Agricola, 153
Corporación de Abiquiú, 13, 120–22, 159, 165; civil lawsuits against, 127; as Colonia Mejicana, 131–33; elected assembly of, 23; establishment of, 85, 192n3; eviction orders of, 125–26; injunction against, 128, 131; surveillance of, 14; tactics of, 86–119, 125, 194n46
Courthouse raid, 2, 13, 14; account of, 136–40; significance of, 4
Cover, Robert, 9, 10

Cruzada por Justicia, 142
Cueto, Maria, 149

De Leon, Daniel, 151
DeVargas, Antonio "Ike," 152–58
Development: logic of, 12, 14, 41, 173; and underdevelopment, 173–75
Dispossession (land grant): as event versus as struggle, 4–9, 13; and law, 84–119; and law's violence, 11; patterns of, 1, 14, 28, 47–68; resistance to, 8, 13, 29, 69–83
Dominguez, Fray Atanasio, 15; and Dominguez-Escalante Expedition, 15–20
Dominguez-Escalante Expedition, 15–20; failure of, 20

Ebright, Malcolm, 4, 5, 29
Ellison, Samuel, 54–57
Escobar, Arturo, 175

FALN (Fuerzas Armads de Liberación Nacional), 146
Federal Bureau of Investigation (FBI), 3, 14, 126; ADEX list, 148; as agents of socio-spatial control, 121; and courthouse raid, 140; Domestic Terrorism Unit of, 148, 205n102; illegal activities of, 144, 145; investigations by, of Alianza, 128–31; investigations by, of La Raza Unida in New Mexico, 151, 152; investigations by, of land grant activists as terrorists, 147–49, 166; racialized tactics of, 129–31, 143; surveillance of Tijerina by, 140–45; use of undercover agents by, 130
Fellion, Tiny, 143
Fence cutting, 9, 13, 68–71, 82, 113–14, 124
Fiske, Eugene, 64–66
Flores, Amador, 14, 159–66
Flores, Rafael, 95, 99, 159
Flores, Roque, 95–101, 159

Flores v. Brusselbach, 94–101, 118, 159
Foreign Agents Registration Act, 130, 131
Forest Service, U.S.: dispossession by, 95, 173–75; opposition to, 1
Frente Internacional de Humanos Derechos, 131
Frost, Max, 53
Fuerzas Armads de Liberación Nacional (FALN), 146

Gallegos, Manuel, 114
Gardner, Richard, 75, 86
General Land Office, 52–55, 64, 65; investigation by, 59
Genízaros, 19–21
Gente Unida Para El Progreso Controlado, 153
GI Forum, 122
Gonzales, Corky, 132, 142
Gorras Blancas, 74, 75, 181n4, 190n20
Great Western Sugar Company, 81
Griffith, D. W., 78
Guadalupe Hidalgo, Treaty of (1848), 6, 28, 37, 50, 51, 183n4

Hall, H. L., 68–70
Hatch, Carl, 103–5
Heirs, land grant: claims by, 14; conflict of, with law enforcement, 9; Las Vegas, 74, 75; legal tactics of, 5, 8–13, 84–119; as migrants, 81; rejection of, 60; removal of, 66; speculation by, 65; as squatters, 67, 71; tactics against, 29, 53; as terrorists, 145, 163, 166; and Tijerina, 2, 123–44; as trespassers, 99, 121
Heirs of Manuel Martinez (organization), 165
Heron, Kenneth, 70–72, 75
Herrera, Herquilano, 95–97
Herrera, Steve, 160, 161
Hijuelas, 37–39, 62–66, 84, 85, 91, 100, 104; legal effects of, 110–17

Hispanic Affairs Commission, 148
HND Land Company v. Suazo, 88–94, 118, 178, 192n15
Holzem, Peter, 160–63, 204n84
Homestead Act (1862), 49, 51
Hoover, J. Edgar, 3, 126–31, 136, 140; and John Birch Society, 142, 143
Horse Lake Ranch, 178
Howard, George Hill, 56

Indian Affairs Bureau, 7, 41–46
Indian Agents, 41–46; as mining boosters, 43
Indian nations: captivity of, 17; equestrian power of, 16; federal policy on, 42–46; removal of, 7, 8, 12, 40–46
Isaacs, John, 65

Jacales, 20
Jackson, Jesse, 3, 164
Jenkins, Myra, 132
John Birch Society, 142–44
Johnson, Lyndon, 133
Julian, George, W., 52, 59, 60

Kauffman, Bruce, 159, 160–63
Kearney, Steven, 27
Kennedy, Robert, 125
Kinderman, William, 95, 193n35
King, Martin Luther, Jr., 3
Klan, Ku Klux, 73–83, 190n20, 191n74
Klesko, Ryan, 167–71

La Follette, Robert Hoath, 90–94, 104, 178
Land grants: adjudication of, 3, 6, 31; and ceremonies of possession, 25, 26; and common property, 1, 3, 34–37, 105–18; *expediente* for, 22–24; heirs of, 2; heirs of, as terrorists, 149, 150; historiography of, 4; loss of, 1, 4; and Piedra Lumbre, 56; rationale for, 1, 26; speculation of, 2–5, 12, 13, 47–68

Land Title Study, 3
Larrazolo, Octaviano, 69, 70
Law: Anglo, 5; common, 87; and land grants, 5–9, 84–119; repression of, 3, 9; as struggle, 7, 13, 76; and violence, 6, 9–11, 145, 158, 166
Locke, John, 31–35
Locke, John Galen, 79
Los Alamos National Laboratory, 134
Lumber (industry), 63–67

Mabry, Thomas, 93, 94
MacPherson, C. B., 34, 35
Maez, Wilbert, 160
Mano Negra, 13, 69–76, 190n31
Manos muertas (*mortmain*), 92–94, 118
Manzanares, Francisco, 110–13
Marshall, Thurgood, 178
Martínez, Danny, 166
Martínez, Eusebio, 66
Martínez, Felix, 135; arrest of, 137
Martínez, Fernanda, 154
Martínez, Francisco, 30, 32, 37–40, 65, 90–92, 98–103, 110–13, 120
Martínez, José María, 106–17, 128, 134; arrest of, 137, 138
Martínez, José Remigio, 114
Martínez, Juan, 123, 134; arrest of, 137
Martínez, Lionel, 114
Martínez, Manuel, 21, 36, 37, 64, 65, 90, 91, 99, 125
Martínez, Sesto, 66
Martínez v. Mundy, 105–18
Martínez v. Rivera, 101–5
Martínez y Lopez, Juan, 99
McBroom, William, 53
McManus, John, 117–19
Medina, Benny, 155
Mercantilism, 60–67
Mercure, Henry, 39, 40
Merrion v. Jicarilla Apache Tribe, 178
Mexico: colonial expansion of, 1; independence of, 20; property law of, 20, 22, 36, 37; Ute relations with, 24
Monero Coal and Coke Company, 58
Montoya, Alcario, 69
Montoya, Maria, 5, 8, 30
Morales, Moises, 147–58, 164
Morris, Roger, 173
Movement: Chicano/a, 3; civil rights, 4; property rights, 5; Puerto Rican independence, 146–47
Movement for the Territorial Reintegration of Mexico (MTRM), 131
Movimiento de Independencia Revolucionario, 146
Movimiento de Liberación Nacional, 148
Muhammad, Elijah, 3, 140
Muller, Frederick, 65
Mundy, Bill, 105–17, 126, 127, 134, 168
Mundy, Jim, 168, 172, 175, 176, 177

Naranjo, Benny, 138, 139
Naranjo, Emilio, 152–58
Nativism, 78–83
Navajos, 1, 16; raids of, 17
Neblett, Colin, 99–101
Night riders, 68–76, 82, 109

Oficina de Ley, 153
Oñate, Juan, 15

Pacheco, M. C., 97
Palmer, William Jackson, 57, 58
Parish, William, 187n64
Parkview, 64
Partido, 60–64
Patronage, 152; and Emilio Naranjo, 152–58
Pelham, William, 37
Peña, Juan José, 151
Peñasco Amarilla Ski Corporation, 159
Peonage (debt), 60–64
Petaca, 25, 26; legal claims to, 54

Planning: logic of, 14, 173–76; politics of, 173
Plant, Mike, 167–76
Police: brutality, 151; political nature of, 158; and violence, 150, 154–58; violence directed at, 157
Poor People's Campaign, 3
Prince, L. Bradford, 34, 52, 55
Property: common versus private, 5, 7, 29–37, 84–119; enforcement of, 121–45; of Genízaros, 19; labor theory of, 33–37; as legal construction, 87–119; liberal theories of, 31–37; as mirage, 180; as object, 6, 117–19, 121, 172; as performance, 32, 37–40, 87; persistence of common property relations, 9, 87–119; as persuasion, 86, 87; and planning, 173; and police violence, 150; politics of, 9; as racialized, 13, 73–78, 109; as relation, 7, 172, 173; relations of (land grants), 25–27, 35, 36, 117–19; rights of, 4, 7; as social struggle, 7, 13, 14, 30, 117, 173; and state, 121; as unfinished project, 173; violence inherent to, 9–11, 121, 173; and whiteness, 77, 78
Proudfit, James, 53, 54
Pueblo Revolt, 15
Puerto Rico, 146; independence movement in, 146–47

Quiet title, lawsuits regarding, 66, 88–119, 120

Rabble Rouser Index (of FBI), 3, 130, 140, 141
Race, 73–83; and FBI, 129–31, 149, 150; and geography, 173
Railroads, in New Mexico, 57, 58
Rancho del Poso, 88, 178
Raza Unida, 14, 150–58, 164; as terrorist organization, 157
Ring, Santa Fe, 28–31, 48–60

Rivera, Bernardo, 120
Rivera v. Brazos Lodge Corp., 196n6
Rogers, Waldo, 120
Rosenstock, Richard, 155, 161, 163
Ross, Edmund, 59
Rowland, Brother, 115, 116
Rusk, Dean, 133

Sabota, 45, 46
Sais, Nick, 138
Salazar, Eulogio, 127, 139
Sanchez, Alfonso, 2; as attorney for La Corporación de Abiquiú, 122–23; as district attorney, 131–45; informants for, 137, 138
Santa Fe Ring, 28–31, 48–60
Sargent, Ed, 94
Scarborough, Paul, 137–39
Serrano, Amarante, 124
Seth, Theodore, 64–67
Sheepherding, 60–64
Sierra, Fred, 102
Simmons, William, 78
Slavery: and borderlands violence, 16; and sexual labor, 18; trade in, 17
Socialist Labor Party, 151
Southern Non-Violent Coordinating Committee, 142
Spain: colonial expansion of, 1; first settlement of, in New Mexico, 15; Indian diplomacy of, 15; reconquest of New Mexico by, 15; Ute relations with, 16, 20
Speculation, land grant: as investment, 5, 28; patterns of, 12, 47–68; resistance to, 2, 5, 8, 13, 30; tactics of, 50–60
Stang, Alan, 142
Stapleton, Benjamin, 79
State Police, New Mexico (NMSP), 2, 3, 14, 121, 143; confidential reports of, 126, 127; investigation of Alianza by, 134, 135; roadblocks of, 137; undercover agents of, 124, 203n64

Surveyor General (N.Mex.), 30, 31, 37, 52, 53
Swadesh, Frances Leon, 11, 74

Tackett, Paul, 128, 131, 160
Tameling case, 93
Taos, attacks of, 16
Terrorism: land grant activism as, 71–82, 142, 145, 147–50; and Puerto Rican nationalist movement, 146–48, 202n2
Tierra Amarilla (land grant), 2, 4; adjudication of, 37–39; "battle of," 41, 45, 46; development of, 14, 153–58, 168–80; diplomatic importance of, 18; legal claims to, 37–40; occupation of, 162–64; official requests for, 20–24; origins of, 7, 18; resources of, 4; speculation over, 39, 47–68; struggle over, 7, 8, 11–14; survey of, 65, 187n77; takeover of, 4, 136–40; Ute claims to, 22; valley as trade corridor, 18; violent struggle for, 69–76
Tijerina, Anselmo, 124, 126, 136; arrest of, 137
Tijerina, Cristobal, 124; arrest of, 137
Tijerina, Reis Lopez, 1–4; arrest warrant for, 137; arrival of, in Tierra Amarilla, 123; attacks against, 143, 144; citizen's arrests of, 2; as civil rights leader, 140–45; FBI investigations of, 128–31; land grant advocacy of, 123–45, 205n102; NMSP investigations of, 124; and People's Constitutional Party, 151; as rabble rouser, 126, 140–42; on trial, 143
Tijerina, Rose, 138
Title: color of, 87–119; quiet, lawsuits, 66, 88–119, 120
Torres, Carlos, 147, 148, 202n11
Trade: outposts (N.Mex.), 16; Spanish-Indian, 15
Treaty of Guadalupe Hidalgo (1848), 6, 28, 37, 50, 51, 183n4
Trujillo, José, M., 99

United Slaves, 142
U.S.-Mexican War, 6, 27, 28; consequence of, 1
Utes, 1, 7, 11, 12, 32; Capote band of, 17, 18, 27, 32, 33, 40–46, 180; geography of, 17; Mexican relations with, 24; Mouache band of, 17; Spanish coalition of, 16; in Tierra Amarilla, 24; treaty of 1868, 43–45; Weeminuche band of, 17, 44

Valdez, Ernesto, 155
Vélez de Escalante, Fray Francisco Silvestre, 15; and Dominguez-Escalante Expedition, 15–20
Violence: and COINTELPRO, 129; as lawmaking, 158; by police, 150; and property, 9–12; racialized, 122, 149, 150; state-sponsored, 122
Vista del Brazos, 159, 160
Vista del Brazos v. Flores, 159–66

Willow Creek Ranch, 178

Zapata, Emiliano, 164, 205n102

GEOGRAPHIES OF JUSTICE AND SOCIAL TRANSFORMATION

1. *Social Justice and the City*, rev. ed.
   by David Harvey

2. *Begging as a Path to Progress: Indigenous Women and Children and the Struggle for Ecuador's Urban Spaces*
   by Kate Swanson

3. *Making the San Fernando Valley: Rural Landscapes, Urban Development, and White Privilege*
   by Laura Barraclough

4. *Company Towns in the Americas: Landscape, Power, and Working-Class Communities*
   edited by Oliver J. Dinius and Angela Vergara

5. *Tremé: Race and Place in a New Orleans Neighborhood*
   by Michael E. Crutcher Jr.

6. *Bloomberg's New York: Class and Governance in the Luxury City*
   by Julian Brash

7. *Roppongi Crossing: The Demise of a Tokyo Nightclub District and the Reshaping of a Global City*
   by Roman Adrian Cybriwsky

8. *Fitzgerald: Geography of a Revolution*
   by William Bunge

9. *Accumulating Insecurity: Violence and Dispossession in the Making of Everyday Life*
   edited by Shelley Feldman, Charles Geisler, and Gayatri A. Menon

10. *They Saved the Crops: Labor, Landscape, and the Struggle over Industrial Farming in Bracero-Era California*
    by Don Mitchell

11. *Faith Based: Religious Neoliberalism
    and the Politics of Welfare in the United States*
    by Jason Hackworth

12. *Fields and Streams: Stream Restoration, Neoliberalism,
    and the Future of Environmental Science*
    by Rebecca Lave

13. *Black, White, and Green: Farmers Markets, Race,
    and the Green Economy*
    by Alison Hope Alkon

14. *Beyond Walls and Cages: Prisons, Borders, and Global Crisis*
    edited by Jenna M. Loyd, Matt Mitchelson, and Andrew Burridge

15. *Silent Violence: Food, Famine, and Peasantry in Northern Nigeria*
    by Michael J. Watts

16. *Development, Security, and Aid: Geopolitics and Geoeconomics
    at the U.S. Agency for International Development*
    by Jamey Essex

17. *Properties of Violence: Law and Land Grant Struggle
    in Northern New Mexico*
    by David Correia

18. *Geographical Diversions: Tibetan Trade, Global Transactions*
    by Tina Harris

19. *The Politics of the Encounter: Urban Theory and Protest under
    Planetary Urbanization*
    by Andy Merrifield

Printed in the USA
CPSIA information can be obtained
at www.ICGtesting.com
LVHW031634270823
756438LV00022B/1286

9 780820 345024